Skill Development
for Generalist Practice

Quotable Quotes

"This book provides real-life case vignettes that will engage students and introduce them to the social work profession." —**Allison Sinanan, Stockton University**

"The simplified nature of this book will help students focus on what is most important in the chapters and advancing their social work practice knowledge, values, and skills in an accessible and easy to read format." —**Elizabeth Russell, The College at Brockport**

"A successful career must be built on a solid foundation. Invest in students' future as generalist social workers." —**Gloria Davis, University of AR at Pine Bluff**

"This book presents social work practice in a logical, progressive format." —**Jim Boyd, Walla Walla University, Wilma Hepker School of Social Work and Sociology**

"This textbook has co-joined classroom instruction and practical skills and presented both to the student in a comprehensive and entirely relatable manner." —**Tanya Johnson-Gilchrist, University of South Florida**

Sara Miller McCune founded SAGE Publishing in 1965 to support the dissemination of usable knowledge and educate a global community. SAGE publishes more than 1000 journals and over 800 new books each year, spanning a wide range of subject areas. Our growing selection of library products includes archives, data, case studies and video. SAGE remains majority owned by our founder and after her lifetime will become owned by a charitable trust that secures the company's continued independence.

Los Angeles | London | New Delhi | Singapore | Washington DC | Melbourne

Skill Development for Generalist Practice

Exercises for Real-World Application

Christina E. Newhill

University of Pittsburgh

Elizabeth A. Mulvaney

University of Pittsburgh

Bobby F. Simmons

University of Pittsburgh

Los Angeles | London | New Delhi
Singapore | Washington DC | Melbourne

FOR INFORMATION:

SAGE Publications, Inc.
2455 Teller Road
Thousand Oaks, California 91320
E-mail: order@sagepub.com

SAGE Publications Ltd.
1 Oliver's Yard
55 City Road
London, EC1Y 1SP
United Kingdom

SAGE Publications India Pvt. Ltd.
B 1/I 1 Mohan Cooperative Industrial Area
Mathura Road, New Delhi 110 044
India

SAGE Publications Asia-Pacific Pte. Ltd.
18 Cross Street #10-10/11/12
China Square Central
Singapore 048423

Printed in the United States of America

Library of Congress Cataloging-in-Publication Data

Names: Newhill, Christina E., author. | Mulvaney, Elizabeth A., author. | Simmons, Bobby F., author.

Title: Skill development for generalist practice / Christina E. Newhill, University of Pittsburgh, Elizabeth A. Mulvaney, University of Pittsburgh, Bobby F. Simmons, University of Pittsburgh.

Description: Los Angeles : SAGE, [2020] | Includes bibliographical references and index.

Identifiers: LCCN 2018044859 | ISBN 9781506384887 (pbk. : alk. paper)
Subjects: LCSH: Social service–Practice. | Social work education. | Social service–Vocational guidance.

Classification: LCC HV10.5 .N49 2020 | DDC 361.3/2–dc23
LC record available at https://lccn.loc.gov/2018044859

This book is printed on acid-free paper.

Acquisitions Editor: Joshua Perigo
Editorial Assistant: Noelle Cumberbatch
Production Editor: Kelle Clarke
Copy Editor: Diana Breti
Typesetter: Hurix Digital
Proofreader: Tricia Currie-Knight
Indexer: Beth Nauman-Montana
Cover Designer: Dally Verghese
Marketing Manager: Katherine Hepburn

19 20 21 22 23 10 9 8 7 6 5 4 3 2 1

BRIEF CONTENTS

CONTENTS

ACKNOWLEDGMENTS

The development and evolution of *Skill Development for Generalist Practice: Exercises for Real-World Application* has occurred over the course of more than two decades of teaching undergraduate and beginning graduate social work students the basic knowledge, skills, and values for entering practice. Over those years, the exercises and cases examples have been revised in keeping with the changing nature of practice, but the fundamental mission of teaching students the foundation essential to good practice has remained the same. We want to acknowledge here the many individuals who contributed to this book. First, we want to acknowledge the countless students who taught us about how these exercises work, gave us feedback, and made suggestions to revise and refine them. We also must acknowledge and thank the many clients who taught each of us how to practice social work and inspired many of the circumstances and ideas in the exercises and cases. Finally, we would like to thank our colleagues Tracy Soska and Shaun Eack for sharing their ideas and materials as part of the development of Chapters 11 and 12, and the many adjunct faculty, including Dean Leahy and Kathy Connolly, who have taught classes using our book and have made suggestions over the years for refining many of the exercises.

We also want to thank our respective families. From Christina Newhill: I would like to thank my husband and fellow social worker, Dean Leahy, for his input and collaboration on how to most effectively teach beginning students using experiential methods, and my daughters Eva and Tiffany, who were great cheerleaders and supporters but are glad the book is now completed. I also want to thank my late father, Esko E. Newhill, who taught me the hard realities as well as the joys of academic writing.

From Beth Mulvaney: I would like to thank Chris and Jamie Ramsey for their support. They certainly tolerated my working on this book evenings, weekends, and during trips and visits in Evanston over these last couple of years—thank you! Many thanks to colleague Rafael Engel for his mentorship, guidance, and encouragement to pursue a book project.

From Bobby Simmons: I would like to acknowledge support from my family, Jan, DeMarcus, and Devin, and my friend Tom S. Mead. Special thanks to you, Christina; the lab manual that you started many years ago has been invaluable in helping me teach the next generation of social workers.

Finally, we also want to thank the many wonderful folks at SAGE who supported and guided us through the reviews and revisions that strengthened our book and readied it for publication. These include our first editor, Nathan Davidson; current editor, Joshua Perigo; copy editor, Diana Breti; project editor, Kelle Clarke; and editorial assistant, Noelle Cumberbatch. We gratefully acknowledge the following reviewers for their kind assistance:

Joseph Anderson, California State University, Sacramento

Lisa Anger, University of Georgia, School of Social Work

Jim Boyd, Walla Walla University, Wilma Hepker School of Social Work and Sociology

Gloria Davis, University of Arkansas at Pine Bluff

Jacqueline Garrison, Grambling State University

Tanya Johnson-Gilchrist, University of South Florida

Lorri McMeel, University of St. Francis

Susan Parlier

Elizabeth Russell, The College at Brockport

Allison Sinanan, Stockton University

Marie Sossou, University of Kentucky

Santos Torres Jr., California State University, Sacramento

Michelle Tucker, Carver School of Social Work, Campbellsville University

INTRODUCTION FOR INSTRUCTORS

Welcome to *Skill Development for Generalist Practice: Exercises for Real-World Application!* This book is designed for social work students to use in their foundation or generalist practice courses at the bachelor's (BASW/BSW) or master's (MSW) level and offers a range of competence-building exercises addressing basic social work knowledge, skills, and values across micro, mezzo, and macro areas of practice. The exercises are designed to be actively used during class time, rather than expecting students to do them on their own, and have been thoroughly field tested successfully with students at the undergraduate and graduate levels with multiple instructors and different social work practice textbooks for more than 20 years.

The primary author wrote the first edition of the book in 1991. Since that time, the three authors have incorporated many changes and updates over consecutive years of use due to a number of factors. First, as many of you know, social work practice has changed significantly over the past 25 years, reflective of how society has changed. Over this period of time, our social safety net (e.g., public assistance supports, state hospital care) has gradually shredded or been curtailed considerably at the same time that the need for social work services has increased as a function of a variety of societal pressures, policy trends, population growth, and crisis events, such as the 2008 economic recession. Our population has become increasingly racially and ethnically diverse, which has impacted how services are and should be delivered, and this has underscored the need for agency and practitioner cultural sensitivity, humility, and competence. Finally, there is the monumental impact of technological developments, which have profoundly changed how people communicate and how social work services are configured and provided.

Students and their learning styles and needs have also changed. Today, faculty teach students who may bring greater challenges to the classroom. This greater spectrum of abilities and challenges includes learning, physical, and psychiatric disabilities; family and social problems; and, particularly in public universities, economic challenges and poor prior academic preparation. Attention spans have decreased for a significant proportion of students due to the impact of technology and multitasking and the overstimulation and increased pace and stress of modern life (Nickless, 2012). As a result, instructors must strive to develop curriculum material that is strategic and powerful enough to capture and sustain students' attention sufficiently so they can learn. Finally, as in many other disciplines, the proportion of part-time social work faculty who teach practice classes has increased dramatically. Such adjunct faculty may have little lead time to prepare their teaching materials, and, thus, a comprehensive flexible book of exercises can be helpful. The exercises and approach used in the book have been modified extensively over the past 25 years to accommodate these changes and current needs.

CONCEPTUAL FRAMEWORK

A range of terms are used in the social work practice literature to refer to the knowledge and skills inherent in the basic social work helping process, including "the helping process" (Hepworth, Rooney, Rooney, & Strom-Gottfried, 2017), the "problem-solving model" (Compton, Galaway, & Cournoyer, 2004), and "planned change" (Kirst-Ashman & Hull, 2015). Although somewhat different in form and emphasis, all incorporate the same basic knowledge and skills at the generalist level. This book also incorporates the recognition that social workers work with a wide range of clients from diverse identities, experiences, and backgrounds, and such clients include individuals, families, small groups, communities, and organizations. Furthermore, these exercises reflect social work's unique commitment to serving those who are the most vulnerable, at-risk, disadvantaged, and marginalized in society, recognizing the importance of understanding and respecting human diversity and achievement of cultural humility, cultural competence, and understanding. The book emphasizes the social work profession's core values: service, social justice, dignity and worth of the person, the importance of human relationships, integrity, and competence. The exercises provided in the book reflect the latest

Council on Social Work Education (2015) educational policy and accreditation standards. In addition, the conceptual framework that guides the exercises in the book is based on the ongoing work of the National Association of Social Workers (2012) and the global definition of *social work* adopted by the International Federation of Social Workers (2014), which reads as follows:

> Social work is a practice-based profession and an academic discipline that promotes social change and development, social cohesion, and the empowerment and liberation of people. Principles of social justice, human rights, collective responsibility and respect for diversities are central to social work. Underpinned by theories of social work, social sciences, humanities and indigenous knowledge, social work engages people and structures to address life challenges and enhance well-being.

APPROACH TO STUDENT LEARNING

As noted above, this book is designed for social work students to use in their introductory or foundation practice courses at the bachelor's (BASW/BSW) or master's (MSW) level. Foundation or generalist courses are the first social work courses that students take and do not typically have course prerequisites, although some students may have previous work experience in the social services arena. It can be challenging for students to understand the skills they must learn without actually practicing the skills using well-designed exercises. Describing the skills in a didactic manner, which may happen if the instructor has little social work practice experience, is not sufficient because it is passive rather than active learning. Furthermore, including a handful of exercises at the end of each chapter in the primary textbook and expecting students to do the exercises on their own usually does not work.

To address these challenges, the primary approach to student learning embedded in each chapter and exercise is *cognitive scaffolding* (Bransford, Brown, & Cocking, 2000): the exercises are accompanied by a set of procedural guidelines that can be used as support when working on developing a particular skill. When competence- or skill-building exercises are then practiced in the classroom setting, the instructor can observe the students and provide immediate constructive feedback to enhance learning, and students can provide peer feedback to each other. Without this kind of learning experience, students may fear that they will not be able to execute a skill well and that they may "make a terrible mistake." Practicing skills in class shows students that we all make mistakes, that mistakes can serve as valuable learning opportunities, and, furthermore, that skills improve with practice.

APPROACH AND STYLE OF THE BOOK

The book's overall purpose is to help students develop solid, primary practice skills. Our approach is a practical treatment of the material, with an emphasis on building basic and necessary skills using self and peer awareness to shape them. The book cuts across all levels of practice with a strong emphasis on diversity to build students' cultural awareness and humility. Content examples and cases are original for this work and come from the practice experience of the three authors.

Our style is an active approach to learning relying upon cognitive scaffolding and kinesthetic learning. Until students actively attempt to build skills, such skills cannot be fully realized simply by reading about them, listening to descriptions of them, or watching demonstrations of them. Given that self (the social worker) is the most important tool used in helping situations, students need practice in initiating and responding to communication, both verbally and nonverbally. Many topics associated with helping are difficult and sensitive to explore, and only active, repetitive practice improves the comfort level and skills used to facilitate use of self. Diversity issues are infused throughout the book, which is more effective than separating such issues into their own section.

The book is divided into topical sessions in a format and sequence similar to the way an academic semester is laid out and the way most introductory social work practice core textbooks are configured, and instructors can pick and choose chapters in the order that best fits their curricular model and needs. The first 15 chapters organize the in-class exercises by topic for 15 consecutive class sessions, a typical semester. The 16th chapter presents lengthier, more challenging cases that can be used for in-class case analysis discussion in small groups, as in-class exams, or as take-home case analysis papers.

Chapter 17 consists of a series of community-based exercises that enable students to get out of the classroom to experience various aspects of the real world of social work. Although materials in the book are offered in a certain order by topic, instructors have flexibility in organizing the chapters in a different sequence and/or pulling out exercises from a chapter and using them at a different point in their particular course.

We hope you enjoy working with your students on developing their knowledge, values, skills, and competencies through the exercises provided in this book.

INTRODUCTION FOR STUDENTS

This skills development book is a training tool for use in your foundation social work courses. The foundation courses are exciting because they prepare you for the academic and professional journey that lies ahead. This book is designed to give you the opportunity to practice skills using experiential exercises in the classroom under the supervision of the class instructor. At the generalist level, the classroom is an ideal, safe environment where the instructor and peers can share feedback. Also, we all make mistakes, even the most experienced social workers; new social workers, naturally, make many. The classroom provides the opportunity for you to make mistakes and learn from them in a safe space. The more you practice, the more you will improve your social work skills and knowledge.

Social work is a practice-based profession that requires confidence, knowledge, skills, and the ability to communicate effectively. All are needed to help bring about change in a variety of social interactions and problem-solving situations. The content of this book is essential to developing generalist social work knowledge, skills, and values across micro, mezzo, and macro areas of practice. All of the chapters have experiential exercises to help foster learning and growth. Many of the case scenarios are adapted from years of social work practice. The case scenarios are diverse in content, giving you a snapshot of what is required to help bring about change in a real-world situation. This book not only provides in-class learning experiences but community-based exercises that will take you out of the classroom and into the community. Having community knowledge and exposure is critical to your social work education.

Your class instructor will help guide you through this learning process. This book has been successfully field tested with students at the undergraduate and graduate levels with multiple instructors and different social work practice textbooks for more than 20 years. Although you may be reluctant to practice a skill in front of an instructor and peers, our experience has been that students see the value in doing the exercises by the end of the term. It may be awkward or you may feel self-conscious at first; we encourage you to make a good faith effort and work through this awkwardness. Imagine how similar your feelings may be to those of clients when they are asked to try something or to practice an unfamiliar skill. Even your reaction to doing the exercises can teach you how to do social work.

We are confident you will find this book helpful throughout your social work foundation education. Please take advantage of all it has to offer.

INTRODUCTORY EXERCISES

The following three exercises are most effectively used as ice breakers during the first session of class, to get you thinking about social work, talking with your classmates, and feeling comfortable participating in class discussion. These exercises ask you to develop a definition of generalist practice, examine why you have chosen to pursue a social work degree and a social work career, and think about what strengths you will bring to the class and what challenges you anticipate.

As you may already know, social workers today work with a wide range of clients in very diverse settings including government agencies, schools, hospitals, mental/behavioral health clinics, children and youth welfare agencies, aging services, business and industry, and private practice. However, what all social workers have in common is a strong commitment to the welfare of those who are poor, oppressed, disenfranchised, and disadvantaged in one way or another.

How do social workers view their work? Most social workers will say that their work can be rewarding, frustrating, satisfying, sometimes discouraging, at times stressful, but, most of all, always challenging. Let us spend some time getting to know each other and begin thinking about what the social work profession is all about.

EXERCISE 1.1: DEFINING GENERALIST SOCIAL WORK PRACTICE

Put away all papers and information on the class.

1. Pick one index card from the deck that is passed around to the class.

2. Do not put your name on it.

3. Using all you know to date about social work, write a concise definition of *generalist practice*.

4. Return your card to the instructor.

5. Receive a card back (it does not matter if it is your own; no one but you will know).

6. Report the ideas found on the index card you receive to the instructor, who will record themes/ideas/terms and then moderate creation of a class definition.

Compare the class's definition to your school's definition. What is the same? What is different?

EXERCISE 1.2: WHY PURSUE SOCIAL WORK?

Form groups of five or six to address and discuss the following four questions:

1. Why have you chosen social work as your career?

2. What do you think it means to be a social worker today? What are the pros and cons of working as a social worker?

3. How do you think the general public perceives the social work profession?

4. What are the most pressing issues that the social work profession should address as we move further into the 21st century?

Each group should appoint a spokesperson to take notes. After a half hour of discussion, reconvene with the rest of the class to share the highlights of each group's discussion.

EXERCISE 1.3: WHAT WILL YOU BRING TO THE CLASS?

Form groups of four to six. One by one, introduce yourself to each member of your group and then briefly interview the classmate to your right for five minutes by asking the following questions:

1. What excites and interests you about taking this class?

2. What resources, strengths, skills, and experiences do you bring to this class?

3. What questions, worries, or concerns do you have about taking this class?

After 10 minutes, the class reconvenes, and then you each briefly introduce the classmate you interviewed, providing at least one answer to each of the following three questions:

1. What excites and/or interests your classmate about taking this class?

2. What resources, strengths, and experiences does your classmate bring to this class?

3. What questions or concerns does your classmate have about taking this class?

After the individual introductions, everyone will try to identify the common themes that have cut across your classmates' comments and discuss what these themes suggest about social work practice and social work education.

THE PURPOSE AND NATURE OF GENERALIST SOCIAL WORK PRACTICE

LEARNING OBJECTIVES

1. Understand and analyze the purpose, core elements, and major objectives of social work practice.

2. Integrate the principles of cultural humility and cultural competence in the purpose and goals of social work practice (Exercise 2.1).

3. Compare and contrast the five main social work practice roles, and determine which role you would assume in each of the case vignettes (Exercise 2.1).

4. Evaluate the advantages and disadvantages of the ecological systems model.

5. Practice analysis of an ecological context and create a representative eco-map (Exercise 2.2).

6. Identify which step of the helping process each vignette represents (Exercise 2.3).

This chapter begins with a concise outline of the roles and responsibilities of social workers and the goals and objectives of social work practice. The generalist helping process is explained. Following this information are three laboratory exercises. The first exercise challenges you to think about different ways to help clients and what social work roles might be assumed for each form of helping, using case vignettes representing micro, mezzo, and macro levels of practice. The second encourages you to create an eco-map to understand ecosystem influences, and the third helps you identify stages of the generalist helping process.

DEFINITION OF GENERALIST SOCIAL WORK PRACTICE

Social work is the professional activity of helping individuals, groups, and communities enhance their well-being, meet basic human needs, and create societal conditions favorable to these goals, with particular attention to the needs of vulnerable, disenfranchised, and oppressed individuals and groups. These goals are accomplished by social workers pursuing a mission of social and economic justice and pursuing social change targeting poverty, unemployment, discrimination, and other forms of injustice.

The International Federation of Social Workers' statement of ethical principles (IFSW, 2012) declares that it is the responsibility of social workers to promote social justice in relation to society and their clients by challenging negative discrimination, recognizing diversity, challenging unjust policies and practices, and working in solidarity. This commitment is also reflected in the current National Association of Social Workers *Code of Ethics* (NASW, 2017a).

SOCIAL WORK: KEY CONCEPTS AND DEFINITIONS

Core Elements

There are four core elements of the social work profession:

1. The purpose and objectives of the profession
2. The core values, *Code of Ethics*, and philosophy of social work practice
3. The knowledge base of social work practice
4. The practice methods and processes employed

A primary goal of the practice of social work is to enhance clients' bio-psycho-social-spiritual functioning within the mission of social justice.

Social work's primary focus is the person and the environment in reciprocal interaction.

Objectives

There are six major objectives of social work practice:

1. Help people enhance their competence, exercise their right to self-determination, and increase their problem-solving and coping abilities.
2. Help people obtain resources and provide advocacy on their behalf.
3. Advocate to make organizations and institutions responsive to people and their needs.
4. Facilitate interactions between individuals and others in the environment.
5. Act to influence interactions between organizations and institutions.
6. Act to influence economic, environmental, and social justice policy efforts.

Knowledge Base

The knowledge base of social work practice includes the following:

1. Human behavior in the social environment

2. Social welfare policy and services

3. Research

4. Social work practice methods at the micro, mezzo, and macro levels

5. Field placement/practicum

Cultural Humility and Cultural Competence

Cultural humility and cultural competence are essential to social work practice:

1. Cultural differences essentially reflect fundamental variations in what people hold to be important and worthwhile and include the thoughts, communication patterns, actions, customs, traditions, beliefs, values, and institutions of a racial, ethnic, religious, or social group.

2. Culturally different clients are entitled to competent, professional social work services, as are all the individuals who we serve as social workers.

3. As social workers, it is our ethical responsibility to be respectful of cultural differences and not participate in perpetuating the history of gross insensitivity to the cultural differences of our clients.

4. Examining cross-cultural issues in social work practice relates to how our profession has conceptualized its involvement with, and commitment to, culturally diverse communities.

5. Maintaining cultural competence and cultural humility in practice is an ongoing, always-evolving aspect of social work practice.

6. Cultural competence embraces a bio-psycho-social-spiritual model, recognizing that spirituality and/or religion is part of any cultural system to some degree and, for many although not all, bears a strong relationship to health and well-being.

7. The concept of cultural humility is a guiding framework for understanding cultural differences and provides the lens of "intersectionality," which enables social workers to understand overlapping social identities while examining and confronting systems or institutions that enable and maintain oppression, discrimination, and domination.

8. Both cultural humility and cultural competence are required components of professional social work practice across micro, mezzo, and macro domains.

9. Thus, as practicing social workers, we must ask ourselves the following on an ongoing basis:

   • What is the cultural background of the clients we serve?

   • How do their community values and affiliations affect how services are provided, utilized, and accessed?

   • What is the cultural setting in which our clients' family and social lives are embedded?

   • What actions can we take to make our services more culturally relevant, sensitive, and humble to those we serve? (Fisher-Borne, Cain, & Martin, 2015; NASW, 2001, 2017b)

The Ecological Systems Model

The ecological systems model posits that individuals are engaged in constant transactions with other human beings and with other systems in the environment. These various persons and systems reciprocally influence each other. People are not just reactors to their environments; they act on their environments, as well (Siporin, 1980).

- Advantage: broad in scope and flexible

- Disadvantage: can present as vague and weak if the parameters are not clear

There are four primary types of systems in the person and environment:

1. Intra-individual subsystems, including the biological, cognitive, emotional, psychological, motivational, and spiritual

2. Interpersonal systems (e.g., marital, sibling, family, cultural, religious, and other social networks)

3. Institutions, organizations, and communities (e.g., government institutions and services)

4. The physical environment (e.g., climate, geography, and human-created structures)

Criteria for Selecting a Practice Approach

1. The extent to which a given approach has been supported by empirical research

2. The extent to which the approach supports client self-determination, empowerment, and collaborative decision making

3. All things being equal, choose the approach that produces the best results with the least expenditure of time, money, and effort.

4. Is the intervention ethical? Does it emphasize social work's core values?

5. Is the intervention culturally sensitive and appropriate?

6. Does the social worker providing the intervention have the knowledge and skills to competently deliver the intervention? (Hepworth, Rooney, Rooney, & Strom-Gottfried, 2013; Hepworth & Larsen, 1990)

Five Main Categories of Roles of Social Work Practitioners

Social work roles can be grouped into five categories (Hepworth et al., 2013):

1. Direct provider of services

    a. Clinical social work with individuals, psychotherapy, or counseling

    b. Marital and family therapy

    c. Small group work

    d. Educator/disseminator of social work–related information

    e. Advocate

2. System linkage roles

    a. Broker of resources and services

    b. Case manager/resource coordinator

    c. Mediator/arbitrator

    d. Advocate

3. System maintenance and enhancement

    a. Director of a service or agency

    b. Supervisor

    c. Organizational troubleshooter/diagnostician

    d. Facilitator/expeditor

    e. Team/task group member

    f. Consultant/consultee

    g. Advocate

4. Researcher/Research consumer

    a. Consuming and evaluating the merits and limitations of research study findings

    b. Staying currently informed by reading the professional literature

    c. Applying and utilizing research findings in practice

    d. Conducting research studies, including evaluating one's own practice effectiveness

5. System development

    a. Program developer

    b. Planner

    c. Policy and procedure developer

    d. Advocate

EXERCISE 2.1: WAYS OF HELPING

Directions

- Each vignette describes a client situation. Imagine that you are the social worker seeing the client for the first time.

- With a partner, brainstorm all the ways you could help the client(s) described in the vignette.

- Note what type of **role** you would be assuming for each way of helping, and discuss what the **goals** of each type of helping might be. The purpose of the exercise is not to find the "correct" way of helping but, rather, to discover all the different possibilities that could be employed to help your client(s).

Micro Practice Case Vignettes

Practice setting: You are a social worker employed at a child and family services walk-in clinic.

Case Vignette 1

The client is a pregnant teenage single mother of two who uses alcohol and heroin and whose presenting complaint is depression. You notice she has a black eye and her arm is in a sling.

Case Vignette 2

The client is a middle-aged, married African American man with two teenage children who was just laid off from the job he has held for 20 years because of a company reorganization. He will soon be broke and has no idea how he will pay his bills. He tells you that he has talked with his pastor and has prayed for help, but to no avail.

Case Vignette 3

The client is a young man who is homeless and lives on the streets. His clothes are worn and dirty, and he looks very thin. He tells you that he has a history of schizophrenia and admits he is currently experiencing hallucinations. He isn't asking for psychiatric help; rather, he is just asking for a place to stay for tonight and some food.

Case Vignette 4

The clients are a Caucasian mother and her 13-year-old biracial adopted daughter. The daughter has run away from home for the fourth time, and the mother has brought her in to your clinic "to be straightened out." According to the mother, the adoptive father refused to come to the clinic and said, "To hell with that kid."

Case Vignette 5

The client is a 35-year-old single Korean-American woman who wants to talk to someone because her fiancé just broke off their engagement and her "life is over." She is attractive, bright, and has a good job as a high school teacher, but she has been feeling worthless since he left her. Her parents tell her that to break up so close to their wedding date is an embarrassment for the family.

Mezzo Practice Case Vignettes

Case Vignette 6

Practice setting: You are a social worker working for public child welfare, primarily in the child protective services division. One of your responsibilities is to facilitate parenting classes for parents who have been ordered to such classes by the courts because of charges of child abuse or neglect.

Your most recently assigned parenting skills group consists of five single mothers, all of whom have been charged with child neglect because they left their children home unsupervised between the time the children came home from school and the time the mothers got off work. The mothers collectively claim that they couldn't help but leave their children home alone "because we can't afford child care on minimum wage."

Case Vignette 7

Practice setting: You are a social worker in a long-term care setting that cares for many people with dementia. One of your responsibilities is to lead a family caregiver support group twice a month. It has social support and psychoeducational goals. Family members voluntarily choose to participate.

Six spouses and three adult children, ranging from age 52 to 95, attend the group. They are struggling with how to respond to various behaviors, including not being recognized by their family members, repetitive speech, and verbal agitation. One spouse says, "It's like my husband just isn't my husband any more. He's alive but who he *is* is gone."

Macro Practice Case Vignette

Case Vignette 8

Practice setting: You are a social worker employed by a newly funded neighborhood community resources center whose mission is to work collaboratively with neighborhood leaders and citizens to improve neighborhood quality of life. Your primary job is that of a community organizer. This is your first meeting with your client.

The client is the daughter of an 85-year-old woman who lives in the neighborhood. The daughter went to the local police department to complain that her mother is afraid to go out of her apartment, even during the day, because teenagers have begun to gather in greater numbers in the nearby park and on street corners. She adds that many of the elderly folks in the neighborhood are feeling fearful after one older man was teased and pushed around by a couple of teenage boys a month ago. She wants someone to help resolve the situation, so the police referred her to you. After you both sit down in your office, she states, "This used to be a good neighborhood. Then the jobs went away, the drug dealers came in, and the older folks are really scared. Can you help us, please?"

THE ECO-MAP

An "eco-map" is a diagram of the ecological context of the client system (Hartman, 1978; Hartman & Laird, 1983). Eco-maps can be useful tools for both the social worker and the client to grasp the complex interplay of the various systems and subsystems impacting the client's situation. There is no single way to create an eco-map. There are many ideas and versions (Hepworth et al., 2017; Becvar & Becvar, 2009; Carillo, 2007; Hodge, 2005). What is important is to capture the dynamic interaction of a person or family and their environment. Diagram 2.1 illustrates the typical features of an eco-map.

- Client system: Typically in a circle at the center of the diagram, it usually includes a person or a household with identifying information, some indication of relationships, and ages of the parties. At least one of those people is the identified client system.

  ○ Fatima lives with her son and her cousin. Their ages are noted.

- Circles represent other individuals, groups, organizations, or entities that affect the client system. Typical entities might be extended family members, workplace, school, social services or medical providers, friends, congregations, clubs related to hobbies/interests, and neighborhood or community groups.

DIAGRAM 2.1 ■ Sample Eco-Map: The Generalist Helping Process

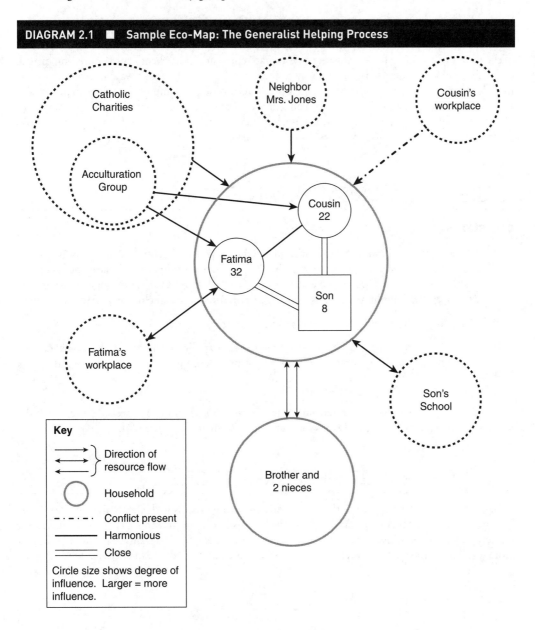

- ○ Fatima, a resettled refugee, has mentioned that she and her cousin are employed (workplaces); her son goes to school; she has a brother and two nieces, a neighbor, and a relationship with Catholic Charities (service provider) as her resettlement agency. Within Catholic Charities, she is connected to an acculturation group.

- Lines indicating something about the nature of the relationships: Are the relationships reciprocal? Are they supportive or stressful? What is the degree of influence or impact of the various parties on the client system?

  - ○ For this eco-map, three types of relationship are referenced—harmonious, conflicted, and close. For example, both Fatima and her cousin have a close relationship with her son, and the whole household is experiencing a conflicted relationship with the cousin's workplace. At the current time, Catholic Charities is having the most influence on the family.

- A key: There should be some type of key to indicate what the various lines, colors, or sizes of the shapes mean.

  - ○ Note that the key for Fatima's eco-map used terms like *harmonious* and *conflicted*. You can allow the client to determine the descriptors of the relationships. As long as the key is present, meaning is clear.

Eco-maps can be used at various phases of the helping process. They can be used as part of assessment to better understand the context and influences on a client-system. They can also be used as part of the planning process. After completing an eco-map representing the client's current life, you can ask the client to draw an ideal eco-map as a way to formulate goals. In the same way, an eco-map can be used during the intervention phase to select particular relationships to improve or resources to develop. It may also be used in evaluation. Perhaps, you and the client redraw an eco-map after the work is complete and compare it to the initial eco-map as a way to document change. The following exercise asks you to create a simple eco-map by interviewing a classmate.

EXERCISE 2.2: CREATING AN ECO-MAP

Directions

- Find a partner and interview each other about the current systems and relationships in each other's lives. These systems and relationships can include one's internal physical and mental health status, friends, immediate and extended family, school, church/synagogue/mosque, neighborhood, community groups, work, transportation, physical climate, and so forth.

- Write down a list of *each other's* systems and subsystems.

- Then, based on the list, collaboratively draw an eco-map for each person with the goal of creating a diagram that provides an accurate picture of each person's current ecological context.

Note: Think about what may or may not be too personal to reveal to your peers. You can limit the responses to one facet of your life if you would prefer not to share all aspects of it.

THE GENERALIST HELPING PROCESS

Generalist social workers engage in the same problem-solving process with clients at all system levels. The approaches and tools may vary with the level of system. However, this base process provides a framework for approaching the variety of challenges clients face (see Diagram 2.2). The steps in this process will be introduced in this chapter and then explored in more depth in later chapters.

Various textbooks on generalist practice use different language for the steps, and some add more steps. After reading through the details, you will realize the activities are basically the same. While this book uses the steps in Diagram 2.2, you should use the steps and language that your program teaches.

Engagement: Before any work can be done, whether the client is an individual or a community, a social worker needs to connect to the client, get to know the client, and establish a relationship. This step involves all the efforts and communication necessary to form rapport with others.

Assessment: Social workers need to understand the nature of risks, challenges, and problems faced by clients as well as the strengths and skills they possess. Social workers also need to understand the environments in which clients live and interact. During this phase of the work, social workers employ a variety of tools to learn about the client system, depending upon the level of system and reason for interacting with a social worker. This collection of information (sometimes called data gathering) is used to move into the next steps in the helping process.

Planning: The social worker partners with the client system to decide what they will accomplish. Together, they set a goal (or several goals) that they want to reach and discuss how they will go about it. The social worker is mindful of his or her competence to help this client and ensures that the client is fully informed so he or she can make good choices.

Intervention: The intervention flows from the assessment and planning. The type of intervention varies depending upon the client system. Intervention includes all the activity used to prevent or solve the issue that the social worker is working on with the client.

Evaluation: This phase of the work has two components and begins during the planning step. The first aspect of evaluation is process evaluation: a regular check with the client about the process of doing the work. The second aspect is outcome evaluation: determining whether the client succeeded in reaching the goal. A well-written goal includes measurement (the way you will know whether the goal has been reached).

DIAGRAM 2.2 ■ The Generalist Helping Process

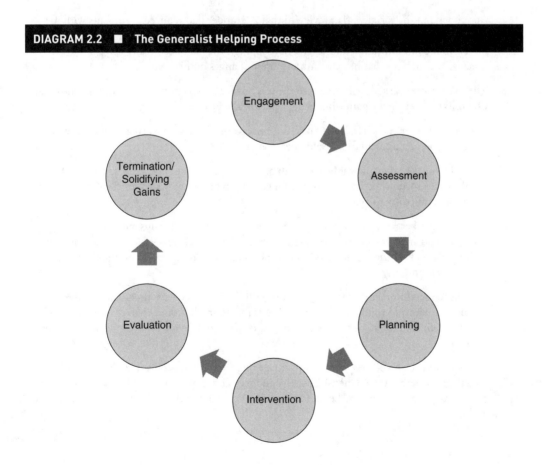

Termination/Solidifying Gains: The final step occurs when a client finishes the work with the social worker. There are a variety of reasons a client finishes. Accomplishing goals is the ideal reason. However, that is not always the case. There are other circumstances that might necessitate ending the relationship.

These steps have been presented as if they occur in a logical pattern, and sometimes they do. However, in reality, social work is not that neat. Many settings require you to engage and assess at the same time. Because clients often need time to truly trust a social worker, they may not fully reveal all information until the client and social worker are in the midst of the intervention. This new information might then necessitate additional assessment and/or revision of the plan. As clients can typically only work on a couple of goals at a time, the process may occur again as new goals are identified and work begins on the new goals. Greater detail about each of these aspects of the work can be found in later chapters.

EXERCISE 2.3: UNDERSTANDING THE GENERALIST HELPING PROCESS

Directions

- In groups or by yourself, read each brief vignette and identify which step in the helping process is occurring.

Case Vignettes

1. Casey and the social worker have visited four apartment complexes and completed six housing applications in the last three weeks.

2. Alexander and the social worker reviewed that Alexander had reduced arguments with his partner and teenage children to fewer than two a week. Alexander reflected that learning more about communication and several new coping skills had been really helpful. He feels reasonably confident that he can maintain these changes on his own.

3. The social worker asked each person in the Caregiver Support group to decide what he or she would like to personally gain from being a part of the group.

4. The social worker and GHI Neighborhood Association members staged a rally at City Hall to call attention to a particularly unsafe intersection.

5. A social worker began a new job at a group home for teens. The supervisor suggested the social worker spend time in the living room getting to know the youth for the first week while becoming familiar with agency policy.

6. The social worker with LMN Agency conducts a series of focus groups with various groups within the organization—employees, clients, and referral agencies—asking questions about their perceptions of the organization, the work it does, and how well it communicates with the wider community.

7. Jo and the social worker discuss Jo's comfort with the way they have been working together to reduce anxiety. Jo thinks she is more comfortable in small groups than before the work began, which is the goal, but a new goal might be needed: to work on being comfortable out in public.

8. Kali and the social worker spend a lot of time exploring all the people in Kali's life, trying to understand whether the relationships are supportive and in what ways. The social worker suggests this information may be helpful in creating a strategy to fix up Kali's home and make it livable again.

Answer Key

1. Intervention

2. Termination/Solidifying Gains

3. Planning

4. Intervention

5. Engagement

6. Assessment

7. Evaluation

8. Assessment

WORKING WITH DIVERSE CLIENTS USING CULTURAL COMPETENCE AND HUMILITY

LEARNING OBJECTIVES

1. Identify some personal biases, ideas, and stereotypes that might interfere with ability to engage others (Exercises 3.1, 3.2, 3.3).

2. Develop a clearer definition of *disability* and *accommodation* (Exercise 3.2, 3.3).

3. Analyze the impact on services provided to people having multiple identity features that may make them more likely to experience disadvantage, discrimination, or bias (Exercise 3.4).

Today's social workers work with a diverse range of clients, with a particular commitment to those who are the most vulnerable, at risk, disadvantaged, oppressed, and marginalized in our society. Developing cultural competence and approaching culturally different clients with cultural humility, therefore, are essential. As beginning social work practitioners, you must be prepared to provide services to all people, regardless of how they differ from you. Furthermore, competence in practice requires not just knowledge and skills but also competence in terms of values awareness. This chapter challenges you by providing several critical thinking and skill development exercises that address working with individuals who are members of vulnerable populations, including analyzing real-life case vignettes portraying individuals with diverse situations in terms of their environmental needs, how others respond to the client's concerns, prejudices or insensitivities from others toward the client, the impact of stigma, what systems are involved in the client's care, and the nature of the client's strengths, abilities, and resources.

THE NASW STANDARDS

The NASW *Standards and Indicators for Cultural Competence in Social Work Practice* (2015) is the updated revision of the *NASW Standards for Cultural Competence in Social Work Practice* (2001) and the *Indicators for the Achievement of the NASW Standards for Cultural Competence in Social Work Practice* (2007). Important concepts that are reinforced by the latest standards are the following:

- **Culture** refers to the set of shared attitudes, values, goals, customs, and practices that characterize people who belong to a particular racial or ethnic group, sexual orientation, gender identity and expression, or religious/spiritual identity. An understanding of culture and its incorporation into professional practice is important at all levels of social work, including the micro, mezzo, and macro.

- **Cultural competence** is and continues to be highly important for social work and refers to attitudes, knowledge, values, and skills that enable effective cross-cultural practice. Cultural competence is not static; rather, it requires ongoing growth, development, and learning.

- **Cultural humility** functions as a guiding stance for bridging cultural differences and recognizing clients' *intersectionality* (Crenshaw, 1991), which refers to individuals' having multiple identities that harbor multiple strengths and may interact with and lead to multiple forms of discrimination and oppression. The new standards also identify *language and communication* issues that must be recognized and appropriately addressed, including limited English proficiency, literacy challenges, and communication-related disabilities/abilities. Social workers also have a larger responsibility to advance cultural competence and humility through leadership within the social work profession, human services in general, and society at large, including challenging and seeking to ameliorate structural and institutional oppression (NASW, 2017b).

- **Cultural competence versus cultural humility:** Cultural competence and cultural humility are both important and complement each other in critical ways. Cultural competence emphasizes the social worker's knowledge, skills, and values, thereby establishing the social worker's expertise and ability to provide culturally appropriate services for diverse clients. Cultural humility, on the other hand, is an explicit stance the social worker embraces that is "other oriented" and views culturally diverse clients as the experts on their culture, values, and worldview, more so than the social worker. The culturally competent social worker achieves expertise; the culturally humble social worker continually enhances that expertise by learning from his or her clients with cultural humility as a lifelong process.

EXERCISE 3.1: AN EXPLORATORY VALUES CLARIFICATION EXERCISE ADDRESSING [VULNERABLE POPULATION X]

This is a flexible "fill-in-the-blank exercise" in which you can choose any vulnerable population to address, such as

- abused and/or neglected children or older adults

- ex-convicts

- LGBTQIA individuals

- immigrants or refugees

- individuals who are morbidly obese

- individuals who are HIV positive

- individuals who are victims of a natural or human-made disaster

- individuals with substance use problems

- individuals who are members of a racial/ethnic/religious minority group

- military veterans

- victims of family or intimate partner violence

This exercise addresses values clarification and can help you explore and identify some of your thoughts, feelings, implicit biases, and stereotypes about the individuals included in the identified vulnerable population, an important preparation for practice.

Directions

- Form groups of four to six.

- Choose a vulnerable population to address.

- In your small group, discuss the following questions.

- Reconvene as a class and share your perspectives with each other.

Questions for Discussion

1. How would you define the terms used for identifying or describing your chosen vulnerable population? What are their parameters?

2. What does it mean today for an individual to be labeled as a member of your chosen vulnerable population? How are such individuals viewed by (a) social workers, (b) other professionals, and (c) our society?

3. What are some of the major issues for the social work profession in the area of services to those who are members of your chosen population?

4. Should members of your chosen population be considered a "minority group"? If so, why? If not, why not? What does your answer mean in terms of rights, power, and the responsibility of the social work profession and society?

5. What types of situations, conditions, or circumstances should be included in how we define your chosen vulnerable population? Which situations, conditions or circumstances should be excluded? Why or why not?

INDIVIDUALS WITH DISABILITIES

In 1990, the Americans With Disabilities Act (ADA; Pub. L. No. 101-336, 104 Stat. 328) was signed into law. This Act prohibits discrimination against individuals with disabilities in employment, transportation, public accommodation, communication, and activities of state and local government. The ADA basically requires that reasonable accommodations in policies, practices, and procedures must be made to avoid discrimination on the basis of disability. Private clubs and religious organizations, however, are exempt from ADA requirements. In response to the development and passage of the ADA, the Council on Social Work Education required that all schools of social work include content on working with individuals with disabilities in generalist courses and, of course, concern for the needs of persons with disabilities directly stems from social work's core values and our appreciation of and respect for the common human needs, worth, and dignity of each person.

Individuals with disabilities often need the services of social workers, and many still face multiple challenges living in a society that may not fully recognize their unique strengths, abilities, and needs. People with disabilities often carry a heavy burden of stigma, which contributes to discrimination socially and in the workplace. Harpur (2012) argues that changing how we use language is one strategy for reducing oppression and promoting strengths and abilities. One way of conceptualizing this for practice is to view each client as having a spectrum of ability within which are both strengths and challenges. People sharing a particular disability, for example, may have a great range of both abilities and disability, and both should be recognized and taken into consideration when providing services. Taking a strengths-based collaborative approach with clients helps to ensure that abilities are recognized and supported. In addition, taking a "capability approach," in which the social worker assesses what an individual can do (capabilities), rather than focusing just on functional impairment, can support capacity development as part of the client assessment and service plan (Saleeby, 2007). The 2017 NASW *Code of Ethics* has also modified its language to reflect this view. For example, at the end of Section 1.05(c), the text "mental or physical disability" now reads as "mental or physical ability." This shift in language appears throughout the *Code* in sections 1.03(g), 1.05(d), 1.06(g), 1.15, 2.01, 4.02, and 6.04(d).

EXERCISE 3.2: AN EXPLORATORY VALUES CLARIFICATION EXERCISE ADDRESSING INDIVIDUALS WITH DISABILITIES

The term *disability* can potentially refer to a wide range of conditions, and social workers may encounter individuals with a vast range of abilities and disabilities in the course of their practice. In light of this reality, this exercise will address values clarification and help you explore and identify some of your thoughts, feelings, implicit biases, and stereotypes about various conditions that may be labeled as disabilities and how the concept of "disability" can be defined.

Directions

- Form groups of four to six.
- Discuss the following questions in your small group.
- Reconvene as a class and share your perspectives with each other.

Questions for Discussion

1. How would you define the term *disability?* What are its parameters? How would you define the term *ability* and its parameters?

2. What does it mean today for an individual to be "disabled"?

3. What are some of the major issues for the profession of social work today in the area of services to those with disabilities?

4. Should people with disabilities be considered a "minority group"? If so, why? If not, why not? What does your answer mean in terms of rights, power, oppression, and the responsibility of the social work profession?

5. Should the following conditions be labeled as disabilities? Why or why not?

   a. Acquired immune deficiency syndrome (AIDS)

   b. Addiction to alcohol, drugs, tobacco, or gambling

   c. Autism spectrum disorder

   d. Cancer

   e. Chronic unemployment

   f. Depression

g. Diabetes

h. Hearing impairment

i. High blood pressure

j. Intellectual disability (formerly called mental retardation)

k. Morbid obesity

l. Post-traumatic stress disorder

m. Poverty

n. Schizophrenia

o. Visual impairment

6. What accommodations do you know about for various disabilities? How does your knowledge compare to your peers'? Are there any disabilities for which you are unaware of accommodations?

EXERCISE 3.3: RANK ORDER—A VALUES CLARIFICATION EXERCISE ADDRESSING DISABILITIES

The goal of this exercise is to help you get in touch with underlying assumptions, biases, and prejudices that you may hold with regard to different types of disabilities (Simon, Howe, & Kirschenbaum, 1995).

Directions

- Form groups of four to six.

- For each question, rank the choices from first choice to last choice, and try to identify the underlying personal values driving your rank ordering sequence for each question.

- Answer each of the rank order questions individually, and then discuss your answers with the others in your small group.

- You may choose to answer the questions provided below, which address individuals with disabilities, or you can make up your own rank order questions addressing a different vulnerable population.

- If you choose to make up your own questions for a different vulnerable group, each group member can make up one question, and then the questions from all the groups can be combined into an exercise for the class to complete.

Questions

1. Which would be the most difficult adjustment for you?

_____ to lose your dominant (right or left) hand or arm

_____ to lose your left leg

_____ to lose both thumbs

2. You would most prefer that your tax dollars go to

_____ build new substance use treatment centers and programs

_____ make all public buildings accessible to those with disabilities

_____ enlarge the range of those considered disabled and eligible to receive government support

3. Which procedure is it most acceptable for a medical insurance company to exclude from coverage?

_____ injuries in which the injured person is at least partially at fault (e.g., head injuries from riding on a motorcycle without a helmet)

_____ gender reassignment surgery

_____ elective cosmetic surgery

4. Which would be the most difficult for you to cope with?

_____ gradually becoming totally blind

_____ gradually becoming totally deaf

_____ a tracheotomy resulting in loss of the ability to speak independently without a voice box

5. As a social worker, you would *least* want to work with

_____ people with terminal medical illnesses

_____ people with severe traumatic brain injuries

_____ children with profound intellectual disabilities

EXERCISE 3.4: WORKING WITH INDIVIDUALS WITH INTERSECTIONAL IDENTITIES BY EMPLOYING CULTURAL UNDERSTANDING AND CULTURAL HUMILITY: THREE CASE ANALYSES

The impact of environmental factors is critical to consider in both assessment and in determining appropriate interventions and mobilization of resources for clients. Social workers must consider the best person-in-the-environment fit between the needs of their client and the resources the environment provides. Such environmental needs include the following (Coulton, 1979, pp. 8–9):

1. Having sufficient opportunities for social relationships

2. Having sufficient opportunities to express feelings

3. Having sufficient sources of emotional support

4. Meeting the expectations of self and others

5. Being able to fulfill responsibilities

6. Having opportunities to engage in interesting, productive activities and achieve goals

7. Fulfilling the demands of certain situations (e.g., job, social events, caring for other family members)

8. Getting information to allow some certainty about the future

9. Having knowledge about one's physical condition, community resources, etc.

10. Knowing where things are, what to expect, and how to behave in new settings

11. Having sufficient financial resources to meet demands and obligations

12. Having help with physical, emotional, and self-care needs

13. Finding the means to move from place to place

In the following case vignettes, these environmental needs should be considered as you work on answering the questions. In these vignettes (all based on actual clients from the first author's practice), the client's situation is described, and then questions are posed for you to answer as if you were the social worker assigned to work with the client. Each client has intersecting identities that combine to increase his or her vulnerability and need for services.

Directions

- Form groups of four to six.

- After reading through all three case vignettes, choose one of the vignettes to analyze as a group.

- Identify the client's various identities and how they intersect to define the client and his situation and needs, and think about how you would approach the client with cultural competence and humility.

- Discuss each of the questions listed below the case, paying particular attention to your feelings and what underlying values may be driving the feelings.

- After 20–30 minutes, reconvene as a class to discuss the cases.

Case Vignette 1

Mr. Jackson is a 62-year-old divorced African American Vietnam War veteran who was escorted to the psychiatric emergency room by police for evaluation. Mr. Jackson uses an electric wheelchair and has been using a wheelchair ever since he lost both legs in the war. He is on full veteran's disability and has been treated multiple times at the nearest V.A. medical center for severe alcohol use disorder. One month ago, he again requested admission to the alcohol treatment inpatient unit, but this time his request for admission was denied. The admission staff told him that until he was willing to follow up with outpatient addiction treatment and involvement in AA (Alcoholics Anonymous), they would not consider another admission. This made Mr. Jackson extremely angry. He immediately returned home, got drunk, then called the alcohol treatment inpatient unit and threatened to kill the admitting physician and the head nurse. The staff who answered his initial phone call hung up on him, which angered him further, and he continued to make threatening phone calls until staff finally called the police. Police went to Mr. Jackson's home. When he refused to answer the door, they broke it down and claim they found Mr. Jackson sitting in his wheelchair holding a bottle of sleeping pills and a bottle of vodka. They interpreted this as an indication he was suicidal, and based on that, plus the earlier threats, they decided to transport him to the psychiatric emergency room. Upon arrival, police stated to the social work evaluator that "nobody really takes his threats seriously because he's in a wheelchair, and so what could he really do?"

Questions

1. How are others responding to Mr. Jackson? Do you think that others' responses to him would be the same if he were not physically disabled and using a wheelchair?

2. Do you identify any prejudices, stereotypes, or insensitivities displayed by the various professionals in contact with Mr. Jackson? If so, what are they exactly? Do you think his race may play a role in how people have responded to him?

3. What are Mr. Jackson's various intersecting identities? How do they intersect and interact in his situation and with his problems?

4. Mr. Jackson is very angry. What are the sources or triggers for his anger? What unmet environmental needs or wants do you identify that are reflected in his anger?

5. What systems are involved in the situation? What systems should be involved that are not?

6. If you were the social worker assessing him in the psychiatric emergency room, how would you feel about working with Mr. Jackson? How would you employ cultural humility in the process of establishing rapport with him and exploring his concerns?

7. What are Mr. Jackson's abilities, strengths, and resources that can be capitalized on in the process of helping him?

Case Vignette 2

Ken is a 27-year-old single, gay Caucasian man who comes to the walk-in counseling clinic asking to talk to someone. He has been totally blind since birth and is accompanied by his German Shepherd service dog. Ken works part time at the sheltered workshop run by the local blind association (which is a struggling nonprofit agency that offers very low pay) and occasionally takes courses at the local junior college where, fortunately, tuition is free to state residents. Upon evaluation, Ken complains of feeling depressed, stating, "I've always been depressed. I've never been happy." He reveals that he lives alone in a rather "seedy" part of town and is often afraid of being burglarized at home or robbed when out walking with his dog. He is angry about his fears and feels that he has been victimized all his life because he is blind. He is lonely and isolated but is resistant to efforts to meet others, stating, "What's the use? All my friends turn on me eventually anyway." He tells the social worker that he is gay but has never had a lasting romantic relationship with another man. Ken sits slumped in his chair, head down, and speaks in a monotone. His service dog lies quietly in front of him and is noticeably dirty with unkempt fur, although she seems well nourished and very devoted to Ken. Occasionally Ken reaches down and pets the dog on the head.

Questions

1. What are the potential obstacles to developing a positive rapport with Ken? How might you overcome them through the use of cultural humility?

2. What avenues of exploration could be initiated with Ken?

3. What environmental needs and/or wants does Ken's situation suggest? What resources might be mobilized to help him?

4. Brainstorm about what role his disability might play in his difficulties, if any. If not, why? If so, what initial directions might you wish to pursue in addressing this?

5. What developmental tasks or issues may be involved in Ken's situation?

6. What are Ken's strengths, abilities, and resources that could be tapped and capitalized on to help him at this time? Where might his abilities and challenges fit on a spectrum of ability?

Case Vignette 3

Leo is a 34-year-old Mexican American man who comes to the medical emergency room complaining of extreme paranoid feelings, auditory and visual hallucinations, extreme nausea and vomiting, and decreased sleep. He is a patient of Dr. B, who has been supplying him with valium to help with his complaints of anxiety. Leo, who is in recovery from heroin addiction, is currently in the methadone maintenance program at the county hospital. However, he is continuing to use crank (injectable amphetamines) and oral amphetamines on a regular basis along with the methadone and valium. According to Leo, he has never been involved in treatment at the county's community mental health center, although, according to county records, he has been seen many times over the past 20 years in the walk-in service. He has never followed up with treatment, however, for any length of time.

Upon evaluation, Leo is angry and morose. At one time he was probably a handsome man, but two years ago he tried to kill himself by putting the barrel of a shotgun under his chin and firing. He was high on drugs at the time, did not aim the gun barrel as he intended, and instead of killing him, the shot destroyed the lower half of his face. Even after extensive plastic surgery, he remains extremely facially disfigured and talks with the use of a mechanical voice box. Currently, it is likely that his complaints—particularly the paranoia and hallucinations—are a direct consequence of drug intoxication. He also appears to have led a fairly antisocial lifestyle, has had numerous arrests since adolescence, and has been in prison twice. Over the course of his adult life, Leo has fathered multiple children with several women but has never stayed with any of the children's mothers nor provided support for them. At this time he denies suicidal or homicidal feelings, is cooperative, and answers questions appropriately.

Questions

1. How would you define Leo's disabilities?

2. What role might his physical disability play in his current difficulties?

3. What unmet environmental needs and wants does he have? What kinds of environmental resources might you mobilize to assist him?

4. What are Leo's strengths, resources, and abilities? How could you capitalize on these in the process of helping him?

5. Leo's facial disfigurement was extreme and at times the evaluator found it awkward and discomforting to look at him. If you experienced similar feelings, how might you handle them in a way that would enable you to remain empathic and culturally humble?

6. Do you think that Leo's disfigurement is his own fault? If so, does this influence your perception of whether he deserves special consideration and rights protections as a person with a disability?

UNDERSTANDING VALUES
AND ETHICS

1. Examine the dilemmas faced by practicing social workers as they strive to achieve the profession's value ideals (Exercises 4.1 and 4.2).

2. Compare and contrast the concepts of values and ethics (Exercise 4.3).

3. Compare and contrast various approaches to learning values, identifying the pros and cons of each approach (Exercise 4.2).

4. Examine your own values priorities through the process of values clarification (Exercise 4.2).

5. Examine your personal values and compare them with social work professional values and the values you hold as perceived by others (Exercise 4.3).

6. Operationalize and apply the social work core values to specific practice situations with clients (Exercise 4.4).

7. Examine and synthesize the six core values of the social work profession (Exercise 4.5).

8. Analyze and synthesize competing alternative solutions to ethical dilemmas (Exercise 4.5 and 4.6).

9. Understand, operationalize, apply, compare, and contrast the concepts of self-determination and paternalism (Exercise 4.6).

10. Analyze and understand conditions under which paternalism may be justified (Exercise 4.6).

11. Using the Ethical Decision-Making Guidelines, analyze and resolve ethical dilemmas presented in realistic client case vignettes representing diverse clients and practice settings (Exercise 4.7).

CHAPTER OUTLINE

- Definitions: Ethical Dilemma vs. Ethical or Clinical Challenge
- Exercise 4.1: Discussion Questions
- The Process of Values Clarification as Preparation for Practice
  - ¢ Defining Values and Ethics
  - ¢ The Six Core Values of the Social Work Profession
  - ¢ Traditional Means of Learning Values

- Exercise 4.2: Rank Order
- Exercise 4.3: Exploring Your Values
- Exercise 4.4: Operationalizing the Core Values of Social Work
- Exercise 4.5: Values Application and Decision Making
- Self-Determination vs. Paternalism
- Summary of Ethical Decision-Making Guidelines
- Exercise 4.6: The Ethics Debate
- Exercise 4.7: Resolving Ethical Dilemmas

The social work profession is strongly rooted in a value base that supports and provides guidance for the NASW *Code of Ethics*, and the *Code*, in turn, provides guidance for practice decisions. Experiencing the complexities associated with social work values and ethics is critical for your professional growth because ethical issues continually arise in everyday social work practice. Professional social workers need knowledge and skills to appropriately resolve ethical dilemmas and make decisions about ethical issues affecting their clients and other stakeholders. Part of professional competence and integrity is the ability to recognize when practice issues are affected by our ethical code (e.g., issues related to client privacy and confidentiality).

In the following exercises, you will be challenged to understand how your value system can impact the helping process, thereby affecting the clients you serve. Although most of the application of ethics occurs in ordinary practice, gaining insight into the decision-making process necessary when confronted with an ethical dilemma is one of the goals for you in this chapter. Multiple exercises introduce the basic concepts related to social work values and ethics. These include a set of critical thinking and discussion questions, a rank-order values clarification exercise, an exercise on operationalizing the core values of the social work profession, an exercise addressing how to distinguish between a clinical challenge and an ethical dilemma, an "ethics debate" exercise, and an exercise on resolving ethical dilemmas. All of these exercises are designed to reinforce the fact that values and ethics impact all aspects of the social work profession and social work practice.

DEFINITIONS: ETHICAL DILEMMA VS. ETHICAL OR CLINICAL CHALLENGE

All social work practice is influenced by ethics in routine ways, so much so that ethical issues may go unnoticed by students who are new to the profession, particularly because ethics are often implemented to the benefit of clients, professionals, and organizations. However, there are times when challenges arise or when ethics conflict with one another, and it is difficult to use them to guide practice. This leads to a distinction between ethical dilemmas and ethical or clinical challenges (see Table 4.1).

Ethical dilemmas occur when two or more ethical standards or duties equally apply to a circumstance, are equally compelling, and conflict with one another when implemented.

Ethical or clinical challenges occur when one or more ethical standards applies to a situation, and it is simply difficult to implement them.

TABLE 4.1 ■ Clinical Challenges vs. Ethical Dilemmas	
Clinical challenges occur when	**Ethical dilemmas occur when**
• differing opinions exist about how to proceed	• information is complete
• information is incomplete, or	• values have been clarified, and
• values have not been clarified	• two or more options/approaches to a situation seem equally compelling and conflict with one another

Part of becoming a social worker involves learning to scan every situation and apply professional ethics. With experience, you will learn how to practice in a manner that prevents most situations from reaching the point of being an ethical dilemma.

EXERCISE 4.1: DISCUSSION QUESTIONS

Directions

- Consider the following questions on ethics and values, and jot down your thoughts about each question on a piece of paper.

- Next, share some of your thoughts with others in the class. This exchange of thoughts and ideas can be done with the class as a whole, or the discussions can be held in small groups of three or four students.

- Reading the article "Values: A Problem for Everyone" (Pilsecker, 1978) can also provide you with "food for thought" as you consider the discussion questions.

Questions

1. Have you experienced ethical dilemmas in your field placement or in your work with clients? If so, can you describe them and how they were resolved? If not, what kinds of ethical dilemmas do you think you may experience in your field placement or future practice?

2. Do you agree that the old social work mandate to be nonjudgmental is, in fact, unrealistic and unattainable? Is *not* making value judgments an impossible goal in social work practice?

3. Are the values and ethical standards that social workers set for themselves sometimes beyond their grasp? If so, why and what should be done? If not, why not?

4. If you have work or personal experience with a social work–related service or have read about social work situations in the press, have you ever observed discrepancies in the social work profession's behavior versus its stated beliefs? If so, how is this a problem? For example,

   - social workers who do not seem very empathic

   - social workers who do not seem truly supportive of client self-determination

   - social workers who tell clients what to do rather than taking a collaborative, facilitative approach

   - social workers who don't treat colleagues with respect

5. What are some of the steps you could take if you find you dislike a client or disapprove of a client's behavior or lifestyle, so that you can still provide good ethical services?

THE PROCESS OF VALUES CLARIFICATION AS PREPARATION FOR PRACTICE

Exercise 4.2 Rank Order (below) addresses the process of values clarification. However, before engaging in the exercise, a few relevant issues need to be addressed. First, we must define what is meant by the terms *values* and *ethics*. Next, we must review the social work profession's core values and discuss some of the ways people approach the process of learning values and the strengths and weaknesses of these various approaches. This is followed by engaging in the Rank Order exercise.

Defining Values and Ethics

Values are preferences with respect to which persons, groups, or societies feel an *affective regard;* values represent individuals' worldviews and core beliefs that, in turn, guide their behavior.

Ethics, though also involving affectively charged preferences, worldviews, and core beliefs, connotes a partiality to certain *actions*.

Thus, values represent verbally or behaviorally expressed preferences, while ethics represents verbally or behaviorally expressed preferences about behavior.

Values may or may not affect other people; ethics always affects other people.

In sum, *ethics are values in action* (Levy, 1976).

The Six Core Values of the Social Work Profession

1. Service

2. Social justice

3. Dignity and worth of the person

4. Importance of human relationships

5. Integrity

6. Competence (NASW, 2017a)

Traditional Means of Learning Values

1. The moralizing or imposing values approach

   Underlying assumption: My life experience has taught me a certain set of values that I believe would be right for you. Therefore, to save you the pain of coming to these values on your own and to protect you from the risk of your choosing less desirable values, I will effectively transfer my own values to you and you will accept them.

   Problems with this approach:

   a. Moralizing or imposing values is not very effective because society is inconsistent and people are exposed to many sets of values.

   b. Moralizing or imposing values doesn't help an individual to learn to develop his or her own choices with regard to values.

   c. Clients may experience painful guilt and conflict if the imposed values run counter to long-standing deeply held values.

   d. Moralizing or imposing values is paternalistic and undermines client self-determination.

   e. Clients may resist the practitioner's efforts to impose values, even to the point of discontinuing services.

   f. Moralizing or imposing values undermines the client's task of self-exploration and analysis.

2. The laissez-faire approach

   Underlying assumption: No one value system is right for everyone. People have to forge their own set of values, and I should not impose mine in any way. No one set of values is any better than any other—it is all relative. So, I'll just let my clients do and think what they want without intervening in any way, and eventually everything will turn out all right.

   Problem with this approach: Everything doesn't always turn out all right.

3. The modeling approach

   Underlying assumption: I will present myself as an attractive model who lives according to a certain set of values. My clients will be duly impressed by me and by my values and will want to adopt and emulate my attitudes and behavior.

   There are some positive aspects to this approach. For example, being a positive role model may provide clients with an example of how one can constructively manage life, akin to the notion of "lending one's ego" to the client. Modeling can also provide consistency and reliability. However, there are problems inherent in this approach and its basic assumption.

Problems with this approach:

a. Such an approach is grandiose and even arrogant.

b. Your clients are exposed to more models than just yours, and these competing models can cause confusion.

4. The values clarification approach

Underlying assumption: The values clarification approach can help the social worker and the client to build his or her own system of values. Values clarification challenges and helps the client or social worker to analyze his or her own values and identify particular areas of conflict and vulnerability. Values clarification can also help the social worker assess the compatibility of personal values with the established professional social work values.

Values clarification gained considerable traction in the 1970s and then fell out of favor in the 1980s. Kirschenbaum (1992) identifies five major reasons for the decline of values clarification during that time: changing times, faddism, stagnation, erratic implementation, and problems related to the theory of values clarification itself. However, beginning in the 1990s, values clarification was again seen as valuable in helping students and emerging professionals prepare for careers working with diverse populations, and it continues to be popular today. All values education has inherent challenges, but values clarification is generally the preferable approach for values and ethics preparation in social work (Simon et al., 1995).

Values Indicators:

Beliefs	Activities	Goals and aspirations
Attitudes	Thoughts	Interests
Morals	Feelings	Hopes and concerns

EXERCISE 4.2: RANK ORDER

Directions

- Form small groups of four or five students.

- Read each question carefully and then rank the choices of answers from first choice to last choice. As you rank each choice, try to identify the most relevant value(s) underlying and driving the choices.

- Each of you completes the exercise on your own, and then your group discusses each item, sharing similar and different answers and discussing the values underlying and driving individual choices.

- Before the class reconvenes, each small group selects the one item in the exercise that generated the most valuable discussion, and a group spokesperson is chosen to report the main points of the group's discussion.

- Alternatively, students complete the exercise individually, and then the instructor asks volunteers to share with the whole class their answers to the questions in the exercise.

Questions

1. If your unwed teenage daughter became pregnant, you would prefer that she

    _____ have an abortion

    _____ carry the pregnancy to term and then place the baby for adoption

    _____ carry the pregnancy to term and keep and raise the baby

2. Which type of change do you think would affect you the most socially, psychologically, and spiritually?

_____ to be a member of a different racial, ethnic, or cultural group

_____ to have a different sexual orientation

_____ to be born with a different gender identity

3. Which would you _least_ like to be?

_____ very poor

_____ very sickly

_____ severely facially disfigured

4. Which do you think is most harmful to one's health and to society?

_____ cigarettes

_____ marijuana

_____ alcohol

5. For which treatment do you think a medical insurance company has the greatest right to refuse coverage?

_____ erectile dysfunction medications (e.g., Viagra)

_____ bariatric (weight loss) surgery

_____ contraception

6. Governments of poor countries to whom we provide economic aid should be required to limit the families of their citizens to

_____ one child per family

_____ two children per family

_____ there should be no limit

7. Which is most important in a friendship?

_____ loyalty and support

_____ empathy and sensitivity

_____ honesty and reliability

8. As a social worker, you would find it difficult to work with

_____ an individual with faith-based or religious beliefs different from your own

_____ an individual who declares he or she holds atheist beliefs

_____ an individual who states his or her beliefs are secular in nature

9. Which of the following do you want most?

_____ to be liked

_____ to be respected

_____ to be envied

10. If you were president of the United States, which domestic issue would you give the highest priority?

_____ the economy

_____ health care

_____ the environment and climate change

11. You have been dating someone for three months. You realize they are not the person for you. How would you communicate this?

    _____ You set up a time to talk over coffee

    _____ You give the person a call

    _____ You send a text message

12. You are married, work full time, and have two small children to raise. Your mother died several years ago, and your father is in the late stage of Alzheimer's disease. What would you do?

    _____ care for your father in your home

    _____ arrange for your father to live in a nursing home

    _____ arrange for in-home care for your father in his own apartment

EXERCISE 4.3: EXPLORING YOUR VALUES

The purpose of this exercise is to explore and assess (1) how similar, or congruent, your self-identified values are with the social work core values and (2) how congruent your self-identified values are with the values that others perceive you hold.

Directions

- Ask five of your friends to list six values they perceive you believe and embrace. Ask them to rank those values from most important to least important.

- Review their lists and answer the questions below.

- Explore the possible sources of the incongruence and discuss with a classmate how such incongruence might be resolved.

- Alternatively, answer the questions as part of a journal entry or reaction paper.

Questions

1. How do your friends' lists compare with the six core values of social work?

2. How do your friends' lists compare with the values you self-identified in Exercise 4.2: Rank Order?

3. Where are the three value sets congruent with each other?

4. Where are the three value sets incongruent?

EXERCISE 4.4: OPERATIONALIZING THE CORE VALUES OF SOCIAL WORK

The goal of this exercise is to assist you in developing skills for operationalizing and applying the social work core values in specific practice situations with clients. It will also enable you to think about how various behaviors by clients can present challenges with communication and motivation that make it difficult to establish rapport.

Directions

- Form pairs or small groups with an even number of students.

- One group member reads each client statement aloud.

- Identify which of the core values are germane to the situation and which of the behaviors involved in the client's message interfere with building rapport, acceptance, and respect (see Table 4.2).

- With a partner, take turns playing the role of the client and the practitioner. The practitioner tries to formulate a response to the client's statement that addresses the challenges and also implements the relevant social work core value(s).

- Reverse roles and repeat.

- If you and your partner(s) are having difficulty with the exercise, ask your instructor to perform a demonstration by taking on the role of the practitioner and then role playing the scenario.

Client Statements: Micro Vignettes

1. Rural mother living in dilapidated but neatly kept home; her children are shabbily dressed but appear adequately nourished and healthy:

   "You city folk don't seem to understand that you don't have to have a fancy home and tons of luxuries to have a good life and raise good kids."

2. Adult client as interview ends and next appointment is discussed:

   "Oh, just work me into your schedule where it's convenient for you. Just let me know when you want me to come, and I'll get there somehow I guess." (hangs head and looks at the floor)

3. Adult client as interview ends and next appointment is discussed:

   "I can't wait a whole week to see you again—please, please—I feel so awful—can't I come back again tomorrow?" (begins to cry)

4. Female client arrives at walk-in clinic asking to talk to somebody, but after giving her name, she is silent, staring at the floor.

5. Young adult client has seen social worker for one month and sends the following text message:

   "I don't think this is helping. I don't think you care, so I am not coming back."

Client Statements: Mezzo Vignettes

6. Adolescent male client is a new client in a solution-focused group that is part of the treatment program in a juvenile justice group home. During introductions of each member at the beginning of the session, client slouches in the chair and crosses his arms over his chest:

   "I don't want to be here, and I got nothing to talk about."

TABLE 4.2 ■ Core Values and Client Behavior Challenges	
Six Core Values of Social Work (NASW, 2017a)	**Client Behavior Challenges in Building Rapport (Hepworth & Larsen, 1990)**
1. Service	1. Perceives self as helpless
2. Social justice	2. Silence or withdrawal
3. Dignity and worth of the person	3. Aggression or sullen behavior
4. Importance of human relationships	4. Uses patterns which may be seen as manipulative or exploitive
5. Integrity	5. Makes self-effacing statements
6. Competence	6. Responds passively
	7. Shows "normal" resistance to change

7. Group member in first group session for convicted sex offenders:

   "Yo, look people, the only reason I'm here is because I was framed, man. But, hey, you guys look like you need help—just ask me anything, and I'll give you some good advice." (laughs in a sarcastic manner)

8. Group member in a smoking cessation group takes a Snapchat image of a fellow group member, noting how "hot" the person is, thinking no one in the group will see it. Another group member gets a screenshot of it and reports it to the social worker.

Client Statement: Macro Vignettes

9. Hillside Community Association community member says to the social worker,

   "I hear you had a pop-up protest about the police incident three days ago. You know, I would have been there, but I didn't get the message. A lot more people would have been there. Everybody is not on Facebook!"

10. Older adult client during a tenant organization meeting:

    "You've come here to help straighten up this neighborhood? Hah! As if someone like you knows anything about what we're going through!"

EXERCISE 4.5: VALUES APPLICATION AND DECISION MAKING

The goal of this exercise is to help you better identify which values and standards apply to situations and whether the situation involves a clinical/ethical challenge or an actual ethical dilemma. The exercise also asks you to think about how you can keep the work at the level of a clinical challenge.

Directions

- Form groups of three to five.
- Select a spokesperson.
- Read the case vignettes one at a time and identify the values, standards, and mandates that apply to the situation.
- Determine whether the vignette presents an ethical dilemma or clinical challenge.
- Explore what you might do in this situation.
- Reconvene as a class and have the spokespersons share what the groups decided.
- Explore whether perspectives shifted after hearing from other groups.

Case Vignette 1

You are an intake worker in a small community mental health center's outpatient clinic. You are midway through the initial interview with a person who looks vaguely familiar, but you cannot place the person. The person mentions using exercise to cope in the past, and you recall that you have seen the person at the local fitness center where you and your family belong. In fact, your children and the person's may have been in some of the same activities. You may have to interact in that setting.

Case Vignette 2

You work as an elementary school social worker in a well-regarded school district. Two major employers have recently left the area. Quite a few families have one or more adult members out of work, leading to financial and housing hardships. Students who had lived in the district are now "staying with" relatives elsewhere yet wish to stay in the district schools. The McKinney-Vento Act should allow them to, as homeless youth. There are additional costs to the district in terms of verification, coordination, and transportation when working with homeless youth, and the state has not offered additional financial support to do this work. The district knows that these students are not performing as well, which could impact their scores on state tests and meeting No Child Left Behind progress and attendance standards. You think the pressure from these policies and their implementation has created a barrier to continued district enrollment for many students, thus further marginalizing them.

Case Vignette 3

You are working with an 83-year-old woman in her home, providing care management services. In your quarterly assessments, you are noticing a pattern of memory loss and decreased cognitive functioning. You are concerned that it is increasingly unsafe for her to live alone. You have suggested she have a formal cognitive assessment from her family doctor or from a specialty clinic. She has refused. Her adult children live nearby but only see her a few times a year.

Case Vignette 4

You and Marcel are employed by ABC Counseling Services. You have been colleagues for six years. Lately you have noticed that he is arriving late a few times per week. He has asked you to cover his on-call several times and even a therapy session with a family that used to be assigned to you, which he forgot. When you asked if anything was wrong, he said "no." Last week, you fielded an emergency call from one of his clients. When you pulled up her record, his last note didn't match the date she told you they last saw one another or the content she reported. She also didn't seem to know how the agency's clients are supposed to get help for emergencies. You have never had that experience with one of Marcel's clients before.

Case Vignette 5

Students have access to electronic medical records as a part of their field placement in a larger health system. During some downtime at field, one student looks up an aunt's medical record, wanting to find out if a family rumor was true that she had an "oops" pregnancy and an abortion. You walk in and ask what that student is doing. When you realize it is not related to his or her assigned patients, what do you do?

SELF-DETERMINATION VS. PATERNALISM

As social workers, we highly value and seek to foster client self-determination. However sometimes, under certain circumstances, a decision or action that is paternalistic may be warranted. How do we decide when paternalism, which limits self-determination, is warranted? The goal of the next two exercises is to provide an opportunity for you to address and resolve such challenging and often complex ethical dilemmas using realistic practice situations. Prior to commencing the exercises, the following concepts and issues should be discussed.

Self-determination may be defined as the right and need of clients to be accorded freedom in making their own choices and decisions about important issues in their lives. The social worker's role in relation to supporting self-determination is to allow clients maximum control over their destiny and, when there are limits, safeguarding clients' interests and rights.

Paternalism implies, "I know what is best for you." There are conditions under which paternalism may be justified:

1. When the client is a minor child and is thus assumed to lack the developmental capacity to make an informed decision

2. When the client is considered mentally incompetent or lacking in rationality, to the extent of being unable to comprehend the results of decisions

3. When the potentially negative consequences of a client's action are far reaching and may be irreversible

4. When temporary interference with liberty insures future freedom and autonomy

SUMMARY OF ETHICAL DECISION-MAKING GUIDELINES

Whenever considering two or more options in resolving an ethical dilemma, the social worker must choose the option that

1. Adheres to the social work profession's *Code of Ethics*

2. Is guided by the social work profession's core values

3. Is more efficient (relative cost to achieve stated objective)

4. Is more effective (the degree to which the desired outcome is achieved)

5. Protects the worth, dignity, and opportunities of all persons

6. Protects society's interests and/or furthers the welfare of society as a whole, rather than that of any one segment

7. Protects the client's rights and furthers his or her welfare

8. Causes the least harm, the least permanent harm, and/or the most easily reversible harm (Lowenberg & Dolgoff, 1988, pp. 108–127)

EXERCISE 4.6: THE ETHICS DEBATE

Ethical conflicts often present alternatives that are diametrically opposed. This exercise is designed to give you the experience of dealing with such a situation, comparing and contrasting alternative actions, deciding on a course of action, and developing a rationale for your choice of action utilizing critical thinking skills. What ought to emerge from the discussion is the recognition that to resolve an ethical dilemma, one must think beyond the literal "rules" of the NASW *Code of Ethics* to base the choice upon its underlying values. This exercise should also provide the experience of publicly affirming a particular position and defending it, a common experience you will face in "real-world" social work practice.

Directions

- Form groups of four to six.

- Read through the two case vignettes and then choose one of them to analyze.

- Determine which ethical standards apply and whether any other obligations apply.

- Analyze how the social worker ought to respond to the issue, taking either position A or position B. If your group cannot support either position, it may develop its own position and course of action.

- Develop and write up a defense of the position on the basis of the *Code of Ethics*, the Six Core Social Work Values, and the Ethical Decision-Making Guidelines.

- Choose a spokesperson to take notes. After working on the task for 20–30 minutes, reconvene the class, and the spokesperson from each group will share the group's work with the rest of the class.

Case Vignette 1

Ms. Jasmine Brown, an adoption social worker, is doing a private adoption home study. Her job is to prepare the home study results and make a recommendation to the Family Court judge. The child, 10-year-old DeShawn, was born six months prior to the marriage of his biological mother and her husband. The husband, Mr. Tyrone Jackson, is seeking to formally adopt the boy, although he is not DeShawn's biological father. DeShawn carries his mother's maiden surname, Jones. Ms. Brown learns that DeShawn wants his name changed to Jackson but is not aware that the only father he has ever known is not his biological parent. Mr. and Mrs. Jackson insist that the social worker, the judge, and the attorneys maintain the fiction that Mr. Jackson is the biological parent and that they are simply going to court to "set the record straight." The social worker has found no other compelling reasons for a negative recommendation to the judge but is concerned that this dishonesty would create problems in the family eventually, which could have a serious impact upon the child's development and his relationship with his parents.

What should the social worker do?

A. Recommend approval of the adoption petition. The judge has stated that it is legally possible to approve the petition without destroying the "fiction" because DeShawn's biological father has not been heard from since before DeShawn was born.

B. Recommend that approval be denied unless or until DeShawn has been given full and accurate information.

Case Vignette 2

Mrs. Irma Johnson, a 92-year-old, alert, very wealthy widow, living alone without children, has fallen frequently in the last five years, on one occasion breaking her hip. A public health social worker, Ms. Rosario Gonzales, was called to her home by neighbors because of their concern that she should not live alone, and during this visit, as they walked around the house, Mrs. Johnson fell once and stumbled while walking several other times. Mrs. Johnson wants to continue to live independently in her home, she refuses to hire a home health aide to live with her, and she is supported in this by her priest, who feels it is her right to make these decisions. Although she does not have much experience with technology, she saw a TV ad for a fall sensor system that can be installed in homes. Mrs. Johnson's oldest nephew and his wife, who have periodically taken care of her in their condominium, are no longer able to do so because they have become quite frail in health. The nephew wants to have Mrs. Johnson placed in a nursing home or have an aide live with her for his aunt's own safety.

What should the social worker do?

A. Accept Mrs. Johnson's wish to live alone, without a home health aide, even though it is obvious she is not able to care for herself.

B. Work with the nephew to have her placed in the nursing home, or to hire someone to stay with her, even though she resists this, saying, "I can take care of myself." This will require having her declared incompetent by the court so that someone else can control her finances and make these arrangements for her.

EXERCISE 4.7: RESOLVING ETHICAL DILEMMAS

In this exercise, you are going to explore situations in which values, ethical standards, regulation, and laws suggest taking different actions. These actions will affect the various parties (social worker, client, colleagues, organization, or community) differently. Choices will, in all likelihood, have some negative outcomes. Practice at this point may be about figuring out how to maximize positive outcomes, minimize negative outcomes, and maintain relationships.

Directions

- Form groups of four to six. Each group can choose or be assigned one of the case vignettes.

- Analyze the chosen or assigned vignette, and imagine you are the social worker depicted in the case.

- Guided by your answers to the questions following each vignette, outline the steps you would take in resolving the ethical dilemma(s) presented in the case and the actions you would take as the social worker.

A suggestion: Some of the vignettes are quite challenging, and if you have little to no previous social work practice experience, you may want to ask your instructor to collaboratively work with your group to resolve the ethical dilemmas.

Case Vignette 1

Yolanda is a licensed social worker at the local faith-based refugee resettlement program. One day she interviews a young Laotian couple who complain of stress and economic problems. They have their 7-year-old son with them. In the course of the interview, Yolanda notices that the boy's legs are bruised. She asks the child how he got hurt, and he acts frightened and clings to his mother's skirt. Eventually it is revealed that when the father drinks and is under stress, he beats the boy with a stick. Both parents agree that they need help and say that they will follow through with counseling, but they beg the social worker not to report them to Child Protective Services. The father is afraid it would result in their child being taken away from them, "and he is all we have." Plus, they are concerned that such a report would place continued receipt of services at risk, and they fear deportation because they are undocumented. However, the husband refuses to get help with his drinking and states that he doesn't have a problem there. The mother is very passive, not really stating her own opinion and allowing her husband to speak for her. The session ends with the family's stating that they will refuse counseling if there is a report "because that will mean you really don't want to help us."

Questions

1. Which NASW core values, ethical principles, or standards and regulatory/statutory codes are applicable and relevant to this vignette?

2. What cultural issues are embedded in the family's situation and presentation in the interview?

3. Should Yolanda report the family to Child Protective Services?

4. How should the issue of the father's drinking be addressed?

5. What possible consequences might ensue with your plan? What actions would you recommend to minimize negative consequences and to maintain a helping relationship?

Case Vignette 2

Jack is a mental/behavioral health agency social worker in the role of "officer of the day" for crisis situations. One day, several people come to the agency to complain about their neighbor, a young man named Bob who is well known to Jack and the mental health center and has been treated for years, off and on, for paranoid schizophrenia. The neighbors report that Bob has been hanging empty milk cartons from all the branches of the trees in his front yard. He also has tied brightly colored bows on the trees along with other odd ornaments. He has been piling old junk and garbage in his yard; the neighbors complain the whole thing is an eyesore, and it smells bad. Bob has been seen sitting on his fence and talking to himself, and the neighbors state that they are "just sure he is going to do something." Later in the day, Jack makes a home visit to see Bob, and Bob is the same as he always has been, although he seems more anxious and admits to hearing voices. He denies any suicidal or homicidal thoughts, and Jack concludes that Bob does not qualify for civil commitment. It is left that Bob will take the bus to the clinic to meet with Jack tomorrow and see the crisis psychiatrist for a medication evaluation. When the neighbors are informed of this, they threaten to make sure Jack is fired. Agency policy is to provide clients with the least restrictive alternative and to keep community relations positive as well.

Questions

1. Which NASW core values, ethical principles, or standards and regulatory/statutory codes are applicable and relevant to this vignette?

2. Should Jack "stretch" the civil commitment criteria and hospitalize Bob anyway and thus pacify the neighbors—and perhaps Bob would improve a little?

3. Should Jack interpret the civil commitment criteria strictly, respect Bob's right to live as he pleases, and work out some other course of action? If so, what alternative actions could be taken?

4. How should Jack balance the need to respond to the community with Bob's individual needs and rights?

5. What possible consequences might ensue from your plan? What actions would you recommend to minimize negative consequences and to maintain all relationships?

Case Vignette 3

George, a BASW social worker attending an MSW program part time, works in a secured unit in a nursing facility. One day, he observes that in the course of responding to physical aggression by one of the residents, one of the aides surreptitiously kicks the resident in the stomach. This particular resident suffers from late-stage Alzheimer's disease and has been labeled a "screamer" by the staff because he goes through times when he yells for no discernable reason, which annoys the staff. Later, after the kicking incident, the resident begins to cough up blood. The nursing home doctor asks the staff if they observed any injuries occurring because the large black and blue bruise on the resident's stomach area is obvious and was not noted in the medical record. All the other staff present during the incident deny they saw anything unusual. The social worker is not sure what to do. He has had problems achieving cooperation with the aides and is the only social worker in the facility, but it seems to him that this resident was abused, although no serious physical damage was sustained, according to the examining doctor's report. Reporting the aide would result in outside agencies opening an investigation in the facility.

Questions

1. Which NASW core values, ethical principles, or standards and regulatory/statutory codes are applicable and relevant to this vignette?

2. Should George speak to his direct supervisor and leave the decision up to him or her?

3. Should George report elder abuse to the appropriate authorities, even though the resident is unlikely to be able to help with an investigation and other employees are reporting that they saw nothing?

4. What possible consequences might ensue from your plan? What actions would you recommend to minimize negative consequences and to maintain all relationships?

Case Vignette 4

Adrian is a licensed clinical social worker who works in the outpatient department of a large community mental/behavioral health center. Six weeks ago a client, Gary, was referred to her for treatment with the goal of helping him to improve his interpersonal relationships. He stated that he could not seem to make and keep friends and wanted help. Over the course of treatment, it was revealed gradually that Gary is actually quite paranoid, and Adrian thinks that he probably has a paranoid personality disorder. He is not psychotic and does not use drugs. During the most recent session with Gary, the subject of his recently estranged wife surfaced. Upon broaching the subject, Gary became very agitated and began talking about how he feels his ex-wife has been trying to plot to have Gary lose his job. With clenched fists, he tells Adrian that he is going "to take care of her once and for all. She'll never bother me again, that's for sure." Upon further questioning, Gary reveals he has several guns and plenty of ammunition. He shows her an app on his phone that he is using to track his estranged wife. While looking at his phone, Adrian realizes that she could activate the smart phone's tracking app so others could track him. He concludes by telling the social worker that if she tells anyone about this, he'll kill himself.

Questions

1. Which NASW core values, ethical principles, or standards and regulatory/statutory codes are applicable and relevant to this vignette?

2. Should Adrian break client confidentiality and warn the ex-wife about Gary's threats?

3. Should Adrian activate the tracking device on Gary's phone?

4. How should Adrian handle Gary's suicidal threat?

5. What about Adrian's own safety?

6. What possible consequences might ensue from your plan? What actions would you recommend to minimize negative consequences and to maintain all relationships while ensuring the safety of all?

Case Vignette 5

Pepita is a medical social worker in a rural public hospital emergency department. The hospital also houses a 12-bed psychiatric inpatient unit. Around midnight, a thin bedraggled young man rings the ED buzzer asking for a place to stay. The man is dirty, says he hasn't eaten for days, shows evidence that he is on Social Security disability, but is not showing overt psychiatric symptoms. He denies suicidal or homicidal ideation as well, although he is depressed about his situation. Pepita calls all over the county to all the shelters; at this time at night they are all full, and resources in this particular area are very scarce to begin with. It is pouring rain outside (though it is a warm night), and the client pleads with Pepita to let him in the hospital, claiming that the cold he has will turn into pneumonia if he has to sleep under the freeway overpass (as he has been doing the past few nights). There is one bed available on the psychiatric unit, but it is strict hospital policy that patients should not be admitted unless they are in need of acute psychiatric care, which this individual does not appear to require. It is a busy night in the ED with medical emergencies, and the admitting MD says to Pepita, "I will admit him if you want, but you have to take the flack from administration if there is any pushback."

Questions

1. Which NASW core values, ethical principles, or standards and regulatory/statutory codes are applicable and relevant to this vignette?

2. Should Pepita recommend admission and get the MD to sign the order?

3. Should Pepita recommend against admission and take some other course of action with this man?

4. What possible consequences might ensue from your plan? What is the impact on the man, the collegial relationships, and the hospital?

Case Vignette 6

Joe is a medical social worker in a large university teaching hospital. Joe's primary job is to work with terminally ill patients and their families, helping them adjust to the illness and prepare for the eventual death of their loved one. Currently he is seeing a patient who was recently diagnosed as having a large malignant brain tumor. The tumor is of the kind that does not produce much pain, and, therefore, the patient is perplexed by the fact that his doctor is advising that he remain in the hospital when he doesn't feel sick. The tumor is inoperable, and there is no question the patient will die within the next six months. The family is adamant about not telling the patient that he is terminal. The patient is insisting that Joe tell him the truth. The doctor tells Joe to do "whatever you think is best, but don't upset my patient." Joe believes that patients have the right to know the truth; he firmly believes in an individual's right to work through death and dying issues but feels caught between a rock and a hard place.

Questions

1. Which NASW core values, ethical principles, or standards and regulatory/statutory codes are applicable and relevant to this vignette?

2. How should Joe balance the patient's needs and questions, the doctor's position, and the request posed by the family?

3. What possible consequences might ensue from your plan? What actions would you recommend to minimize negative consequences and to maintain all relationships?

COMMUNICATING: EMPATHY AND AUTHENTICITY

LEARNING OBJECTIVES

1. Recognize and apply the core facilitative conditions necessary for the development of positive rapport during in-class role plays (Exercise 5.1).

2. Achieve a beginning level of skill in communicating empathy by practicing the application of empathic communication skills during in-class role plays (Exercise 5.1).

3. Compare and contrast the concepts of empathy and sympathy (Exercise 5.2).

4. Evaluate the various ways empathic communication can be useful in helping relationships (Exercises 5.1, 5.2, 5.3).

5. Analyze the impact of poor empathic and authenticity skills (Exercise 5.2).

6. Analyze handling challenges in rapport building using content-to-process shifting (Exercise 5.3).

CHAPTER OUTLINE

- Key Concepts for Discussion
    - ¢ What Is Involved in Empathic Communication?
    - ¢ What Is the Difference Between Empathy and Sympathy?
    - ¢ How Empathic Communication Is Useful
- Exercise 5.1: Developing Empathy and Rapport
- Exercise 5.2: "Of Course I Want to Help You"
- Exercise 5.3: Handling Challenges in Rapport Building: Content-to-Process Shifting
- Technology and Communication
- Exercise 5.4: Some Tech Play

This chapter addresses the first building block of skill development, which is how to communicate with clients in an authentic and empathic manner in order to develop rapport. Developing rapport involves gaining the client's trust and fostering open, effective communication, which is critical to any form of social work, whether you are working with an individual or working with a community neighborhood group. Developing rapport successfully with a client depends on certain practitioner characteristics, including a nonjudgmental attitude and accepting the client as a person with inherent worth and dignity.

KEY CONCEPTS FOR DISCUSSION

The following are some key concepts for you to discuss with your classmates and instructor prior to working on the exercises.

Core or facilitative conditions that must be present for a successful helping relationship to develop:

1. Respect, warmth, and unconditional positive regard drawn directly from employing the social work core values

2. The communication of empathy to the client

3. Presenting oneself with authenticity or genuineness, which refers to the sharing of self with another person in a natural, sincere, spontaneous, and open manner

What Is Involved in Empathic Communication?

Empathy is essentially the emotional and cognitive reactions that an individual has to the observed experiences of another (Davis, 1983). Carl Rogers (1961) defined *empathy* as "accurate understanding of the [client's] world as seen from the inside. To sense the [client's] private world as if it were your own, but without losing the 'as if' quality—this is empathy" (p. 284). Empathy, then, is the social worker's "ability to perceive and communicate, accurately and with sensitivity, the feelings of the client and the meaning of those feelings" as the client shares and describes his or her situation and concerns (Fischer, 1973, p. 329).

Empathic communication involves the accurate perception of and the ability to clearly communicate with the client about his or her inner feelings and emotional state at the moment, with respect and without judgment. Empathy nurtures and sustains the helping relationship, creating an accepting, nonthreatening, and supportive atmosphere. Empathy is essentially the means by which the practitioner and client become emotionally significant to each other, thus fostering a reciprocal attachment and a mutual commitment to the helping process.

Sympathy, on the other hand, engenders either (1) a feeling of care or sorrow for another's circumstances or (2) a common understanding when different people share the same interests. Although a close kin to empathy, sympathy does not require the social worker to gain an accurate understanding of the client's perspective, nor is it reasonable to expect the social worker to share the experiences of all his or her clients.

For example, a client tells the social worker that her husband just announced that he wants a divorce. The social worker responds:

Sympathy: "Oh my gosh, I feel so bad for you. When my husband left me, I was devastated."

Empathy: "I imagine you are feeling shocked and both sad and angry about what has just happened."

Empathy involves the ability to communicate the following to the client:

1. Your perception and understanding of the client's immediate surface feelings related to their situation and concerns

2. Your perception and understanding of the client's underlying deeper feelings and emotions

3. Your perception and understanding of the client's verbal and nonverbal communications

What Is the Difference Between Empathy and Sympathy?

Sympathy connotes "I would feel and do the same as you have in the same situation" and, thus, provides no guidance for the client.

Empathy means genuinely understanding and accurately perceiving the other person's feelings and situation without taking that person's position, thus retaining one's separateness and objectivity, but also without becoming cold or distant. Empathy also "throws out a rope" to the client and provides support.

How Empathic Communication Is Useful

1. Empathy facilitates the development of positive rapport and a supportive therapeutic alliance with the client.

2. Empathy facilitates bridging ethnic and cultural differences, by communicating the desire to understand and appreciate clients' unique views and perceptions.

3. Empathy enables the social worker to "start where the client is" and keep attuned to changes in clients' moods, feelings, and reactions.

4. Empathic communication helps in gathering assessment data therapeutically and assessing clients' strengths and problem areas more accurately.

5. Empathy enables the social worker to accurately perceive and respond to clients' nonverbal messages as conveyed by their body language, tone of voice, etc.

6. Empathy softens and makes more palatable the delivery of bad or unwelcome news to clients.

7. Empathy facilitates engaging involuntary and resistant clients.

8. Empathy facilitates developing rapport with clients we may not like. For example, the client may have engaged in behavior contrary to our personal and professional values, but separating the person from the behavior and empathizing with the person can facilitate connection without condoning the behavior.

9. Empathic communication helps in engaging, de-escalating, and working with suicidal and angry/aggressive clients.

10. Empathic communication helps in facilitating family, group, and community discussions.

11. Empathy facilitates clients' self-exploration of wants, needs, feelings, and goals.

EXERCISE 5.1: DEVELOPING EMPATHY AND RAPPORT

Directions

- In pairs or groups of three, one member of the pair plays the role of the practitioner, one plays the role of the client, and the third (if present) is an observer.

- Begin with the "client" saying the client statement and then the "practitioner" responding to the statement. The observer will note what the practitioner does well and generate ideas for alternative ways to connect empathically to the client.

- Keep role playing back and forth, with the goal of utilizing empathic communication to establish rapport. Switch roles of client, practitioner, and observer so all have the experience of each role.

- Each group will be assigned one client statement and answer the questions posed below in relation to that statement.

- After a half hour of practice, the class will reconvene and each group will role play its client statement, including a few responses of dialogue, for constructive feedback.

Note to Instructor: There are more scenarios than the class can do in a half hour. Please choose those that best fit the needs of your students. In the large group discussion, explore how diversity in gender, race, socioeconomic status, sexual orientation, and faith might impact the establishment of rapport and the social justice issues that impact the circumstances.

Questions

Questions to consider as you role play and when choosing what to show to the class for your assigned client statement:

For the Client and the Observer

1. Do you feel your partner has responded empathically?

2. Has your partner accurately reflected the types of feelings and level of intensity of feeling that you implied in your side of the dialogue?

3. Did your partner's responses encourage you to share further?

4. Did your partner respond well in terms of nonverbal messages (e.g., tone of voice, eye contact, gestures)?

For All Roles

1. What are the apparent surface feelings? What are the probable deeper feelings?

2. How could your partner have responded better to your initial statement and other parts of the dialogue?

3. What level of empathy is being displayed?

4. Do the person's features of diversity impact how you respond? Do your features of diversity impact your response?

Client Statement 1

Young Hispanic man, age 21, on probation for motor vehicle theft and reckless driving. His probation officer has sent him for counseling because the probation officer is concerned about the client's inability to control his temper:

"Look, man, I don't need no social worker. I've got to find me a job and a place to crash—the courts have messed me over enough already. I don't have nothing to talk about."

Client Statement 2

South Asian American man, age 36, practitioner of Hinduism and a new member of an alcohol rehabilitation group:

"Hey, you know, I don't know why I'm here really. I used to drink, but I don't anymore and things are going real great. You people look like you've got problems though—well, maybe I can help you—you, know, give you advice and stuff." (Client continues to talk in this manner for a while longer; speech is a bit loud and pressured, hands clasped together tightly; client sits forward rigidly in his chair.)

Client Statement 3

Chinese American man, age 87, who has recently been diagnosed with cancer and is the primary caregiver for his 83-year-old wife, who has Alzheimer's disease:

"I came today because Dr. Smith said that I need to come. I really don't understand why or what you can possibly do for me. My days are very busy, and I don't like to leave my wife alone, even in the waiting area. She needs me at all times. In fact, some of the doctor's ideas for treatment are not going to work for me at all."

Client Statement 4

Caucasian man, age 40, referred for anger management classes by his parole officer. He is on parole after serving 20 years in prison for the brutal rape of his 7-year-old stepdaughter. He glares at the social worker, and the social worker feels revulsion:

"Look, b**ch, you and my PO [parole officer] can just go to hell. I served my time and I'm done with this sh*t. And I'm supposed to register as a sex offender? Forget it—I'm out of here."

Client Statement 5

Hispanic woman, age 24, at the community mental health center outpatient clinic for the first time for "nerve problems." She talks in a very soft, barely audible voice, eyes downcast, hands clenched in her lap:

"I don't know why I'm here. I don't know what you can do for me. I feel awful; I can't think anymore. Sometimes I hear things—*mi mama* says I'm *volviendo loca*—you know, that I'm crazy. . . . I think I just have bad nerves, not *loca*."

Client Statement 6

Middle class African American woman, age 70, talking to social worker at senior citizen center:

"Dear, I know you mean well, but I just can't seem to get interested in the activities here. Ever since Chris died—you know, my late partner Chris—I just don't have any energy anymore. I don't think there's anything here for me. Besides, I don't drive, and it is hard for me to take the bus all the way over here."

Client Statement 7

Caucasian woman, age 35, mother of five children aged 7 to 18 years old. As she talks, she is teary eyed and wrings her hands:

"I just can't handle my kids anymore. My 15-year-old son, Brent, is the worst. He back talks me, stays out at night, and sleeps all day. Couldn't you have somebody come out and talk to him? I just can't do anything right. I need help—my nerves are shot."

Client Statement 8

Caucasian person, age 17, with dropping grades and who seems increasingly unhappy at school. Ze may also be exploring zir sexuality: as you have heard student rumors of zir dating people of both genders,

"Look, I know you want to help me with my grades and stuff, but really I don't know how you and my parents can expect me to learn in this school. Everyone is so lame and closed minded. The kids say such stupid things all the time, and everyone is running around pretending to be some 'big' thing. It is not like anyone can be real here or that you or my parents can even get this."

Client Statement 9 (Mezzo Example)

A child welfare social worker is meeting with a group of police officers about how to improve agency-police working relationships. After the social worker introduces himself, a police officer says,

"I've got to be honest here. I'm sick and tired of spending most of my time on social work–type calls—domestic violence, abused kids—my job is to deal with crime. The kind of calls that should go to you all take up too much of an officer's time."

Client Statement 10 (Macro Example)

A group of neighbors (some white, some African American) are meeting with the social worker at the small community center in their poverty-stricken neighborhood at the request of the Neighborhood Watch program:

"I know you mean well, but you're driving a nice car, you're educated, and you've probably had a real good life. I don't see how you can understand where we're coming from or why you'd really care. We've had social workers come in before to help us, and they don't do much; they leave, and we're back where we were before."

EXERCISE 5.2: "OF COURSE I WANT TO HELP YOU"

Listening and responding empathically are two important skills a social worker must learn in order to establish therapeutic relationships. Clients can communicate powerful emotional content that can leave an inexperienced social worker searching for the appropriate way to respond. It is equally as important for social workers to show authenticity or genuineness throughout communication with a client. The ability to respond in a natural, open, and caring manner is crucial to the growth of the therapeutic relationship and the growth of the client.

Directions

- This case scenario can be demonstrated in front of the entire class, with one student playing the role of the social worker and the other the client.

- Each student in the class should answer the following questions and be prepared to engage in the class discussion about this case scenario.

Questions

1. Is the social worker more sympathetic or empathetic in his or her responses?

2. What are the differences between the two concepts?

3. Is a therapeutic relationship being established? If so, why? If not, why not?

4. Do you think the social worker is empathic/authentic in response to the client's situation?

5. What are the missed empathy/authenticity cues?

6. What might you do differently?

Case Scenario

Charles is a 26-year-old Caucasian single male. He has a history of depression and drug abuse. He has only had one hospitalization due to suicidal ideation that occurred after a night of heavy drug use. He has limited family support and often moves back and forth between his parents' home and friends' apartments for shelter. He is on medication for depression, and he attends NA meetings regularly. He is a bright young man with aspirations to be an auto mechanic. He has been unable to complete his education due to depressive episodes and drug abuse. This is Charles's second meeting with the social worker.

Social Worker:	Hello, Charles. It's good to see you again. Glad you're able to make it. Take a seat.
Charles:	Thanks, I am feeling a lot better and ready to give the auto mechanic training program a try once again; I can't wait to get started. I really am ready this time.
Social Worker:	Are you sure you're ready and can you afford it? It's my understanding that a job was your top priority.
Charles:	I haven't felt this good in months, my motivation is high, and I am determined to stay out of trouble and away from negative influences. Yes, a job is important, and I will find something part-time. I can do two things at once, you know.
Social Worker:	That's what my son said a couple of months ago when he tried taking on too much. Well, we shall see. Where are you staying now? Are you with your parents or with your friends?
Charles:	Right now, I'm with my parents. I feel bad depending on them. You know, it's hard for them. I can see the sadness in their eyes. I know I am a failure. I should have achieved so much more at this point in my life.
Social Worker:	Well, at least you have a place to stay. We don't have many homeless shelters in this city, so count your blessings. Oh, and you should be thankful that your parents are still around.
Charles:	I love my parents. Do you think I want to be a burden to them?
Social Worker:	That's encouraging to hear. They have gone through a lot lately. Other than your desire to continue the auto mechanic program again, what else is on your mind? I have worked with many young men just like you, struggling trying to find their way.
Charles:	Well, I am unique with my own set of problems, and everyone is different, right?

Social Worker:	Of course, but with my experience, I should be able to help you move on with your life in a positive and productive manner.
Charles:	I really don't want to rush things. It's important that I take advantage of all you have to offer. I have been in so much pain over the past two years and have disappointed not only myself but friends and family.
Social Worker:	No one escapes pain in this world, Charles. The question is what do you do with your pain? Do you let it keep you out of the game of life or do you confront it head on? Only you can decide. Did you watch the game last night?
Charles:	What does basketball have to do with what we're talking about? Are you sure you want to help me?
Social Worker:	Of course, I want to help you, Charles. I was about to use a basketball analogy but changed my mind. You seem to be a little upset. Feel free to share your feelings; after all, that's why I am here.
Charles:	Hey, the more I think about it, I don't have much more to say today, maybe at the next appointment. I need to leave now.
Social Worker:	Ok, Charles, I am sorry you have to leave so soon; let's make an appointment two weeks from today.
Charles:	I will try to make it, but it all depends on what I am doing.

EXERCISE 5.3: HANDLING CHALLENGES IN RAPPORT BUILDING: CONTENT-TO-PROCESS SHIFTING

Sometimes, despite very good effort by the social worker, it is difficult to establish rapport or for the client to recognize and respond to empathic communication. A variety of factors can contribute to this reality. When this occurs, the interaction can become very frustrating for the social worker and the client alike. It may have to do with the social worker, the client, or the two together in that moment. This will present itself in many ways. It may seem as if the conversation is going nowhere, as if the client is not connecting to the social worker, or the social worker is misreading (failing to accurately "tune into") the client's feelings. The social worker may notice feelings that suggest discomfort, "stuckness," frustration, or even anger toward the client when his or her effort is unsuccessful. Rather than persisting with the interaction, shifting away from the topic (content) of the conversation to the way the conversation is happening (process) is often a way to address the moment and reconnect in an authentic way. For example, the social worker might say something like,

> Michael, I am noticing that we aren't connecting well today. It seems as if I do not really understand what you are trying to tell me and that you and I are both feeling frustrated as a result. Can we talk about that instead of how to solve the challenges with your teacher at school?

Notice that you still have an empathic statement (connecting the poor quality of the interaction to the here-and-now dynamic) in this switch to process and a self-involving response (admitting your own frustration), which is very authentic. Talking about how the talking is not going well often, but not always, leads you back to the topic in a more productive and connected manner.

Directions

- In pairs or groups of three, one member plays the social worker, one plays the client, and the third (if present) is an observer.

- Begin with the "client" and "social worker" reading the scripted statements in the case scenarios. At the end of the script, the social worker will make a content-to-process shift.

- The pair should then talk about their experience when they were not connecting well. The social worker will try to establish rapport utilizing empathic statements while discussing process.

- The observer will note what the practitioner does well and generate ideas for alternative ways to connect to the client.

- Group members should switch roles for each case scenario, playing each role at least once.

- After practice, the class will reconvene and discuss the experience.

Note to Instructor: Each case scenario has a slightly different factor contributing to the lack of connection. There is an opportunity to discuss how a physical condition can interfere in Case Scenario 1, how unresolved trauma impacts Case Scenario 2 and intersects with social worker burden, and how past bad service can interfere in Case Scenario 3.

Case Scenario 1

A social worker in a medical setting is meeting with Karen, 36 and recently diagnosed with stage 2 breast cancer. The meeting immediately follows her chemotherapy appointment that day and focuses on how to save money on transportation. She has had to stop working, and finances are tight.

Social Worker:	Hi, Karen; it's good to see you. Thanks for stopping by to talk about transportation options today. How's the chemo going?
Karen:	Yeah, it is good to see you, too. The chemo is fine, I guess. So, do you have an answer on the transportation stuff?
Social Worker:	Well, yes and no. It turns out there are no easy options, but I think there may be four or five different ways to access some less difficult options. Let me explain them.
	[Imagine social worker is talking for about 10 minutes, trying to check in with Karen so as to cover all the options. Karen's attention is fading. Karen is minimally responsive and not really focusing.]
Karen:	So, is this going to take much longer? I really need to leave.
Social Worker:	Karen, I thought this was important to you. These are choices you are going to have to make, and you cannot make them without this information. You don't seem as interested today.
Karen:	It is important to me. I just need to go.

Case Scenario 2

A social worker at community social service agency is meeting with Steve, a 62-year-old U.S. Army veteran, who lost his housing due to a recent fire. Steve has struggled with trust and relationships since leaving the service and may have untreated post-traumatic stress disorder (PTSD). The social worker is overwhelmed with all the families impacted by this fire.

Steve and the social worker have been talking for about 20 minutes. For the last 10 minutes, they have been discussing housing options. This conversation picks up midway through. Steve has been responding in vague and noncommittal ways.

Social Worker:	With the Red Cross funding, you will have about a week in the hotel, so you may want to jump on these veteran options right away.
Steve:	I suppose that's a good idea (not making eye contact).
Social Worker:	If this isn't what you want to do, you don't have to do it.
Steve:	Yeah, I know (a shudder in his body).

Social Worker:	I am just trying to get everyone some options. I can't do it without your input.
Steve:	Okay, I get that.

Case Scenario 3

A social worker at an LGBT community center meets with Gregory Jones, a 20-year-old gay man who is homeless and without reliable income. Gregory has sought help before from other agencies, and it has not gone well.

Social Worker:	Hi, Mr. Jones, it is nice to meet you. What would you like me to call you?
Gregory:	You can call me Gregory, I guess.
Social Worker:	Okay, Gregory, I got a little bit of information from the person who did your intake. She shared that you are 20 years old, living on your own, and currently without any income or work. Is that accurate?
Gregory:	Yes, it is.
Social Worker:	Okay. While that is a lot of information, it doesn't tell me all about you as a person. Can we spend some time getting to know each other better?
Gregory:	Sure. Why not?
Social Worker:	Would you like to tell me about you first, or vice versa?
Gregory:	Tell me something about you.
Social Worker:	I am a licensed social worker in this state. I have been practicing for about eight years at this agency. I work with people who need to find jobs or places to live regularly; probably about 50% of my clients have a job or a housing issue. With some of the other people who work here, we are often successful in helping people. That's me professionally. What else would you want to know?
Gregory:	Do you get it?
Social Worker:	Do I get what?
Gregory:	Never mind. Most places don't get it.
Social Worker:	Are you sure? I am happy to answer anything.
Gregory:	Yeah.
Social Worker:	So, tell me something about yourself?
Gregory:	I'm from the country, just north of the city. I moved away when I was a teen. I can basically take care of myself, but my friend Gina insisted I come here. I could use a job and a place to live.
Social Worker:	Okay, do you have any hobbies or interests?
Gregory:	Not really.

TECHNOLOGY AND COMMUNICATION

Increasingly, clients and settings want to use means other than face-to-face meetings to communicate. The rationale and justifications for increased use of technology include distance, professional expertise, convenience, and/or costs. Technology, like phones, has been a part of social work practice for many years. Technologies may make social work services more readily available, but they may also make certain information more difficult to ascertain. Without the visual clues of a face-to-face interaction, the practitioner must rely on tone of voice and other

TABLE 5.1 ■ Technologies Useful in Social Work

Technology	Description	Possible Purposes
Telephone (audio)	Discussion without visual images/voice only	To get information, build rapport, provide therapy
Video	Discussion at distance with visual images via a phone or computer application	To get information; build rapport; provide therapy, coaching, or other services
E-mail/Text	Written communications	To communicate information, convey details, follow up, remind, reinforce
Smartphone apps	Behavior logs, mood logs, journals, dysfunctional thought records, geolocation for triggers, etc.	To collect baseline data or progress data, to provide with feedback, to cue skills use, to give feedback
Biofeedback devices	Heart, sleep, step, exercise monitors	Collect information about client biological functioning
Laptop computers/ tablets	Computer tools that may include some of the above technologies or be used to collect and transmit information	To create client records in real time, to allow clients to access online resources or send feedback

cues to a greater degree. It may also be more difficult to convey empathy effectively in written formats. There are also applications and software that may be used as a part of the helping process. Multiple technologies are now quite portable and all on a single device, the smartphone. Table 5.1 lists some technologies to consider.

When using technology, social workers must also consider ethics and the ethical implications of using the particular technology (NASW et al., 2017). How do we use these technologies in a manner that is consistent with HIPAA and other standards for privacy and confidentiality? How do we assure that e-mail or text communications are secure and not compromised? How do we stay up to date with a rapidly changing field of technology and security? In most cases, social workers or the agencies that employ them will need to collaborate with tech professionals. Social workers must ask these questions, but the ability to answer them is often outside our scope of practice.

Evidence is limited on the impact of the presence of these technologies in face-to-face interactions. It is also emerging for how to communicate using text and e-mail. The next exercise asks you to consider communicating about, with, or through technology.

EXERCISE 5.4: SOME TECH PLAY

Directions

- In pairs or groups of three, one person plays the social worker, one plays the client, and the third (if present) serves as an observer.

- Consider how technology affects the interaction in each of the case vignettes below.

Case Vignette 1

Gilbert Trees experiences anxiety disorder and has a history of delusions and some paranoia that he is not liked by others. The social worker is a service coordinator for the local mental health provider. This is the first meeting with him, and the social worker is supposed to enter data into the agency's system using a tablet with air card technology during the intake. Role play how you would introduce the use of the tablet with this client. (Students may pull out a laptop to do this role play.)

Case Vignette 2

Kathryn Closter lives in a remote part of the state (more than 60 miles from the nearest provider) and has lost her license due to driving while intoxicated. Part of her court order is to get therapy.

She is reluctant to get help and does not think she has a problem. The social worker is connecting with her for the first time on the phone. The social worker's agency has a protocol that allows for the possibility of video therapy services. However, before that can begin, some type of face-to-face full assessment must take place to rule out suicidality and ensure the appropriateness of remote services. Role play a telephone call to engage the client, placing your chairs back to back to eliminate the use of visual cues.

Case Vignette 3

Tanzi Walise's father was diagnosed with ALS about three months ago, and the family's whole life seems to be turned upside down. Tanzi posts the following in an online ALS discussion forum:

My dad has Lou's disease, and it seems like my whole family has turned upside down. My mom is sad but pretending to be happy. My sister doesn't come home much anymore, and my dad is trying not to lose his job. What am I supposed to do?

The social worker is the moderator for this forum today and responds to Tanzi's post. For this exercise, write responses to one another on a piece of paper. Keep in mind that other people could type in this forum, too.

COMMUNICATING: VERBAL FOLLOWING/ACTIVE LISTENING SKILLS

This chapter focuses on exercises to build and strengthen the communication skills that are essential for effective engagement, interviewing, assessment, and intervention with clients, including individuals, families, small groups, communities, or organizations. The terms *verbal communication skills, active listening skills,* and *verbal following skills* all refer to the same basic set of skills that facilitate connecting with clients, enabling clients to talk about their concerns, and establishing rapport. The umbrella term *active listening skills* includes restating, summarizing, minimal prompts or encouragers, reflecting, giving feedback, probing, validating, effective use of silence, "I" messages, and redirecting. Verbal communication skills use similar terms. In this book, the term *verbal following skills* is used, and this group of skills includes the following: furthering (minimal prompts and accent responses), paraphrasing, closed-ended responses, open-ended responses, seeking concreteness, summarizing, and providing and maintaining focus (Hepworth et al., 2017).

FUNDAMENTALS OF COMMUNICATION AND FEEDBACK

Communication in all forms, and particularly spoken communication, is the cornerstone of social work. Most social work students communicate so easily that they do not think of all its components. Before exploring the specific skills, it is good to recall the elements of communication, and, that as social workers, it is your duty to assure that you are communicating effectively with your clients, whether your client is an individual, a group, a family, or a community.

Communication involves several actions that usually occur without much conscious thought (see Diagram 6.1). The first person to begin the communication decides upon a message to send. That person has to encode the message and determine how to send it. Will it be sent via words, actions, or both? Think about when you were a child and a parent or other adult communicated with a look indicating that you had stepped out of line—no words were necessary. As another example, the authors of this book want to teach you about communication and have chosen to use English words to do it. Next, the person must choose a medium for the communication. Will it be oral or written? Will it be in person or via technology, such as telephone, video, blog, letter, books, or other options? There are pros and cons to each medium and the various ways of encoding the message. In the case of the authors, they are using written words in a book format. It is not an interactive medium (a con), but it allows the authors to communicate with many people at different times (a pro). The second person in the communication must then decode the message (i.e., try to understand what is meant by the message) using the entire context of the message and the medium through which it travels. In the case of this book, if a student does not know English or has difficulty reading, it will be difficult for that student to decode the book's messages. When the second person decodes the message, he or she responds as if he or she understood and wants to further the communication or indicates he or she wants to clarify the communication. In the case of this book, if the student does not fully understand this book, the medium does not easily allow the student to create a communication loop with the authors. The student can, however, create communication loops with fellow students and the instructor.

People's skill at encoding and decoding messages play a role in how well they communicate. Additionally, past experiences with communication may connect with emotional or behavioral responses to communication. These past responses impact the way people decode and encode information now, leading to the possibility of miscommunication. Social workers will bear more responsibility in client interactions to check on their own encoding and decoding, as well as to decipher whether clients are struggling to encode or decode messages. Social workers also need to consider what mediums of communication are preferred by clients. By understanding this feedback loop, social workers can begin to work with clients to improve aspects of the communication feedback loop that are not effective for them.

Consider this example of Edgar (person 1) texting (medium) Chris (person 2) the following message:

> Late????

What does that mean? How should Chris interpret (decode) this? Is Chris late? Is Edgar late? Is this a sincere inquiry or an irritated confrontation because there are four question marks? How should Chris respond (encode the next message)? Should Chris text back or phone (medium)? Think about the complexity of ordinary spoken and written communication and become amazed at how well we manage to do it as often as we do.

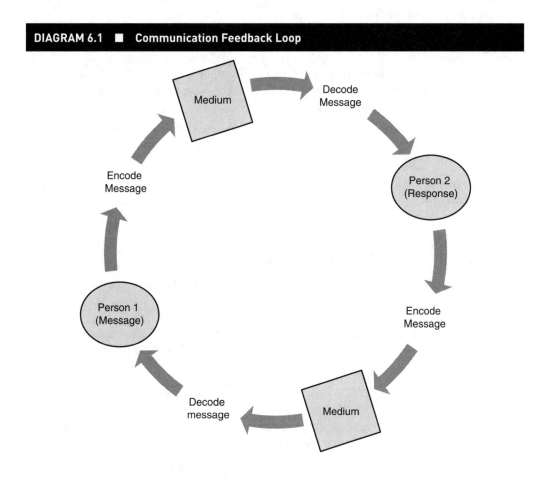

DIAGRAM 6.1 ■ Communication Feedback Loop

FURTHERING, PARAPHRASING, CLOSED-ENDED RESPONSES, AND OPEN-ENDED RESPONSES

Furthering responses communicate attentive listening and encourage clients to verbalize further. There are two main types of furthering responses. Minimal prompts, sometimes referred to as "encouragers," are short but encouraging responses, such as "I see," "Then what?" and "but," with the nonverbal counterparts including head nods and other gestures indicating attentiveness.

The second type of furthering response is an accent response, which involves repeating in a questioning manner a word or short phrase, to prompt further elaboration by the client. For example, the client states, "My son drives me nuts," and the practitioner responds with, "Nuts? In what way?"

Paraphrasing involves succinctly restating the client's message in fresh words to provide further clarity and convey understanding. You want to avoid repeating the client's words exactly, as that can result in a parroting impression.

Closed-ended responses are questions or responses that are used to elicit specific data or define a topic. They are effective for gathering concrete information but can block open communication and, if overused, they can result in the interview taking on the flavor of an interrogation.

Open-ended responses invite expanded expression and leave the client free to share whatever seems most relevant and important. Open-ended responses, which can be structured or unstructured, can yield rich data and enhance the flow of the interview. However, open-ended responses may be inefficient in soliciting factual data.

EXERCISE 6.1: CLOSED- VS. OPEN-ENDED INTERVIEW

This exercise illustrates how a client interview using primarily closed-ended questions differs from an interview using primarily open-ended questions.

Directions

- The instructor plays the role of the practitioner, and a student volunteer plays the role of the client. It is helpful if both players know that they will be doing the exercise ahead of time, so they can prepare by briefly reviewing the scripts.

- Role-play the closed-ended interview (Take 1) first, and then role-play the open-ended interview (Take 2). During the role play, the class should try to identify the differences between the two interviews.

- After the two role plays are completed, discuss the differences you noticed between the two interviews and answer the following questions.

Questions

1. Which interview seemed to work best? Why did it work best?

2. Which verbal following skills were employed, and where were they were used in the two role plays?

Setting: The practitioner is a clinical social worker in private practice. The client, Joe, is a 23-year-old single African American man who made an appointment with the social worker after seeing her website. This is the first interview.

Interview Take 1

The practitioner and client introduce themselves and then sit down. The practitioner sits in a chair turned toward the client and away from the desk. The client sits down across from the practitioner.

Social Worker:	Okay, I need to ask you some questions.
Client:	Okay.
Social Worker:	How old are you?
Client:	23.
Social Worker:	Ever been in counseling before?
Client:	No.
Social Worker:	So, what's your problem?
Client:	I don't know, really. I just think I need some help.
Social Worker:	For what?
Client:	I don't feel so good.
Social Worker:	So what's the matter? Do you have aches? Pains? What?
Client:	No, none of that.
Social Worker:	Then what?
Client:	Look, maybe I just better go.
Social Worker:	Are you sure?

Client:	Yeah.
Social Worker:	Okay, then. Come back anytime.

Interview Take 2

The practitioner and client introduce themselves and then sit down. The practitioner sits in a chair turned toward the client and away from the desk. The client sits down across from the practitioner.

Social Worker:	Let's begin by your telling me why you are here and how you would like me to help you.
Client:	Okay. I guess I'm here because I think I really need some kind of help. I probably look normal to you on the outside, but I'm just a mess inside.
Social Worker:	Sounds like you're feeling pretty bad. I'm glad you came in to see me. Are you feeling kind of confused and mixed up inside—like, tied up in knots?
Client:	Yes, yes—that's what it is. It's like I'm all tied up inside—like a big lump or something.
Social Worker:	Could you tell me more about what that feels like?
Client:	Oh, I don't know. . . . I just feel really down and blue, and I don't have any energy. . . . I just hate myself sometimes. . . . I feel like I'm a bum or something. Sometimes, I feel like I don't want to go on. My family tells me to pray more, and I do, but I still feel bad.
Social Worker:	It must be terribly painful to have such feelings. I gather you're feeling pretty helpless and hopeless.
Client:	I am. I just don't know what to do. I feel I'm falling into this black hole, and I just can't crawl out again. Sometimes I . . . [stops]
Social Worker:	Sometimes you . . .
Client:	This probably sounds to you like a crazy person . . . maybe I am crazy . . . but . . . sometimes I think that life just isn't worth it . . . that life just isn't worth living, you know?
Social Worker:	Are you feeling that way now?
Client:	No, I don't think so.
Social Worker:	You don't think so, but sometimes you do think of it?
Client:	Yes, but I wouldn't do anything. Suicide's a sin. But, I don't know how to get to feeling better.
Social Worker:	How to feel better is something we can work on together. It sounds like you may have depression, and the good news is that depression is very treatable. Most people with depression get better with the right treatment, and getting the right treatment is something I can help you with.
Client:	That sounds great. I feel a little hopeful now.

SEEKING CONCRETENESS, SUMMARIZING, AND FOCUSING

The next three verbal following/active listening skills are seeking concreteness, summarizing, and focusing. Below, these skills are defined and then followed by two skills development exercises. The first exercise focuses on the skill of seeking concreteness, and the second exercise illustrates a blending of the skills of seeking concreteness, summarizing, and focusing.

Seeking concreteness involves recognizing clients' general abstract messages and coaching them to express themselves in more specific terms. It also involves teaching clients to be concrete, specific, and clear in their communications with others. Seeking concreteness is an important tool in establishing clearly defined goals and selecting appropriate interventions. There are four subtypes of seeking concreteness:

1. Checking out perceptions

2. Clarifying the meaning of vague or unfamiliar terms

3. Exploring the basis of conclusions drawn by clients

4. Assisting clients to personalize their statements

Example 1

Client: My daughter never does what she's told.

Practitioner: (seeking concreteness by exploring the basis of the client's conclusion along with checking out perceptions) Joan, you seem irritated and frustrated because your daughter doesn't follow through with what you ask her to do. It sounds like you think that she doesn't respect your requests, and you're not sure what to do about that.

Example 2

Instead of saying to a client (modeling the use of concreteness in language) "You really did better in our session today," which is vague and general, you could say, "Today, I noticed that you seemed more at ease talking with me. You expressed some real insight into how you play a role in your arguments with your husband, and you succeeded in deciding on what first steps to take to work on improving your communication with him."

There is a three-fold purpose to seeking concreteness:

1. Clients become clearer about what is expected of them and how they are perceived.

2. It reduces potential misunderstandings.

3. It models clear communication.

Summarizing is a skill that involves pulling together, succinctly, large amounts of information and lengthy client messages. Summarizing can also provide focus and continuity within sessions and between sessions with clients.

Focusing is important because in today's world of brief interventions and limited resources and time, staying focused is pragmatic and employs your expertise and guidance efficiently. There are three essential functions of focusing skills:

1. To help select topics for the social worker and client to address

2. To help the social worker and client explore topics in depth

3. To help the social worker and client maintain their focus and keep on topic

EXERCISE 6.2: SEEKING CONCRETENESS

Directions

- Form groups of two or three.

- One of you plays the role of the practitioner, one plays the role of the client, and the third (if present) is an observer.

- First, the "client" reads the client statement; then the "practitioner" responds to the statement. The client statements are purposefully vague and general. The goal of the practitioner is to seek concreteness, that is, to help the client express himself or herself in more specific terms (see the Guidelines for Seeking Concreteness provided below).

- Keep role playing back and forth. In responding to each statement, try verbal following:

  ○ First, respond with the goal of seeking concreteness and specificity.

  ○ Next, try to combine seeking concreteness with the use of open-ended responses and questions.

  ○ Third, add focusing.

Guidelines for Seeking Concreteness

1. Check perceptions of client messages.

2. Clarify the meaning of vague or unfamiliar terms that the client uses.

3. Explore the basis of conclusions clients draw about themselves and their situation.

4. Assist clients to use "I" statements.

5. Elicit specific, rather than vague, feelings.

6. Help the client focus on the here and now.

7. Elicit richer details about clients' experiences and interactions with others.

Client Statements

1. Teenager: "My mother bugs me all the time. Nothing I do is right."

2. "Yesterday was the worst day of my life. Everything went wrong."

3. Client whose gender is other than the practitioner's: "I don't want to offend you, but I don't want to see a [gender identity of practitioner] therapist. [Gender identity of practitioner] don't understand me."

4. "I don't know why I came back to see you this week. I mean, you don't care about me—nobody does."

5. "I'm so depressed. My whole life's a mess."

6. "I'm not the one who should be here. My husband's the one with problems; he's a lazy, drag-ass, self-centered bastard. Oh hell, my marriage is over. I don't know why I'm wasting your time."

7. Neighborhood citizen to community organizer practitioner: "Why should I believe you can help us? You don't live here. You organizers don't know nothing about the mess this neighborhood is in."

8. Program director to assistant director: "We're just not getting the funding we need. This program's a mess—there's no hope for us anymore. Heck, I probably won't have a job a month from now."

EXERCISE 6.3: BLENDING OPEN-ENDED, CLOSED-ENDED, EMPATHIC, AND CONCRETE RESPONSES TO MAINTAIN FOCUS

The purpose of this dialogue exercise is for you to observe and be able to identify the technique of blending the skills of open-ended responses, closed-ended responses, and seeking concreteness with empathic communication to maintain focus in an interview.

Directions

- Two students can play the roles of practitioner and client, or the instructor can play one of the roles with a student playing the other role.

- After watching the performance, the rest of the class should analyze the practitioner's responses and identify where in the dialogue verbal following/active listening skills are used—and which ones—and where empathy is employed.

Case Scenario

The client, Ramon, is a 27-year-old Mexican American man with schizophrenia who was brought into the mental health clinic by Maria, his board and care operator, for evaluation because of recent problems with his behavior. Ramon and the practitioner meet to assess the situation.

Ramon: I don't know why I'm here. I know Maria wants me put in the hospital, but that's just cause she doesn't like me.

Social Worker: You say you think you're here at the clinic just because your care operator doesn't like you?

Ramon: Yeah.

Social Worker: How do you know Maria doesn't like you?

Ramon: She picks on me all the time and is real mean.

Social Worker: That must be really hard for you. It would help me to understand how best to help you if you could describe a particular situation in which she picked on you and was mean.

Ramon: Well, okay. Like this one time she yelled at me because I wanted to take a nap.

Social Worker: What were the words she used?

Ramon: Oh, she told me to get up, that this was no time to take a nap.

Social Worker: What time was it?"

Ramon: I don't know. I guess it was around 8 in the morning.

Social Worker: What else did she say?

Ramon: I can't remember. Oh, I guess she wanted me to get up and go to my partial program. The van was there, but I didn't want to go.

Social Worker: I gather that you don't like the partial hospitalization program. Am I correct in that?

Ramon: Yeah.

Social Worker: Okay. Could you tell me a little about what you don't like about it?

Ramon: They pick on me there, too.

Social Worker: Could you tell me how they have picked on you?

Ramon: They yell at me for eating stuff and doing stuff.

Social Worker: Could you be more specific?

Ramon: I don't know . . . sometimes I eat cigarette butts, paper, and stuff.

Social Worker: You know, Ramon, it doesn't seem to me as though Maria and the staff at partial don't like you. It sounds like Maria didn't want you to take a nap because she didn't want you to miss your partial program, which she thinks is helpful to you. As for the partial program staff, well, eating cigarette butts can make you awfully sick to your stomach, and I'm sure they don't want that to happen to you because they care about your well-being. I know that having others telling you to stop doing things you want to do is a hard thing to hear, but I think it is all coming from concern for you, not to be mean to you.

Ramon: Well, maybe . . . but I don't like it sometimes.

INTERPRETATION, ADDITIVE EMPATHY, AND CONFRONTATION

Interpretation, additive empathy, and confrontation are better used once relationships are established because the social worker needs to know the client well enough to determine that they may be helpful and to sustain the relationship if they are not on target.

Interpretation involves understanding the implied patterns, goals, or hopes of clients that they are not fully expressing. Interpretation helps improve the client's insight, and its origins are in psychodynamic approaches to helping. Here, it is not being suggested in the way it is used by trained psychodynamic therapists. Instead, for the generalist social worker, interpretation is a way to make an inquiry about some idea the social worker believes to be true about the client and that is at the edge of the client's awareness, to help her to better understand her situation, see it differently, or clarify goals. It may take the form of *relabeling or reframing* something the client has said, such as "Joe, in what you are calling 'failure,' I see a lot of initiative and stick-to-it-iveness." It may also take the form of a *positive reinterpretation* of a circumstance, as in "Audrey, it sounds like you might be saying that, as awful as it was, the hardship of losing your home has really helped you build new skills to negotiate and be assertive with business owners in the community. Have you thought of it that way?" The final comments by the social worker in Exercise 6.3 above is another example of this form of interpretation and positive reframing of the client's situation.

Additive empathy is an empathic statement that goes beyond what the client has stated and obvious observable emotions to those that the social worker suspects might be present. It is a form of interpretation that is more focused on the emotional state of the person. The client may be somewhat aware of the emotions but may not be admitting them, for a wide variety of reasons. It requires some degree of inference on the part of the social worker. When such statements are made, the social worker always leaves room for the client to disagree and correct the ideas.

Example:

The client's parent has recently died, and family tasks and roles are being fulfilled by others, which troubles the client. The social worker says, "I may be wrong, but I wonder if your feelings of resentment toward your siblings and cousins aren't so much about the specific way they are doing things but about a fear that you are getting closer to death yourself and the loss of a generation? Any possibility that fear of dying is part of this?"

Confrontation asks clients to consider an aspect of their behaviors, thoughts, or feelings that is contributing to the challenges they face. The social worker asks the person to consider this aspect of self, which may be uncomfortable. For many people, hearing about a personal "negative" naturally sparks a defensive reaction, possibly anger. They key to successful confrontation is to do it from a place of concern and, like interpretation and additive empathy, to give the person a chance to disagree. Many students identify confronting as a skill that makes them feel very uncomfortable. In part that comes from having experienced or witnessed confrontation that is done in an aggressive rather than assertive manner. Hepworth et al. (2017) suggest that there are four components to an effective confrontation.

1. "I" statement

2. Concern related to the client's goal

3. Clear explanation of the incongruent behavior, thought, or emotion

4. Inclusion of probable consequences

Example:

"Elijah, we have talked a lot about your wanting to support your son and how important being a good father is to you. I am concerned that you won't be able to do that if you are staying out late four to six times per week partying with friends. You just shared that you have been late to work several times in the last month after a night out and received a verbal warning. Do you think that the partying could be jeopardizing your job and your ability to provide for your son?"

One note of caution on the use of these techniques. If people have a history of trauma, there may be thoughts or feelings that they are not ready to explore, and reflecting them using one of these techniques may not be helpful. That might be work better done in therapy than generalist work. So, think carefully about using these when trauma is present.

EXERCISE 6.4: ADDITIVE EMPATHY, INTERPRETATION, AND CONFRONTATION

Directions

- Form groups of three.

- One of you plays the role of the practitioner, one plays the role of the client, and the third (if present) is an observer. Take turns so you each play all three roles.

- Imagine that this is not the first, or even second, time you have met the client—there is some level of relationship present.

- The practitioner will work to use additive empathy, interpretation, and confrontation appropriately. Therefore, the client must disagree with, resist, and push back *a bit*.

- As you role play or observe, consider the following questions.

Questions

1. Did the relationship seem strong enough to employ additive empathy and/or confrontation? Did using the skill increase trust, create more distance, or produce some other reaction?

2. Were interpretations intermittent? Were they phrased tentatively to allow the client to disagree with them without feeling threatened?

3. Were confrontations related to the client's goal?

4. Did the practitioner acknowledge possible errors when the client disagreed?

5. Did empathic communication follow responses to confrontations?

6. Did the practitioner encourage self-exploration and self-confrontation? If so, how?

Case Vignette 1

You are a high school social worker working with a biracial, female youth from a fairly chaotic family. For the past few years, you have interacted on a variety of issues related to school attendance, relationships with peers, and poor academic performance. Dad has been imprisoned twice for drugs and theft. He recently was released from prison on parole, and the home chaos has increased. Mom has struggled with addiction, and the family has past involvement with Children, Youth and Family Services due to parental neglect. Your student has been dating a similarly aged peer who has a really "nice" family. Her boyfriend's home life is completely different from hers. Although his parents are not crazy about their dating, she "knows" that if she were to get pregnant, they would welcome her and the baby into their home. A teacher overheard her say this to a peer in the hallway and referred her to you.

Case Vignette 2

Lorraine (age 55) and Damian (age 48) are the children of Audrey (age 79) and Robert (age 85). Damian has Down Syndrome and resides with his parents. Lorraine lives about 200 miles away. You are the social worker for the employment site where Damian works daily. He has worked there for a decade, and you have known the family for some time. Both parents have had health-related challenges in the past year and a half. Recently, Robert has had to stop driving, and this impacts Damian, as his father transported him each day to and from the employment site. You have tried on multiple occasions to get the family to do some planning to ensure Damian's needs will be met should one or both of the parents become incapacitated. Lorraine dropped Damian off today and has come to your office about the transportation issue specifically.

Case Vignette 3

You are the social worker in a specialty clinic for diabetes. Anders is a 28-year-old man diagnosed with Type 2 diabetes one year ago. Since he got the diagnosis, you have been seeing him monthly as part of a lifestyle change group. Despite faithful attendance at the group, he has been reluctant to adopt most recommended diet changes and has been inconsistent in checking his blood sugar or taking his medications. He says he is trying. He, however, believes he is "doing pretty well by comparison to the other folks [he] knows." He is overweight—obese, according to his BMI. He has hypertension and is at high risk for cardiac problems. His father and grandfather both had diabetes, as do his maternal aunt and four cousins. A 34-year-old cousin just had a heart attack. All were diagnosed with diabetes as adults. His grandfather ended up with three amputations as a result of not following through on diet and lifestyle changes. His father lost his sight due to diabetic retinopathy. The physician is concerned that Anders will end up with the same complications and increased debility over time. Oral medications have not been sufficient to manage his blood sugars to date, and the MD has prescribed insulin. You were asked to do an individual session about this recent change, to explore the barriers to his embracing treatment recommendations including diet changes and medication adherence.

ENGAGING CLIENTS WITH MOBILE AND DIGITAL TECHNOLOGY

Social work is a profession that depends on communication. Developing active listening and verbal communication skills are essential in establishing a therapeutic alliance. The traditional way of helping clients has been in the office/agency via face-to-face contact or visiting clients in their community environment. With advances in technology over the past 20 years, significant changes in how we communicate as a society are rapidly emerging. Digital and mobile technology have made it possible to instantly have contact with another person practically anywhere in the world. Social workers are now able to communicate with clients using their desktop computers, laptop computers, electronic tablets, and smartphones. According to the Pew Research Center (2017), eight out of ten adults in the United States own a desktop or laptop computer. Ninety-five percent of Americans own a cell phone, while 77% own a smartphone (Pew Research Center, 2017). Social workers are embracing technology as a means to provide therapy and support to clients. The prevalence of technology has made it possible for treatment to occur anytime and anywhere. Engaging clients electronically can take place using e-mail, videoconferencing, instant text messaging, real-time chat, and internet phone (Freese, 2015). Therapy apps are available for download on smartphones and tablets. With technologies similar to Skype and FaceTime, social workers can schedule live video therapy sessions with clients. The U.S. Department of Veterans Affairs (2017) is a leader in the use of Clinical Video Telehealth. The use of this technology has allowed veterans to receive quality health care and case management throughout the country.

Legal and ethical guidelines must be followed to protect the information and privacy of the client. Training and supervision will need to be developed to ensure competence of social workers using digital and mobile technology to engage with and provide services to clients. Understanding that technology is being used to both help the client and aid the social worker in providing services is critical to the helping process. The 2017 revision of the *Code of Ethics of the National Association of Social Workers* provides additional guidelines to address the increasing use of digital and mobile technology in the social work profession, as do the *NASW, ASWB, CSWE, & CSWA Standards for Technology in Social Work Practice* (2017). Table 6.1 shows potential risks and benefits of using digital and mobile technology.

TABLE 6.1 ■ Risks and Benefits of Digital and Mobile Technology

Risks	Benefits
Internet security	Flexibility
Technical issues	Ease of use in technology
Confidentiality	No traveling
Insurance may not cover online therapy	Convenience/comfort
Limited ability to manage emergency situations	Cost
Difficult to observe and evaluate nonverbal cues	Privacy
Voice tonality/sound quality	Minimize stigma
Legal guidelines may vary from state to state	Increase access to rural communities
Complex/complicated situations	Increase access to individuals with limited mobility

Source: Freese (2015).

MULTIDIMENSIONAL CLIENT ASSESSMENT

- Exercise 7.5: The Role of Culture in an Initial Assessment
- Exercise 7.6: Screening for Depression and Suicide
- Home Assessments and Safety: The Home Visit
- Exercise 7.7: A Student's First Solo Home Visit
- Generalist Social Work Assessments
- Exercise 7.8: Comparison of Generalist Assessments

Once you have the capacity to listen and communicate effectively, you are ready to begin to collect information about why a client is seeking help. Assessment is a critical part of helping because it sets the foundation for the types of interventions that will be used to solve clients' problems. Obtaining information for a multidimensional assessment often begins before encountering the client or community problem. There may be old records from a previous visit or a referral from another professional available for review. A competent assessment addresses problem areas; it also focuses on evaluating the strengths, resources, healthy functioning, and other positive factors of the client, family, or community. At times, completing an assessment will require more than asking open-ended or closed-ended questions; use of evidence-based assessment tools is essential to the multidimensional assessment. Social workers should be knowledgeable about these tools, especially when assessing for suicidality, depression, or substance abuse. Assessment tools vary based on the age group of the client(s) and the system level. Therefore, the selected tool should match the system level, such as choosing a community assessment tool (macro) to determine the needs of the community or the effectiveness of social policies. You must also be prepared to integrate technology into assessment, as many agencies are now using electronic records or digital tools to collect and help manage client data, improve diagnosis and treatment decisions, and to make client information available to other providers. Regardless of the agency or client situation, a thorough assessment requires knowledge, skills, and practice.

KEY CONCEPTS AND DEFINITIONS

Assessment can be defined as "the process of gathering, analyzing, and synthesizing salient data [about clients and their situations] into a formulation that encompasses the following vital dimensions: the nature of the clients' problems," their motivations, their coping capabilities and strengths, and relevant systems and resources (economic, legal, medical, cultural, religious/spiritual, political, educational, social, or interpersonal) (Hepworth & Larsen, 1990, p. 193).

An assessment can be a product, such as a one-time evaluation in the emergency room, or an assessment can be an ongoing process, as in case management or service coordination. Depending on the mission of the agency and the problem presented by the client, assessments can gather a great deal of data. These data enable the social worker to get a full picture of who the client is and what social systems may or may not be involved. Information for the assessment can be obtained in multiple ways. In most cases, the information is given by the client. However, there are situations in which information must be obtained from a secondary source, such as a family member, friend, or other involved individuals.

Information Often Obtained in a Micro-Level Assessment

Micro-level assessment is also known as a bio-psycho-social-cultural-spiritual assessment.

- Client information
- Challenges and/or disabilities
- Cultural history
- Daily living skills
- Educational history

- Family history
- Legal history
- Leisure/recreational interests
- Medical history
- Other relevant information
- Presenting or current problem
- Psychiatric history
- Referral source
- Sexual history
- Spiritual history
- Strengths, abilities, and goals
- Substance use history
- Work/vocational background

Social work practice emphasizes the importance of the strengths perspective, arguing that overemphasizing pathology serves to

1. undermine the process of tapping client strengths

2. impair the ability to discern clients' potential for growth

3. undermine the process of enhancing clients' self-esteem

The social worker strives to achieve a balanced view by identifying strengths and positive potential while recognizing where there are challenges, vulnerabilities, problems, or pathology.

The ability to carefully collect, analyze, and synthesize client or community information is an important skill for a social worker. An understanding of systems theory is critical in assessing how the client and the environment influence one another in positive and negative ways. A balanced assessment identifies strengths and deficits as well as which system levels might be the best target for intervention. This is crucial in deciding which treatment modality or intervention approach might address the client's problem(s). The balanced assessment matrix (Figure 7.1) is helpful in organizing strengths, resources, deficits, and challenges.

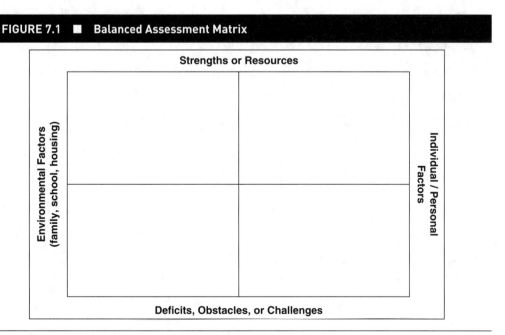

FIGURE 7.1 ■ Balanced Assessment Matrix

Strengths or Resources

Environmental Factors (family, school, housing)

Individual / Personal Factors

Deficits, Obstacles, or Challenges

Source: Cowger (1994), Saleebey (2013).

Information Sources Relevant to Formulating an Assessment

1. Background information and historical case records

2. Assessment tools, psychological tests, measures/scales, or other client self-report forms, which may be cross-sectional or repeated on an ongoing basis to monitor client progress

3. Clients' verbal reports about their situations and concerns

4. Social worker's direct observation of interactions between the client and others

5. Social worker's observation of the client's strengths, resources, and coping capacities

6. Verbal information and observation of nonverbal communication gleaned from collateral contacts (e.g., family, friends, neighbors, clergy)

7. The personal experiences and observations of the social worker based on direct interactions with the client(s)

Preliminary Inquiries That Can Quickly Identify Key Issues

1. What do the potential clients perceive as their main concerns and problems?

2. Are there any relevant current or pending legal mandates that may affect the interventions or services provided?

3. Are there any serious or imminent health or safety issues relevant to potential clients' situations?

Questions to Aid in Further Specifying the Client's Problems in an Assessment

1. What are the specific indications or manifestations of the problem(s)?

2. What persons and systems are involved in the problem(s)?

3. How do the clients and systems interact to produce and maintain the problem(s)?

4. What unmet needs and wants are involved in the problem(s)?

5. Is a particular developmental stage or life transition relevant to the problem(s)?

6. How severe is the problem, and how does it affect clients?

7. What meanings do the clients ascribe to the problem(s)?

8. Where do problematic behaviors occur?

9. When do problematic behaviors occur? When are they not occurring?

10. What is the frequency of problematic behaviors?

11. What is the duration of the problem(s)?

12. What are the consequences of the problem(s)?

13. Have other issues (e.g., drug abuse) affected the functioning of clients or family members?

14. What are the clients' emotional reactions to the problem(s)?

Questions to Enhance Cultural Competence in Assessment

1. What are the clients' cultural identities?

2. What are the clients' cultural explanations of their situations, problems, and/or concerns?

3. What are the cultural factors related to clients' environments which affect their functioning?

4. What are the cultural factors impacting the relationship between clients and the social worker?

5. What are the cultural factors that must be considered in the assessment of clients and their situations? (American Psychiatric Association, 2000)

EXERCISE 7.1: WHERE SHOULD WE START, MR. M?

Often when clients present to a social worker, their problems are multifactorial and complex. As noted in earlier chapters, good listening skills are imperative to the helping process. It is equally important to have excellent observation skills when conducting assessments. Clients are often in distress when a social worker is involved. Observing body posture, facial expressions, and communication (emotion) congruency can help validate the information provided throughout the assessment.

Note to Instructor: This case vignette is designed to foster insightful discussion not only about the importance of observing body language during an assessment, but being prepared for the unexpected information that may result in the social worker's taking a different course of action.

Directions

- Form groups of four to six.

- Read the case vignette of Mr. M and discuss the questions below.

Case Vignette

The setting is a walk-in counseling clinic staffed by social workers who do intake assessments. Mr. M is a 52-year-old, single, Latino male who recently lost his construction job. He is legally mandated to attend treatment services by a local judge due to several violent incidents. In the middle of your assessment, he says, "I miss my son. We are not speaking because I yelled at him for getting into trouble and taking my money. He left me all alone." The social worker notices that Mr. M is teary eyed when talking about his son. The social worker inquires further about the relationship, but Mr. M refuses to share additional information. Instead, he reports he had a doctor's visit two weeks ago. He has some "serious" health challenges to face over the next months. He does not verbalize any additional concerns about his health but puts his head in his hands and holds it there for several seconds. Before the social worker can ask further questions, Mr. M states with a grin that he will be "evicted" from his apartment tomorrow morning.

Questions

Based on the information received thus far,

1. What are Mr. M's three concerns?

2. Which of the three identified concerns is Mr. M most distressed about? Explain your choice.

3. What role did body posture, facial expressions, and/or communication congruency play in your answer?

4. Given what you know at this point, would you continue with the assessment? If yes, why? If no, why not?

5. What, if anything, is missing from this brief but significant conversation?

6. What would be the ideal question to ask Mr. M at this point?

EXERCISE 7.2: THE ASSESSMENT OF ANTONIA

Directions

- Form groups of four to six.

- Answer the questions and complete the balanced assessment diagram at the end of the case vignette.

Case Vignette

Antonia Garcia is a 23-year-old Mexican American transgendered woman who lives with her sister in a small town in the agricultural region of central California. Five years ago, after a suicide attempt secondary to being relentlessly teased and bullied in high school, Antonia (then using her birth name Antonio and living as a man) told her parents that she felt she was a woman living in a man's body and that she was going to begin exploring the process involved in transitioning from male to female. Antonia's parents, who immigrated to the United States from Mexico 20 years prior, are strong Catholics and socially conservative. Upon hearing this from their only son, Antonia's mother burst into tears, and her father told Antonia that he disowned her. The only family member willing to support Antonia was her sister, Maria. Maria invited Antonia to live with her and helped her find a part-time job in a flower shop. Antonia began living as a woman, but it was very difficult. Young people who knew her as Antonio continued to harass and tease her, and, in response to the stress and her increasing social isolation, Antonia began using drugs—marijuana and cocaine. Soon after, she suffered her first psychotic break.

Antonia was hospitalized and given the diagnosis of schizophreniform disorder. During her hospitalization, Antonia experienced considerable hostility from both staff and other consumers on the unit. One staff member complained that "it is impossible to find this person a roommate because of their sexual identity problems," and many made transphobic and homophobic comments intentionally within earshot of Antonia. When Antonia told the unit social worker about what was going on, the social worker immediately took action and held meetings with both staff and consumers to talk about the issue of transphobia and educate participants about gender identity, gender nonconformity, and sexual orientation to help them better understand such issues (see, e.g., Institute of Medicine, 2011). This seemed to help a little. By the time Antonia was discharged, her clinical status was stable, and her sister welcomed her back into her home.

A couple months later, Maria announced she was getting married and her new husband-to-be was not supportive of the idea of having Antonia live with them. Antonia's job in the flower shop did not pay enough to live independently, and Antonia's depressive symptoms began to return. Feeling like she was falling into a hole of despair, Antonia made a suicide attempt. This time, her admitting diagnosis was Bipolar II disorder, and she was placed on a mood stabilizer and an antipsychotic medication. On the third day of hospitalization, Antonia met with the unit social worker, Janice. Antonia says, "I don't know what to do anymore. Most of my family hates me. I have nowhere to go. I know my sister still loves me, but I can't live with her anymore. I am transgendered, you know, and I want to move to the next step. I know I want to start on hormone therapy and think I will want the surgery eventually, but I have nobody to talk to about this. Sometimes I think I am better off dead, but then I pray to God for his guidance, and he tells me to go on living, that I do have something to offer the world. I try to take care of myself, but I know I won't remember to take my meds once I leave the hospital. Please help me; what should I do?" (Newhill, 2015).

Questions and Balanced Assessment Matrix

Develop a general assessment of the case, including answers to the following:

1. What are Antonia's Strengths/Resources from an environmental perspective?

2. What are Antonia's Strengths/Resources from an individual perspective?

3. What are Antonia's Deficits, Obstacles, or Challenges from environmental perspective?

4. What are Antonia's Deficits, Obstacles, or Challenges from an individual perspective?

5. What, if any, issues of diversity exist with the client?

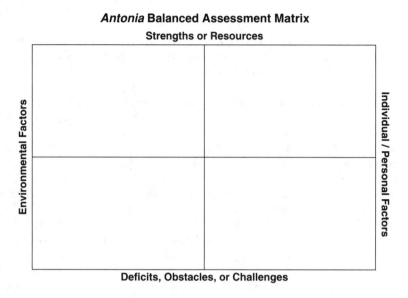

***Antonia* Balanced Assessment Matrix**

Find the Answer Key to Antonia's Case on page 82 at the end of this chapter.

EXERCISE 7.3: ADDRESSING MULTIDIMENSIONAL ASSESSMENT, MR. B

Directions

- Form groups of four to six.

- After reading the case vignette, answer the questions that follow, using the given information.

- If there is insufficient information in the vignette to answer the question, discuss what steps you might take to access the missing information.

Case Vignette

Mr. B, a 33-year-old married African American railroad engineer, walked into the psychiatric emergency service to request "legal advice." Upon evaluation, he was neatly attired, polite but very guarded with the evaluator. He asked to speak with a black, male doctor, but because none were available, he reluctantly agreed to talk with a triage clinician who was a white, female, clinical social worker. Initially, he told the social worker that he wanted legal advice to help him pursue a complaint of racial discrimination. He explained that he had come to the conclusion that the company management of the railroad where he worked had a conspiracy of prejudice against him because of his race, since all of his white colleagues had succeeded over the years in securing promotions while he was continually passed over for promotion. The social worker's reaction was that this seemed to be a reasonable perception in light of the facts Mr. B was citing, along with the social worker's awareness of the reality of racial prejudice and discrimination in this country. The social worker asked Mr. B, however, why he had come to a psychiatric emergency service if all he wanted was legal advice. He was visibly uncomfortable with the question and again asked whether a black male clinician was available. When told that there were no black male clinicians employed by the emergency service, and although the social worker offered to make a referral to a black male clinician at another mental health service, Mr. B said he would go ahead and talk anyway.

In a very guarded manner, Mr. B stated that he had with him substantial evidence indicating that his wife had been having affairs with several men, both black and white. His suspicions had begun two years ago when he found a business card with a man's name on it in his wife's purse. Immediately he accused her of having an affair, which she denied. Over the ensuing months, he continued to collect more "evidence" including (1) shopping lists he claimed proved his wife was meeting her lover at the local grocery store, (2) books of matches "proving" they had been at a motel together, and (3) some blurred photographs of streets and buildings that he claimed were clear evidence of a tryst, but that, when examined by the social worker, showed nothing overt. Mr. B admitted he had reached the point to insist that either his wife must admit to the infidelities or he was going to have to kill her. This was compounded by the fact that the white men he suspected were all work colleagues. Remarkably, during all this time he had maintained a good work record and avoided any significant interpersonal conflict with his fellow workers. Mr. B exhibited no schizophrenia or affective symptoms but was clearly very suspicious and angry about both the racial discrimination issue and his wife's suspected infidelity. He told the social worker that he is "a very religious man, close to my personal God" and had recently met with the minister of his church to discuss his concerns about work and about his wife. The minister had then suggested that Mr. B see someone at the mental health clinic for help.

The social worker concluded after a thorough assessment that Mr. B's complaint of racial discrimination was probably based in reality and should be pursued via legal channels. The complaints about his wife, however, appeared not to be reality based, particularly after the social worker called Mr. B's wife to warn her of Mr. B's threats per the Tarasoff mandate. During their conversation, Mrs. B adamantly insisted that she was not involved with any men and never had been, stating that she was at her wits end with her husband's threats and accusations. The social worker, therefore, concluded that Mr. B was experiencing both a functional paranoid reaction, in terms of his suspicions toward his wife, and a "healthy cultural paranoia" (Grier & Cobbs, 1968) in terms of his perceptions about his work situation. After referring him to an affirmative action complaint board for the work-related problems, the social worker worked with Mr. and Mrs. B to try to help them resolve their marital conflicts, including his suspicions of her infidelity. This short-term intervention consisted of two sessions at the clinic, at which time the social worker was able to convince Mr. B to see the psychiatrist and take some antipsychotic medication. Subsequently, however, he refused to return to the clinic because he did not like the side effects of the medication. He did, however, contact the social worker from time to time by telephone. At last contact, he told her that his homicidal urges had remitted but that he could not give up the suspicions about his wife, although he had "learned to live with it" (Newhill, 1990).

Questions to Be Answered in Assessment

1. How does the client define and understand the present situation and concerns?

2. What does the client say he wants at this time?

3. How extensive and serious are the problems at this time? If the problems are not resolved successfully, will the consequences be damaging and irreversible?

4. What persons and systems other than the client are involved in the problems?

5. How is each of the participants involved in the problems?

6. What unmet needs or wants are involved in the problems?

7. What developmental stage and/or life transition is relevant to the problems?

8. What social, psychological, or spiritual meaning does the client ascribe to the problems?

9. What are the client's cultural norms within which the problems are situated?

10. Where does problematic behavior occur?

11. When does problematic behavior occur? When doesn't it occur?

12. How frequently do the problems occur?

13. What is the duration of the problems?

14. What are the client's emotional reactions to the problems?

15. How has the client attempted to cope with the problems so far?

16. What efforts have produced positive results, and what efforts have not worked?

17. What are the skills and strengths of the client?

18. What external/environmental resources are needed to help the client?

IDENTIFYING SKILLS AND STRENGTHS FROM A BIO-PSYCHO-SOCIAL-SPIRITUAL PERSPECTIVE

1. What has been observed in terms of the client's skills, strengths, capabilities, and resources?

2. What is the client's perception of his skills, strengths, capabilities, and resources?

3. How do factors related to the client's gender, ethnicity, race, culture, socioeconomic status, religion, and social class connect to the presenting problem in terms of strengths and resources?

4. What is the client's motivation for making changes in his or her life? What is the source of that motivation, and how can it be sustained?

5. What is the client's readiness and capacity for change?

6. What positive coping skills does the client have? What is the client's perspective about his coping skills?

7. What strategies does the client employ to manage changes and stresses in his life?

8. How has the client successfully handled and resolved problems in the past? What has worked well? What has not worked well?

9. Is the client willing and able to accept and utilize help from others? Does the client have assistance from others in the environment?

10. What skills does the client have that could apply to addressing the problem (e.g., social skills or work skills)?

11. What support systems exist or need to be created for the client?

12. What external or environmental resources are needed by the client?

13. Which external or environmental resources already exist, and which need to be created?

14. What internal resources can the client draw upon?

EXERCISE 7.4: CREATING A CULTURALLY RELEVANT MULTIDIMENSIONAL ASSESSMENT ECO-MAP FOR MR. B

As noted in Chapter 2, an eco-map is a diagram of the ecological context of the client system and the various other systems that reciprocally affect it, and it can be a useful tool for assessment. The eco-map can also be a tool for enhancing cultural competence and cultural humility in assessment because it can provide a picture of the role of culture in the client's ecosystem.

Directions

- Form groups of four to six and re-read the Case Vignette for Mr. B in Exercise 7.3.

- Begin by identifying the various systems involved in the case, including Mr. B's mental health provider, family, church, work, and others.

- Then, draw an eco-map that illustrates the connections among these systems.

- After creating this initial map, discuss the following questions to examine the role of Mr. B's culture in the expression of his concerns.

Questions to Determine the Role of Culture in the Client's Ecosystem

1. What is Mr. B's racial/cultural identity? What role does his identity play in his current concerns?

2. What are Mr. B's cultural explanations for his suspicious thoughts and ideas?

3. What are some of the cultural factors in the psychosocial environment that may be affecting his situation? Examples of cultural factors are social or work stressors, social supports, or the role of religion and family networks in providing support.

4. What cultural issues can you identify as existing in the relationship between Mr. B and the social worker?

5. How do cultural considerations shape the social worker's recommendations for helping Mr. B?

(American Psychiatric Association, 2000)

EXERCISE 7.5: THE ROLE OF CULTURE IN AN INITIAL ASSESSMENT

Directions

- Form groups of four to six.

- After reading each case vignette, answer the questions that follow, using the given information.

- If there is insufficient information in the case vignette to answer the question, discuss what steps you might take to access the missing information.

Case Vignette 1

Mrs. Gomez, a 35-year-old Mexican American woman who speaks broken English, comes in seeking help with marital complaints. Her husband of 17 years is in a new job at a warehouse. He has been staying out after work off and on, sometimes until midnight, for the past month. He says he's just going out with some co-workers for a beer. She thinks he may even be seeing other women because she smelled perfume on one of his shirts and feels scared for her marriage and their three children. When she shared her concerns with her mother, her mother told her that men are like that so don't say anything or he may leave. Mrs. Gomez says she prays all the time now, but she is sleeping very poorly because of her worries.

Questions

1. What cultural considerations might affect the problem and/or solution for Mrs. Gomez?

2. How will you approach assessing these cultural considerations?

3. What resources might you explore to help Mrs. Gomez?

Case Vignette 2

Mrs. Seng comes in with her husband of 12 years. They are both 32 years old and are Cambodian refugees who came to the United States with their parents 25 years ago. They have two children, and he operates a shoe repair shop. He reports that his wife seems to be down much of the time and is not sleeping very well. Although she speaks English well, they converse in their native tongue when queried and then he answers for her. They both resist her being seen by the social worker without his being these and prefer the present format of interaction. From what you know, their culture is very patriarchal, and the father always speaks for the family.

Questions

1. What considerations might you need to observe in seeing Mrs. Seng?

2. Should you pursue trying to see Mrs. Seng alone without her husband present? Why or why not?

3. How might you find out about other cultural differences that might affect your work with Mr. and Mrs. Seng?

EXERCISE 7.6: SCREENING FOR DEPRESSION AND SUICIDE

Note to Instructor: Select and distribute a depression screening tool, such as the PHQ-9, and some type of suicide assessment tool, such as SAMHSA's SAFE-T.

Directions

- Form pairs or groups of three.

- One of you will play the client and the other the social worker. The third person (if present) will be the observer, providing feedback.

- For each case vignette, the social worker will conduct a depression screening using the tool provided by the instructor.

- Switch roles after each vignette. Read only the information for the role you are playing.

- Tips for social worker role: Use the starter lines as written. You may probe to understand the answer better. If the client endorses suicidal thoughts during the depression screening, use a suicide assessment tool.

- Tips for client role: Answer what is asked. Don't offer all the details unless the social worker inquires.

For the Person Playing the Social Worker

Vignette 1

Julie (age 16) is a Korean American high school student who came in with complaints of being unable to concentrate on her class work.

Starter Lines

Social worker: So, Julie, based on what you have said so far, it sounds like you have had recent change in ability to concentrate and get things done. I would like to ask you some questions about your mood. May I do that?

Julie: Yeah, I have. So sure, I guess so. Go ahead.

Vignette 2

Emilio Lopez (age 82) is a Colombian American retiree who came in with complaints of an inability to sleep, general aches and pains, and irritability. You are doing a screening as part of a multidisciplinary team.

Starter Lines

Social worker: So, Mr. Lopez, we ask all our patients about how they have been feeling. It is a standard set of questions. May I ask you them?

Emilio: Sure, if you ask everyone. That will be fine.

Vignette 3

Katerina (age 55) is a Slovakian American who came in because of recent job loss, divorce, and death of a parent. You are doing screening as part of intake for intensive case management services.

Starter Lines

Social worker:	Given that you have had so many stressors, I would like to do a screening we do with people on their mood. Can I ask you some questions?
Katerina:	Yeah, why not? My mood has been awful.

For the Person Playing the Client

Vignette 1

Julie (age 16) is a Korean American high school student who came in with complaints of being unable to concentrate on her class work.

Starter Lines

Social worker:	So, Julie, based on what you have said so far, it sounds like you have had recent change in ability to concentrate and get things done. I would like to ask you some questions about your mood. May I do that?
Julie:	Yeah, I have. So sure, I guess so. Go ahead.

As the screening happens, incorporate the following information in your answers.

- You feel fine about yourself, except you cannot get the schoolwork done. Otherwise, you are not particularly worried about letting people down. You are not especially sad, but this "studying thing" is really wearing on you. You feel down about it three to four times per week.

- For the past month, you have not felt like hanging out with friends as much, maybe four or five times a week rather than 10 times a week. You still see friends daily. It is just not as much fun to go listen to music or see movies as it used to be.

- You have gained about five pounds in the past month because you have not felt like exercising (only two to three days a week, whereas previously you were exercising daily). Now, you are snacking more—too much snacking, almost every day.

- Your sleep seems about the same, but you feel low energy about two to three days a week.

- You are struggling daily to concentrate in class or to stay focused when reading or writing papers for classes. All the class work is taking about three times as long as it should.

- You have not felt restless or especially slow.

- The question about harming yourself takes you by surprise. Of, course you have never thought about killing or harming yourself.

Vignette 2

Emilio Lopez (age 82) is a Colombian American retiree who came in with complaints of an inability to sleep, general aches and pains, and irritability. You have come in for a health examination.

Starter Lines

Social worker:	So, Mr. Lopez, we ask all our patients about how they have been feeling. It is a standard set of questions. May I ask you them?
Emilio:	Sure, if you ask everyone. That will be fine.

As the screening happens, answer with the following information.

- You are surprised by the question about your mood. But, yes, now that you think about it, you feel sad most days. Getting old has been hard, and it got harder two years ago when your wife died. Now you feel lonely most days.

- You sit around and watch a lot of TV. Your kids have been on you to get out and take care of the garden (something you used to love and did with your wife). You used to walk the dog daily, but you gave the dog to your grandson. You also stopped playing cards with your friends when one of them had a stroke. No one stepped up to plan the games since then, including you.

- You have lost 25 pounds in the past year because you eat less. You just don't have much of an appetite most days and don't really feel like making your own food. You weren't trying to lose weight; it just happened. Anyway, "it is not a big deal" because you think you could stand to lose a few more pounds since you were overweight.

- You sleep more but not well and often in the chair in front of the TV. It probably amounts to about 11 hours a day, but in fits and starts so you never feel quite rested.

- You have not really noticed problems in concentration. Your daughter says that you seem more scattered in conversations, but you think she is wrong.

- Of course, you are moving slowly; you are 82 years old. [Note: this may indicate internalized ageism.] Yes, it bothers you. You have noticed slowing in the past several months. You intend to move faster but cannot seem to make it happen.

- You really feel worthless and a burden to your family these days. You have thought about dying, wishing that you would just not awaken after you fall asleep.

- There isn't a day that these two ideas don't go through your head several times a day. The idea stays with you briefly, about 20 minutes at a time.

- You really don't have a plan. You once thought about walking into the river, as you do not swim, but decided that was a dumb idea; plus that would be suicide. Suicide is forbidden in your faith tradition.

- You don't have firearms or extra pills in the house.

- You have never tried to kill yourself; you have no family history of suicide, and you have no history of mental health problems.

- In the past, you coped with challenges by relying upon family and prayer.

Vignette 3

Katerina (age 55) is a Slovakian American who came in because of recent job loss, divorce, and death of a parent.

Starter Lines

Social worker: Given that you have had so many stressors, I would like to do a screening we do with people on their mood. Can ask you some questions?

Katerina: Yeah, why not? My mood has been awful.

As the screening happens, answer with the following information.

- Of course you feel hopeless every day with all the chaos and change in your life. "How worthless does a person have to be to lose their job and husband all at once?" What a "failure" you think you are.

- You cannot find pleasure in almost anything. The only "bright spot" is your 1-year-old grandson, but you only see him about once a week.

- You haven't noticed a change in appetite or weight, but you find it is expensive to eat healthy. Your diet could improve if you had a bit more money.

- You are not sleeping because you are so worried about losing your house, not finding a job, and living without your husband—you're maybe getting four good nights of sleep a week. Your energy is low and it is hard to initiate any new activities, like looking for a job.

- You are struggling to concentrate a few days a week, especially on the days you are not sleeping. You used to read all the time, but you find you have to read the same page over and over.

- You have not noticed any change in your speech or movement.

- You have thought about killing yourself. Who would "really miss" you anyway? Your kids are busy with their lives, and your ex has moved on. Your mom is gone.

- You think about killing yourself two to three times a week. The thought stays with you for about an hour or two and usually occurs at night.

- You saved a bunch of your mom's left over oxycodone tablets after she died. You have about 30 of them and think that "would do the job." You haven't told anyone this before. You don't have firearms in the house. Your ex got them in the divorce; plus you wouldn't want your daughter to find that mess.

- Your sister died by suicide about five years ago, and depression runs in the family.

- Your cat is the main thing that stops you. You are not sure who would take care of it.

- In the past, you relied on your mom, sister, and former husband for support. They are all gone.

HOME ASSESSMENTS AND SAFETY: THE HOME VISIT

For decades, social workers have been conducting home visits. Every day, individuals from infants to older adults receive services and support in their home environment from a social worker. Home visits are an effective and efficient way to access clients for services and can provide a more complete picture of the client's living situation. These visits are not without risks, however. Social workers must be mindful of their safety and take the necessary steps to avoid potentially harmful situations. Most social service agencies provide safety training. Attending this training is often mandatory and should not be taken lightly.

It is very important to prepare for a home visit. This includes a self-assessment or self-inventory. The self-assessment requires the worker to be emotionally prepared for the home visit, confident in the objectives of the visit, and respectful of the values of the client's home environment. Such preparations include alerting your supervisor or agency that you will be making a home visit and taking a fully charged cell phone. See the *Standards for Technology in Social Work Practice* (NASW et al., 2017) for more information about the use of cell phones in practice. Ensure you have the correct address and directions to the client's home. Some agencies may require you to complete a travel log prior to your visit. Before visiting a client's home, initiate the client assessment by reviewing pertinent intake or referral information. This information can be useful in building rapport and may provide insight into the client's situation. Some home visits are scheduled with an appointment, but not all. It is recommended to call ahead and inform the client when you're on the way. When you arrive at the home of the client, an assessment of the surroundings, both inside and out, should occur. Observation is critical to safety. For additional information on social worker safety, see *NASW Guidelines for Social Worker Safety in the Workplace* (NASW, 2013).

EXERCISE 7.7: A STUDENT'S FIRST SOLO HOME VISIT

Note to Instructor: This exercise is about awareness and safety. A broad discussion should follow this exercise to reinforce the need to comply with agency protocols and safety guidelines.

Directions

- Form groups of four to six.

- As a group, make a list of what you would do differently for each of the three phases of the home visit.

Case Vignette

Amanda is a social work student in the first term of her second-year/concentration field placement. She plans to work with children and families after graduation. After completing the agency's safety training, she is now ready for her first solo home visit. Her client, Mrs. Ridges, is the parent of a child referred for services.

GENERALIST SOCIAL WORK ASSESSMENTS

Social work assessments differ depending on the mission and scope of the agency as well as the system level; therefore, the information collected varies. The social worker's knowledge and skills have a direct impact on the quality of an assessment. Table 7.1 suggests differences and similarities in six broad settings, and as you review it, consider what they are.

Phase 1: Phone Call

Dialogue	Observations & Thoughts
Amanda: Hello, Ms. Ridges, this is Amanda Smith from Best Family Human Services. I am calling to arrange a home visit for next week.	I am a little nervous. I must remember to speak up and be professional.
Ms. Ridges: Ok, my son's school told me someone would be calling. When do you want to come? I am busy, you know. Do you have to come to my home?	I am a good parent. I am not sure why she wants to come to my home. The school could have given me more information.
Amanda: What about next Tuesday at 10 am? Will you be home at that time?	I hope she can do a morning visit. I need time to prepare, so next Tuesday is good for me.
Ms. Ridges: That's early; what about noon? I need to get myself together before you get here, so noon is best for me.	I really don't have time for this, but I have to do it for my son. Why do they have to come to my home? I don't need any trouble.
Amanda: Ok, next Tuesday at noon it is. I look forward to meeting you.	That went well. I can answer all of her questions during the visit. She sounds like a nice person.

Phase 2: Leaving the Office and Going to the Home

Dialogue	Observations & Thoughts
Amanda: Betty, I have a home visit at noon today. I have it listed on the chart in the central office. Wish me luck!	My first solo field visit. Wow, it's exciting to write it on the home visit chart.
Betty: Do you have everything you need?	I hope she remembers her training and follows all of the safety guidelines. I wonder if I should remind her?
Amanda: I think I'm ready. I got the referral information, so I am off. See you later.	I got my phone and referral information and don't think I need to do anything else. I have never been on this side of town before. I can't believe I am 20 minutes late. Where should I park my car? There is no place to park nearby. There are a lot of people hanging around today. Why are they looking at me so intensely? Hopefully, Ms. Ridges will still meet with me. I am 20 minutes late, which is not a good way to start the visit.

Phase 3: The Home Visit

Dialogue	Observations & Thoughts
Amanda: Hi, Ms. Ridges, I am Amanda from Best Family Human Services. Sorry I am 20 minutes late. I got lost on the way here. Is parking always difficult in this area?	I can't believe I am having to apologize for being late. I will definitely be on time the next visit. Maybe I should ask Best Family for a GPS for the agency car.
Ms. Ridges: Come on in. I didn't think you were coming, so I invited four of my friends over. Sorry about the loud music. We can go into the other room and talk. Please excuse all the boxes; I am moving some things around. Can I get you something to drink?	She is late; didn't think she was coming. I got a house full of people visiting now. My house is a mess. Oh, well. She looks so young—probably has no clue what it's like to have kids. I really don't need this right now.

(Continued)

(Continued)

Dialogue	Observations & Thoughts
Amanda: No, thank you. I am fine.	The music is loud. Who are the folks in the other room? Can barely get around in this house. Is she moving? Where are the exits? The safety training said I should be near an exit. I am thirsty but will wait until after the visit. Look at all those pictures of her son; must be hundreds of them.
Ms. Ridges: Hold on for a second, let me tell my friends don't go anywhere.	She is 20 minutes late; I've got things to do. Don't want them to leave; this visit is going to be a short one.
Amanda: Ok, fine.	Who are those people? I really need to get started with this home assessment. I need to focus and not be distracted.
Ms. Ridges: Alright, so tell me why are you here?	Let's get this done.
Amanda: Well, our agency got a referral from your son's school. The school is concerned about his aggressive behavior. Once we receive a referral, the next step is a home visit.	Stay focused and think about your questions. Should I pull out the referral information and read it? I wish she would turn down the music; it is hard for me to concentrate. Her friends are loud.
Ms. Ridges: I see. Wait, let me tell my friends something. I'll be back in two minutes.	How long is this visit going to take? My son will be home from school in about an hour. All my free time will be over for today.
Amanda: What's that loud noise?	Sounds like something heavy fell. I am feeling more nervous about this visit. I have my phone just in case. I need to begin this assessment. Maybe I should ask if we could go to a quieter place in the house.
Ms. Ridges: Oh, my friends are just horsing around; I should tell them to go upstairs!	She looks nervous.
Amanda: Sounds like someone is knocking on your door.	It's pretty busy in this home. I don't think Ms. Ridges understand the seriousness of this visit. Two more people just came in. What's happening around here? I have to begin this assessment.
Ms. Ridges: You know, this may not be the best time for a visit.	I can't sit down with her now. I feel sorry about this, but she can always come back at a different time. I am not going to ask my company to leave.
Amanda: Are you sure?	I didn't get anything accomplished. Maybe I should be more assertive and reinforce the seriousness of my visit.
Ms. Ridges: Yes, call me next week so we can try it again.	There is too much going on right now. I don't need a home visit anyway.
Amanda: Ok, I will be in touch. Thank you for your time.	What just happened? I didn't get any information. I can't believe I had to park two blocks away. Hopefully, I can find my way out of this neighborhood.

TABLE 7.1 ■ Generalist Social Work Assessments

Individual		
Food/Clothing Eligibility	**Medical In-Home**	**Mental Health**
1. Demographic data	1. Demographic data	1. Demographic data
2. Personal	2. Personal	2. Referral source
• Number of household occupants	• Income	• Self-referral/agency referral
• Income source	• Insurance	• Legal status
• Employment status	• Household	• Mandated or voluntary
• Education	• Occupants	3. Presenting problem(s)
• Cultural factors	• Current caregiver	4. Mental status
	• Transportation	• Appearance
	• Referral source	• Behavior

3. Medical problems
   - Physical/mental abilities
4. Other required information
5. Decide eligibility
6. Summary & recommendations

3. Home environment
   - Architectural layout
4. Medical history
   - Diagnosis/prognosis
   - Medications
   - Psychological history
   - Current functions/limitations
5. Activities of daily living (ADL)
   - Walking
   - Dressing
   - Eating
   - Toileting
   - Bathing
6. Summary & recommendations

- Speech
- Mood
- Affect
- Thought process
- Thought content
- Cognition
- Insight/judgment
5. Bio-psychosocial-spiritual assessment
   - Cultural factors
6. Drug/alcohol history
7. Use specialized assessment tools, if warranted
   - Psychological test
   - Neurological test
8. Formulate clinical diagnoses

Family

1. Demographic data
2. Referral source/review existing information
   - School
   - Agency
3. Interview family
   - Parents
   - Children
   - Caregivers
4. Consult with other agencies/ individuals, if necessary
5. Consider additional specialized assessments, if needed (e.g., eco-map, behavior, risk, trauma)
6. Determine course of action
7. Develop service/family plan
8. Monitor progress/needs

Groups

1. Type of group
2. Purpose of the group
3. Goal(s) of the group
4. Group size
5. Group composition
   - Heterogeneous
   - Homogeneous
6. Leadership
   - Facilitator/cofacilitator
7. Determine areas for assessment
   - Individual
   - Roles of group members
   - Individuals' cognitions and behaviors
   - Group's patterns/behaviors
   - Group alliances
   - Group norms
   - Group cohesion
8. Group feedback
(Hepworth et al., 2017, p. 294)

Community

1. Identify the community
2. Plan needs assessment
   - Assessment team(s)
   - Assessment tools/questions
3. Determine assessment methods
   - Door-to-door
   - Telephone
   - Mail
   - Determine assessment locations within the community (e.g., private residences, businesses, schools, healthcare facilities)
   - Identify needs to assess (e.g., playground, grocery store, street lights, community policing, youth programs)
4. Conduct assessment
5. Review and evaluate the data
   - Summarize the data
6. Develop community action plan
   - Implement strategies to meet the need(s) of the community
7. Present to stakeholders
(CDC, 2013; Ohmer, Teixeira, Booth, Zuberi, & Kolke, 2016)

EXERCISE 7.8: COMPARISON OF GENERALIST ASSESSMENTS

Note to Instructor: This exercise is beneficial when your students are completing internships or placements.

Directions

- Form groups of four to six. Try to mix groups so a variety of practice settings are present in each group.

- Each person, using Table 7.1 as a guide, makes a list of information collected and tools that are used as part of the assessment process at the internship or field site.

- Students discuss their lists, noting (1) the similarities and differences, (2) which skills they learn in class, (3) which skills they learn in the field, and (4) their current confidence level in using these skills.

- Students in each group should select three key points from their discussion to share with the class as a whole.

Answer Key to Antonia's Case

Antonia's Balanced Assessment Matrix

Strengths or Resources

Hospital social worker(s) Maria: Supportive; provided housing	Personal beliefs Religion & faith Willing to utilize medication treatment Resilient: Will to live Good work history Accepted self as transgendered woman In good health
Homophobia/transphobia Harassment/bullying Family beliefs Hospital staff hostility Rural community Job not sufficient Rejected by parents Sister's husband-to-be unsupportive	Drug use Past hospitalizations Suicide attempts Social isolation Diagnoses: chronic depression, schizophreniform disorder, bipolar II

Environmental Factors (left axis) — *Individual / Personal Factors* (right axis)

Deficits, Obstacles, or Challenges

DEVELOPING AND NEGOTIATING SMART CLIENT GOALS AND FORMULATING A CONTRACT

LEARNING OBJECTIVES

1. Understand the purpose and functions of goals for clients and for success in the helping process (Exercise 8.1).

2. Using client case vignettes, evaluate several general goals and apply guidelines for creating client-centered, strengths-based SMART goals (specific, measurable, attainable, realistic, and timely) (Exercises 8.1 and 8.2).

3. Translate attainable goals into action steps (Exercise 8.2).

4. Become skilled in writing complete client plans (Exercises 8.3 and 8.4).

5. Understand different types of contracts, the purpose of contracts, and their various components (Exercise 8.5).

CHAPTER OUTLINE

- Formulating and Negotiating Goals: Key Concepts and Definitions
  - The Purpose of Goals
  - The Functions of Goals
  - Guidelines for Creating SMART Goals
  - Goal Negotiation Activities
  - Translating Goals Into Action
- Exercise 8.1: Specifying Global Goals
- Exercise 8.2: Translating Goals Into Action
- Exercise 8.3: Elements of the Plan Worksheet
- Exercise 8.4: Goal or Objective Worksheet

- Formulating a Contract
  - ○ Working Contract Questions
  - ○ Elements of a Working Contract
  - ○ Initial or Exploratory Contract vs. a Working Contract
  - ○ Guidelines to Help in Role Clarification
  - ○ Time-Limited Service Advantages
- Exercise 8.5: Going Beyond the Goals to Create the Contract

So far, you have learned how to communicate empathically with your client to establish rapport and how to collect information about why your client is seeking help in order to formulate a multidimensional assessment. The next task, then, is to learn how to identify and collaboratively negotiate a plan of action, including client-centered goals, which creates a working contract. Through the various exercises, you will develop an understanding of the purpose and functions of goals for clients and for success in the helping process, and you will practice defining and establishing goals conjointly with your client, whether that client is an individual, a family, a group, an organization, or a community. Using real-life client case vignettes, you will be challenged to evaluate several general goals and apply guidelines for developing SMART goals (Doran, 1981). You will learn to make general goals into *s*pecific, *m*easurable goals that are *a*ttainable, *r*ealistic, and *t*imely using a strengths perspective. Finally, you will learn how to translate goals into action steps.

FORMULATING AND NEGOTIATING GOALS: KEY CONCEPTS AND DEFINITIONS

The Purpose of Goals

The purpose of goals is to establish in specific terms what clients want to accomplish. Goals may be individual, shared, or reciprocal. Explaining the purpose of goals to clients

- Demystifies the helping process
- Reduces the threat of committing to change tasks and activities
- Invites them into the process of creating the goals

The Functions of Goals

- Goals assure that practitioners and clients are in agreement about what is to be achieved.
- Goals provide direction and continuity to the helping process.
- Goals facilitate the development and selection of appropriate strategies and interventions.
- Goals assist practitioners and clients to monitor progress.
- Goals serve as outcome criteria in evaluating the effectiveness of the interventions utilized in the helping process.

There are three main goal subtypes:

- Individual goals
- Shared goals (between two or more individuals, e.g., couples, families, groups)

- Reciprocal goals (in which members of a system, e.g., a family or organization, solve relationship or interaction problems by agreeing to each make changes in different behaviors)

Goals state the client's (and practitioner's) desired results. Objectives are the more specific steps necessary to reach the goal. In some planning formats, there may be a third level of steps called tasks, or *tasks* may be used as the terminology instead of *objectives.*

Clients will pursue only those goals in which they are emotionally invested and which they see as directly related to improving their lives. Goals should tap into clients' motivations and life in a strengths-oriented manner rather than a problem-focused manner. Working toward something that is desired is often more motivating than simply solving a problem. The client's goal may be very different from the practitioner's choice; thus, the practitioner's job is to find common ground and negotiate a goal that is agreeable and appropriate. The client, however, has the final decision, and you have responsibility to provide guidance.

Guidelines for Creating SMART Goals

The idea of SMART (specific, measurable, attainable, realistic, and timely) goals dates to business management concepts in the 1980s (Doran, 1981; Day & Tosey, 2011) and has been picked up in other sectors of business and service, including the helping professions (Bowen, Mogensen, Marsland, & Lannin, 2015; Tichelaar et al., 2016; Bovend'Eerdt, Botell, & Wade, 2009). These concepts are present in most social work texts, and the actual SMART acronym is included in some, like Hepworth et al.'s text (2017), as well as in training materials and forms for social service programs, such as materials developed by the Pennsylvania Child Welfare Resource Center (2013) for child welfare personnel. As the model has been implemented and studied, some have altered or changed the language associated with the letters, particularly the letters "A" and "R." There seems to be overlap between something being attainable and being realistic. Those ideas will be reflected below in parentheses.

- Specific: Refine and define a desired outcome in clear, concrete terms. Who will be involved? Where will it occur? What will occur?

- Measurable (measurement/metrics): Determine how you will know that you have reached the desired outcome.

- Attainable (achievable/action oriented/acceptable/agreed upon): For most of the "A" language, select a goal that can be accomplished while capturing a sense of stretch to push and challenge the client system. This necessitates awareness of the skills, knowledge, and resources needed to reach the goal, as those details help shape the steps. For the terms *acceptable* and *agreed upon,* collaborate with the client and ensure the client is interested in and motivated to reach the goal. These ideas are consistent with social work's emphasis on being client centered and promoting self-determination.

- Realistic (relevant/results-focused): The goal is "realistic" if it can be accomplished, again with a focus on the necessary skills, knowledge, and resources. To create a "relevant" goal, focus on whether the goal can make a meaningful impact on the life of the client system.

- Timely (time bound): Determine a time frame that makes sense and use that time frame to create accountability and motivate work.

Given the overlap in some of the terminology between A and R, you should use the guidance provided by your social work program; include the ideas of being able to accomplish the chosen goal and its being meaningful to the client.

For social workers who are implementing the SMART goal approach, focusing on a strengths perspective deserves careful consideration. A strengths perspective views client systems as having skills, resources, and capabilities that can be employed, modified, or enhanced to achieve goals. It is also forward-looking in that the goals state what people are hoping to achieve, not simply what they want to eliminate or find troublesome. Many times, both the client and the social worker can more easily identify a problem focus. Simple questioning techniques can be employed to flip it to a strengths focus. For example, Chris and Taylor J. come to the agency stating that they are yelling at their children all the time and their family is tense. They want to eliminate the yelling. A problem focus might state, "Chris and Taylor J. will stop yelling at their kids." The social worker could ask questions to understand the function the yelling serves and then ask them to imagine how they might communicate with their children to achieve those same ends without yelling. This could lead them to determine what they want. A strengths-focused goal, then, might say, "Chris and Taylor J. will learn and use three new parenting techniques."

In summary, goal setting is a joint, collaborative, client-practitioner process in which mutually agreeable solutions to the problems are developed. These solutions or goals should be specific enough to be measurable and proximate enough to be attainable using their strengths and motivations.

Goals should be commensurate with the knowledge and skill of the social worker and the function of the social worker's agency; goals should also be consistent with social work values and ethics.

When negotiating goals, you have a responsibility to consider four important limitations on practitioner activity: time, skill, ethics, and agency function. No social worker can spend unlimited time with a client; thus, time constraints must be considered as a factor in the service contract. If you aren't clear about time parameters, a client may overestimate what you can do. A common misconception is confusing quantity of service with quality of service. Poor quality service is more likely to be provided when practitioners make commitments they cannot keep. Beyond the duty to practice within our scope of competence and the scope of practice for agencies, the NASW *Code of Ethics* (2017) challenges social workers to act in a socially just manner. Therefore, social workers should be mindful that goals do not replicate patterns of oppression in the wider society and disempower client systems.

The following are examples of measurable goals (time frames are not present in all of these examples):

- Bob will build courage to leave his house and will visit his friends Jim and Betty two to three times a week for 30 minutes.

- Janice will report an improvement in mood (to seven on a 10-point scale) and appetite (eating two meals per day) within the next two months without the desire to return to drug use.

- Janice will visit two of her close friends twice weekly over the next three months and report sleeping a minimum of seven hours each night.

- Nadine will engage in conversation with her parents a minimum of 30 minutes each day without immediately leaving the dinner table.

- Bob will leave his home for 15 minutes each day over the next two months.

- Bob will talk to his friend Don about accompanying him to dinner once monthly.

- Billy will spend 30 minutes alone with his stepfather weekly over the next two months.

- To achieve and maintain a drug-free life, Devin will attend two NA meetings weekly over the next three months.

- Mr. William will find a local eye doctor and make an appointment for an eye exam by the end of the month.

- Before the end of the month, Mr. William will create an emergency list of numbers to keep by his phone.

- Mrs. Johnson will contact the local library within the next two weeks to see if there are any reading programs or book clubs available for senior citizens.

- Mr. Johnson will call his state representative twice monthly to discuss his situation and the need for more services for seniors.

- Debra will find a primary care physician and make an appointment for a complete physical by the end of the month.

- The Garcia family will report improved communication as shown by fewer than three arguments per week and playing two family games per week.

- Members of the Men's Skills group will each gain two or more skills to calm themselves when angry within eight weeks.

- The ABC agency will apply for and get at least two grants to support the family program within six months.

- Westside Neighborhood Group will gain agreement from the town council to add three new stop signs within three months.

Goal Negotiation Activities

- Determining whether the clients are ready to begin the process of negotiating goals

- Discussing the purpose of selecting and defining goals

- Eliciting goals from clients, suggesting other potential goals, and then collaboratively choosing goals that are appropriate

- Defining the goals explicitly along with determining the extent of change that the client is ready for at this time

- Determining whether the goals are feasible and attainable and discussing the pros and cons associated with each goal

- Facilitating the process of clients' making a commitment to work on specific goals

- Rank ordering the goals according to clients' priorities

- Using summarizing responses to feed back to the client your grasp of their problems and situation

- Asking the client whether you are accurate and whether anything should be added

- Asking the client if he/she is ready to proceed to considering goals

Translating Goals Into Action

- Specify who will do what by when using a task plan or time line.

- Specify a specific plan for follow-up.

EXERCISE 8.1: SPECIFYING GLOBAL GOALS

The purpose of this exercise is to challenge you to take a broad global goal and break it down into specific, measurable smaller goals that are feasible for the client to attain.

Directions

- Form groups of four or six and, as a group, address each of the case vignettes.

- Examine each of the broad goal statements and, using the SMART goals guidelines, brainstorm the various ways the global general goal could be broken down into smaller, more specific, measurable, attainable, realistic, and timely goals. Use your imagination and feel free to add details to the client's situation.

Case Vignette 1

The client is a 32-year-old married Korean American woman who is seeing the practitioner because of marital problems. She has identified three general goals:

1. Learn how to be more assertive

2. Improve marital communication with her husband

3. Enhance her self-esteem

Case Vignette 2

The client is a 26-year-old unemployed, single, African American transgender man who is seeing the practitioner because he is lonely and shy. He has identified three general goals:

1. Find employment

2. Improve the quality of his social life

3. Learn how to be more outgoing

Case Vignette 3

The client is a 29-year-old single Caucasian mother with three preschool-aged children. She is seeing the practitioner because she says that taking care of her children is overwhelming, and she gets angry with them frequently. Her identified general goals are as follows:

1. Improve her parenting skills

2. "Get a life" for herself

3. Learn how to handle her emotions better when around her children

Case Vignette 4

The client is a neighborhood church group concerned about the fact that the African American teenage boys in their impoverished neighborhood have nothing to do after school, so they hang around the streets and get into trouble. The group's general goals are as follows:

1. Develop some kind of afterschool program for the boys

2. Improve the employment situation for African American teenage boys

3. Find positive role models for the boys

Case Vignette 5

The "client" is a treatment group for individuals who are court-ordered to substance use treatment following a DWI (driving while intoxicated) conviction. The group's general goals are:

1. "Get the court off our backs"

2. "Get our heads straight"

3. Do something about our drinking (each group member, however, has a different idea about this goal)

Case Vignette 6

The client is a local nonprofit that has a contract with local government to provide family support services. However, families often have needs that the grant funds cannot cover. Its general goals are:

1. Increase its capacity to apply for and get grants

2. Create a program to meet families' unmet needs

3. Develop a plan for assessing family needs across the community

EXERCISE 8.2: TRANSLATING GOALS INTO ACTION

This exercise is an extension of Exercise 8.1 above.

Directions

- Choose one of the client statements from Exercise 8.1 that your group has worked on, and translate the global goals into specific measurable goals.

- Then, for each specific measurable goal, identify (1) how the goal will be measured and (2) the first three steps involved in translating the goal into action. These steps will not necessarily reach the goal but will be steps taken along the way to achieving the goal.

Questions to Guide Translating Goals Into Action

1. Is the action directly related to the goal?

2. Is the action feasible and attainable?

3. Is the decision for a particular action the product of a collaboration between the client and practitioner?

4. Does the action draw on the client's strengths?

5. Is there a high probability of the client achieving success with the action?

6. Is the action compatible with social work ethics and values?

7. Is the action culturally sensitive and relevant?

8. Is the action compatible with what the client wants to do?

9. Does the action specify who will do what by when?

EXERCISE 8.3: ELEMENTS OF THE PLAN WORKSHEET

Goal writing seems deceptively simple. In reality, it is a skill that needs to be practiced. This exercise gives you an opportunity to review goal statements, determine whether they are complete, and rewrite them if they are not.

Directions

- Complete this exercise individually or in small groups.

- For each statement, determine whether it is complete and SMART. If not, mark which element or elements are missing: (1) specific outcome, (2) measurable, (3) attainable, (4) relevant (client centered), (5) timely/time frame, or (6) strengths focused.

Hints: Effective goals and plans are about and belong to the client, not the agency or funder. Plans should be living documents that guide practice and are revised as you and the client work on them. Therefore, client-centered goals should star the client, not the service or the practitioner. Services and practitioners will appear in plans but typically in objectives or action steps rather than the goal statements. Two statements are complete in this exercise.

Worksheet

	Goal Statement	Missing Element(s)
1	Mr. Martin will get a job within 90 days.	_____
2	Marcella will stop annoying her parents in the next 30 days.	_____
3	Suzanna will feel better about herself.	_____
4	Social worker will assist Mrs. Jones to manage emotions better within 10 weeks, as shown by fewer than three crying episodes per month and fewer than two angry outbursts per month.	_____
5	Ms. Gonzales will feel more confident in her ability to parent by the end of 12 weeks, as demonstrated by self-report of confidence at an 8 or higher on a scale of 10 and spending at least three hours per day with her children.	_____
6	The ABC Housing Agency will meet with 95% of potential clients within two weeks of getting an application from them.	_____
7	The case manager will help Ms. Zahara find and move to a new apartment by September 30.	_____
8	The Dunlap family will get along better.	_____
9	Within 10 weeks, members of the grief support group won't feel sad anymore, as measured by self-report.	_____
10	Anytown USA will not have any more negative news stories.	_____

Find the Answer Key on page 95 at the end of this chapter.

EXERCISE 8.4: GOAL OR OBJECTIVE WORKSHEET

Goals or plans always have specific steps to reach them, sometimes called objectives and sometimes called tasks. These can be thought of as smaller goals the client system must achieve to reach the goal. This exercise gives you some practice in identifying goals versus objectives. When plans add either objectives or tasks, they may reflect the approach to helping that the practitioner is using. Below are four of the common approaches to generalist helping:

1. Cognitive restructuring. This approach assists a client system in understanding itself and its relationship to the wider world differently. It uses some of the elements of an advanced practice approach to helping, cognitive-behavioral therapy, but remains focused on altering the client's thoughts. This is best used by generalists when some cognitive insight might enable the client system to solve their own challenges using one of the other approaches.

2. Crisis intervention. This approach presumes that something about the current situation has overtaken a client system's ability to respond. It centers on getting people the support, resources, and information they need to resume their previous level of functioning or even improve on it.

3. Solution-focused approach. This approach attempts to shift the focus from "the problem" to solutions—all those other aspects of a client system's life that are working—and ways to make "the problem" less central to everyday living. Like cognitive restructuring, solution-focused therapy is an advanced practice skill set. At the generalist level, the social worker is not doing full therapy and would refer to someone with those qualifications, if necessary.

4. Task-centered approach. This approach assumes people have the ability to solve their own problems but may lack a skill, a resource, or piece of knowledge to do so on their own. It is a concrete approach to helping in which focused goals are divided into concrete steps, and the generalist social worker assists as the client carries them out.

Note to Instructor: Depending upon the way a class is organized, students may or may not be ready to do this part of the exercise. Students can always come back to it later.

Directions

- Complete this exercise individually or in small groups.
- For each set of statements, determine which statements are goals and which are objectives.
- Then, suggest which approach to helping is reflected in the set.

Hints: Goal statements are broader than objectives. One of the sets has two goal statements in it. Sometimes, the goals in plans will look or sound the same even if different helping approaches are being used.

Worksheet

	Statement	Type
Set 1	Within 3 weeks, Ms. Harun and her sister will visit her top three choices for training and collect information to see which is a good choice for her.	
	Within 6 weeks, Mrs. Harun will start one of the culinary training programs.	
	Ms. Harun will gain new job skills within 90 days.	
	Within 1 week, Ms. Harun and her social worker will create a list of job training programs in the culinary field.	

The Set 1 plan fits which approach to helping? _____

	Statement	Type
Set 2	The Meson family will resume living in their repaired home within 3 months.	
	Social worker will help family locate temporary housing within 1 week of the house fire.	
	Mr. and Ms. Meson will work with insurance company and fire restoration company to set a plan for repair by week 3.	
	Within 60 days, the Meson children will emotionally cope with the fire as shown by discussing it with the social worker and parents and continuing school and other activities without any behavioral challenges.	

The Set 2 plan fits which approach to helping? _____

	Statement	Type
Set 3	Tobias will practice turn taking with the social worker and one other student during weeks three to six; social worker will cue him to use his self-management tools.	
	Tobias will take turns with other children when playing games three times per week within 10 weeks.	
	Tobias will play one game in the classroom with two other students during weeks six to eight without a teacher or social worker.	
	Tobias and social worker will try, practice, and choose two self-management tools that Tobias can use during sitting activities to help him stay focused on the game and to sit during the game within three weeks.	

The Set 3 plan fits which approach to helping? _____

Find the Answer Key on page 95 at the end of this chapter.

FORMULATING A CONTRACT

After exploring problems sufficiently and reaching agreement as to their nature and the systems involved and negotiating goals, you and your client are ready to formulate a contract. Throughout the helping process, there is consistent emphasis on the mutual partnership nature of the interaction. In the contract, this partnership is fully developed and made explicit. Now, in emphasizing mutuality, one must not lose sight of the notion of difference; that is, "partnership" does not mean the practitioner and the client bring the same knowledge, understanding, feeling, and activities to the helping process. Rather, the concepts of partnership and the contract emphasize the unique contributions of each partner to the work to be done.

Maluccio and Marlow (1974) define a contract as "the explicit agreement between the worker and the client concerning the target problems, the goals, the strategies of social work intervention, and the roles and tasks of the participants. Its major features are mutual agreement, differential participation in the intervention process, reciprocal accountability, and explicitness. In practice these features are closely interrelated" (p. 30).

A contract

- Protects the client's uniqueness and maximizes the opportunity for self-determination

- Increases the client's opportunities for meaningful decisions about self and situation

Working Contract Questions

- Is the problem we want to work on the one that was identified when we began work together? If not, why not?

- Why has the problem persisted in spite of earlier attempts to solve it?

- What is the desired solution?

- How will this solution be achieved?

Elements of a Working Contract

Compton and Galaway (1989, p. 473) provide four essential terms of a contract, which should be explicit and detailed so that each party knows clearly what is expected of him or her in the relationship.

1. The goals toward which the social worker and the client(s) shall work. These goals or terminal behaviors should be specific, discrete and, whenever feasible, observable;

2. The specific responsibilities of each party to the contract in terms of rights and obligations;

3. The techniques, interventions, or strategies to be used in achieving the goals;

4. The administrative procedures to be involved: when to meet, where to meet, time, and so on.

Initial or Exploratory Contract vs. a Working Contract

An initial or exploratory contract is an agreement to explore and negotiate the terms of a working contract, and commitment from both parties involved is necessary. A working contract may or may not grow out of the initial contract; this will depend on the negotiation that takes place. Therefore, the sequence is as follows:

1. Development of an exploratory contract

2. Development of a working contract

3. Review and evaluation of the accomplishments of the working contract

4. Renegotiation resulting in a new working contract or termination of services

All contracts should include the following elements (Frankel & Gelman, 2016):

- Goals to be accomplished (ranked by priority)
- Roles of the participants
- Interventions or techniques to be used
- Temporal conditions (i.e., frequency, number, length, and duration of client-practitioner contacts or sessions)

Guidelines to Help in Role Clarification

- Determine the client's expectations
- Briefly explain the nature of the helping process
- Emphasize the importance of being open in sharing feelings, thoughts, and events
- Go over protocol regarding scheduling, keeping and canceling appointments
- Discuss the difficulties inherent in making changes
- Discuss your role as assisting the client to focus on strengths and the incremental growth he or she can hope to achieve
- Clarify how your approach to helping may differ from previous experiences
- Discuss the advantages of time-limited versus open-ended contracts

(Hepworth et al., 2017; Rapp & Goscha, 2012)

Time-Limited Service Advantages

- Often equally as effective as open-ended service
- Less likely to encourage dependency, can foster optimism and support self-determination
- People often intensify efforts when there is a deadline
- More likely to be cost-effective
- More clients can be served with fewer resources
- Facilitates the process of termination because the ending point of service is clear

The formatting and structure of treatment/service/goal plans may or may not include all the elements of a contract. Each student can explore how different agencies and populations include the elements of the contract into plans. In Rapp and Goscha's (2012) work on strengths-based case management, they suggest that plans include many of the elements of a contract and that the plan itself should become a blueprint for the work that is reviewed and revised at each interaction, to help focus both client and social worker and hold them accountable in partnership.

EXERCISE 8.5: GOING BEYOND THE GOALS TO CREATE THE CONTRACT

In this exercise, you will have the opportunity to discuss aspects of the contract that previous exercises have not explored. These may or may not appear in the plan itself, depending upon the agency, funding, and reporting requirements where social workers are employed.

Directions

- In pairs or groups of three people, take turns role playing the social worker and the client.

- In each vignette, you will be given an agreed-upon goal, and you will concentrate on discussing (1) roles of the participants, (2) interventions or techniques to be used, and (3) temporal conditions.

Case Vignette 1

Rianna, a 53-year-old Salvadoran American woman, is at ABC agency for case management assistance with finances following the unexpected death of her husband in an auto accident. Without his income, Rianna does not have enough funds to cover her expenses. She has had two previous experiences with "professional helpers" other than her doctors. One was when she was temporarily on "welfare" (TANF) after the birth of her oldest child (currently age 20). The other occurred 10 years ago when she was laid off from a job and was required to "see an employment case manager" as a part of getting her severance package. The social worker and Rianna agreed to the following goal:

Goal Statement: Rianna will stabilize household finances in 8 weeks by applying for at least two programs to reduce household expenses, learning two new budgeting skills, and securing her late husband's life insurance benefits.

Starter Lines

Social Worker: Now that we have a goal, let's talk about how we will accomplish it. Can you tell me about your past experiences of working with a case manager?

Rianna: Sure. Both times before, I just did what they told me to get the benefits. I will do whatever you say this time.

Case Vignette 2

Marshall is a 20-year-old college student who was sent to the Student Assistance Center at school after getting caught underage drinking in the dorm. Discussing his drinking with a student coach and attending a substance use education program were part of the consequences from his judiciary hearing. He says he has never really seen any professional helpers other than his doctor and, certainly, not a life coach. During intake, he reveals his drinking and weed use has been increasing the last few months, and his school work has suffered.

Goal Statement: Marshall will pass his classes with a 3.0 for the semester and resume using previous study habits within four weeks.

Starter Lines

Marshall: So, what's next, now that we have a goal? How often do I need to come and all that? We won't talk about my childhood and that stuff, right?

Case Vignette 3

Edith, 75, and James, 78, recently sold their home and moved into a senior apartment because they could not afford the house's upkeep, and its layout was hard to navigate after Edith's stroke. They lived in a neighborhood that had not appreciated, and the house had not been kept up. As a result, the sale did not produce the nest egg they assumed. Their only source of income is Social Security benefits. After they moved, the service coordinator for the building, a social worker, visited them. They are not sure what to expect but agreed to try to work together. They have an exploratory contract. Edith's post-stroke rehabilitation is finished, and she is supposed to continue to exercise on her own. Edith can no longer cook for them, and James has never done their cooking and says they need to eat something other than frozen foods.

Goal Statement: Within two weeks, Edith and James will decide whether they want to work with the service coordinator as part of their move.

Starter Lines

Social Worker: It's nice to see you again. We had agreed I would stop by to talk more about whether I can be of help as you transition into the building and community. Have you thought any more about our last discussion? Would you like to talk to today?

Answer Key

	Goal Statement	Missing Element(s)
1	Mr. Martin will get a job within 90 days.	Complete
2	Marcella will stop annoying her parents in the next 30 days.	Not strengths focused, outcome unclear, not measurable
3	Suzanna will feel better about herself.	No time frame, not measurable, not specific
4	Social worker will assist Mrs. Jones to manage emotions better within 10 weeks, as shown by fewer than three crying episodes per month and fewer than two angry outbursts per month.	Not client centered, not entirely strengths oriented
5	Ms. Gonzales will feel more confident in her ability to parent by the end of 12 weeks, as demonstrated by self-report of confidence at an eight or higher on a scale of 10 and spending at least three hours per day with her children.	Complete
6	The ABC Housing Agency will meet with 95% of potential clients within two weeks of getting an application from them.	No time frame to get to the 95%
7	The case manager will help Ms. Zahara find and move to a new apartment by September 30.	Not client centered
8	The Dunlap family will get along better.	No time frame, no measurement, generally broad and vague
9	Within 10 weeks, members of the grief support group won't feel sad anymore, as measured by self-report.	Inappropriate goal for issue, not strengths focused
10	Anytown USA will not have any more negative news stories.	Not strengths focused, no time frame, probably not attainable

Answer Key

	Statement	Type
Set 1	Within three weeks, Ms. Harun and her sister will visit her top three choices for training and collect information to see which is a good choice for her.	objective
	Within six weeks, Mrs. Harun will start one of the culinary training programs.	objective
	Ms. Harun will gain new job skills within 90 days.	goal
	Within one week, Ms. Harun and her social worker will create a list of job training programs in the culinary field.	objective

The Set 1 plan fits which model of change? Task–centered

Explanation: The goal suggests that the person lacks a resource and a skill, making a task-centered approach very appropriate.

	Statement	Type
Set 2	The Meson family will resume living in their repaired home within three months.	goal
	Social worker will help family locate temporary housing within one week of the house fire.	objective
	Mr. and Ms. Meson will work with insurance company and fire restoration company to set a plan for repair by week three.	objective
	Within 60 days, the Meson children will emotionally cope with the fire as shown by discussing it with the social worker and parents and continuing school and other activities without any behavioral challenges.	goal

The Set 2 plan fits which model of change? Crisis intervention

Explanation: Even though longer than eight weeks (crisis intervention is usually brief), the focus is on resolving a crisis, being overwhelmed after a house fire. Family was coping previously.

Statement		Type
Set 3	Tobias will practice turn taking with the social worker and one other student during weeks 3 to 6; social worker will cue him to use his self-management tools.	objective
	Tobias will take turns with other children when playing games three times per week within 10 weeks.	goal
	Tobias will play one game in the classroom with two other students during weeks six to eight without a teacher or social worker.	objective
	Tobias and social worker will try, practice, and choose two self-management tools that Tobias can use during sitting activities to help him stay focused on the game and to sit during the game within 3 weeks.	objective

The Set 3 plan fits which model of change? Solution-focused

Explanation: Solution-focused is the best choice because of the behavioral nature of the issue and because it is really difficult to determine what the issue might be. Rather than resolving "the problem" you are focusing on what the child wants, which is the "solution." One might be able to make an argument that this is task centered because sometimes the same steps can represent more than one approach.

UNDERSTANDING FAMILY FUNCTIONING

LEARNING OBJECTIVES

1. Understand and be able to describe various key constructs for family functioning and family communication patterns (Exercises 9.1, 9.3, 9.4)

2. Identify the stage of family life cycle development and the practical and emotional tasks associated with it (Exercises 9.2, 9.3)

3. Identify rules, roles, and functions within families and the way culture influences them (Exercises 9.1, 9.3)

4. Analyze a scripted case scenario to determine the next steps that you could take to engage the family (Exercise 9.3)

5. Evaluate the case scenario and develop a series of questions for further assessment, if you were the practitioner in the scenario (Exercise 9.3)

CHAPTER OUTLINE

- Definitions and Key Concepts
  - ¢ Family Therapy Concepts
- Exercise 9.1: Exploring Family Roles, Rules, Patterns, and Culture
- Family Development: A Dominant Culture View of the Family Life Cycle
- Exercise 9.2: Identifying Family Life Cycle Stages
- Family Engagement and Interventions
- Exercise 9.3: Analyzing an Initial Family Interview
- Exercise 9.4: Exploring Family Patterns and Structure Using a Genogram

Working with families is a reality for almost all social workers, even those thinking of themselves as working primarily with individuals or communities. When a community struggles, the families in that community are impacted. When one member of a family has a challenge, it impacts the other members. Children, persons needing health and/or mental health services, persons with disabilities, older adults, people with justice system involvement, and veterans often try to resolve problems first within the family; then they reach out to formal providers like social workers. When individuals come for services, their families can support and enhance their efforts, or they can undermine them. And, many social systems depend on families to support the people they serve, such as school or medical systems. Therefore, all social workers should have knowledge of and skills to work with families. Family-focused social workers carry on the profession's legacy of developing and applying interventions to support healthy families. In *Social Diagnosis*, Mary Richmond (1917) described social work techniques for assessing the situation of troubled families, emphasizing that the relationship between the social worker and the client system is the key to success in social casework. From that time on, social workers were key professionals dedicated to working with families, particularly those living in poverty, viewing the family as the most important reciprocal social system in most people's lives because it is, essentially, "the ecological system that nourishes the individual" (Zimmerman, 1980, p. 195). Family casework, now referred to as "child and family practice," or simply "family therapy" or "family intervention," was based on the notion that the family is the nuclear social institution through which the community translates its moral, cultural, and spiritual heritage.

DEFINITIONS AND KEY CONCEPTS

What is a family? A family may be defined as two or more people connected by the bonds of sharing, intimacy, and mutual interdependence. These connections may result from biological relation or choice. The family is the primary social institution that shapes an individual's development physically, psychologically, emotionally, and spiritually. It meets many of its members' social, economic, and educational needs. It transmits values and culture while teaching vital roles and socializing children to participate in the larger society. Families, like individuals, are diverse in terms of race, culture, ethnicity, religion, sexual orientation, and social class. Increasingly, North American families have members who have been raised in different cultures and with different experiences of diversity, including privilege and oppression. Blending different cultures in a family often represents a strength and/ or opportunity and, sometimes, a challenge. Thus, the competent practitioner must approach families with cultural sensitivity, humility, and awareness that does not impose or presume a dominant cultural representation of families as white, middle class, and led by two opposite, cisgender parents who are married (Walsh, 2015; McGoldrick, Carter, & Garcia-Preto, 2011).

Whatever terminology we use to describe this work—family intervention, family team conferencing, family consultation, family preservation, family treatment, or family therapy—social work with families facilitates change and enhances positive development by viewing the family as a system of dynamic interactions and relationships. The social worker and the family come together to look at how the system meets the family's needs collectively and enhances members' individual development. They identify and support families' inherent strengths, find resources, and alter their interactions to enhance family functioning.

The conceptual framework used by most social work family practitioners is systems theory and the ecological model (Goldenberg & Goldenberg, 2007; McGoldrick et al., 2011). From that basis, many family intervention/therapy approaches emerge. Two of the most well-known approaches to working with families are structural family therapy, originally developed by family therapist Salvador Minuchin (1974), and family emotional systems therapy, originally developed by Murray Bowen (2004). In structural family therapy, the therapist intervenes and disrupts family interactional patterns that are not meeting their needs, with the goal of moving the family toward more healthy patterns. In family emotional systems theory, the family is viewed as an emotional unit with patterns of interaction that have developed over generations; the therapist seeks to reduce family anxiety and reactivity. There are key concepts associated with both of these approaches and other family approaches. There are also concepts that are more closely associated with one or the other.

Generalist social workers are not trained to provide family therapy; this work requires additional training. They can and should, however, become skilled in seeing how clients' challenges impact families, understanding common family patterns, reflecting those patterns back to families, and offering information and resources that families can use. This chapter introduces some general concepts about families that students can utilize.

Family Therapy Concepts

- **Boundaries** delineate who is part of the family and who is not, as well as what resources flow into and out of the family. Family boundaries must adapt to the normative changes (such as a member coupling with another person) and other challenges (serious chronic illness of one member) families face by shifting in their degree of openness to the broader environment to meet family needs.

- **Functions** include all of the activities that a family must accomplish to meet its collective needs and the individual needs of its members. These functions are many and varied, ranging from socializing children to understand the family's culture, to bringing in an income, to washing dishes.

- **Roles** reflect who within the family carries out various functions and expectations about how those functions will be carried out.

- **Rules** are shared ideas about how members of the family should interact with one another and people outside the family. They can be facilitative or problematic; they can be explicit and implicit. An explicit, facilitative rule might be that members alternate who takes out the garbage; a problematic, implicit rule might be that no one can share that a family member has an addiction. The importance of the rule may determine the degree to which it is enforced within the family.

- **Subsystems** include certain members of the family who are connected with one another due to function, power, or interest. For example,

  - **Spousal/couple subsystem**: in families that include a couple, this subsystem's function is the emotional care and support of one another.

  - **Executive subsystem**: this is the part of the larger family that has the responsibility/power to lead the family. Who is part of this subsystem varies from family to family, frequently based on culture or family circumstances. In some families, the same two people are the spousal and executive subsystems. In others, these are separate.

  - **Child or sibling subsystem**: there is a generational line that distinguishes this subsystem from the generations above and below it. Over the course of one's lifetime, the longest peer relationships most people have are with their siblings.

- **Structure** encompasses the way roles and expectations about family intersect with culture and circumstances to determine how families live together and interact. For many years, the public expectation in North America was the nuclear family: two parents with young children living in a household. Today, we recognize a wide range of structures, including single-parent families, dual household families, and multigenerational families.

- **Alliances** occur when two or more family members coordinate with one another to influence the functions, roles, and rules of the family.

- **Triangles** occur when tension or anxiety in a relationship of two people or two subsystems within a family pull in a third person or subsystem to relieve it. For example, two parents who are arguing all the time pull one of their children into the issues. Triangles are not good or bad, per se. They can help with ventilation if the primary parties come back together afterward and resolve their tensions. However, if the triangles become a pattern and the original tensions are never resolved, or if the third party is vulnerable or weaker, triangles become problematic patterns. Some alliances are also triangles.

- **Differentiation** is the ability of all persons in a family to develop into healthy, authentic selves who are able to remain emotionally connected and supported by their families. Note that this idea of individual development is very consistent with western cultural notions of family. This concept may not fit all cultures. When a person tries to differentiate and the family is not willing to allow that, it can lead to the following:

  - **Enmeshment:** one member gives up some part of who they are to fulfill the ideas/needs of another person or persons in the family because they fear loss of emotional, concrete, or both forms of support if they assert themselves.

  - **Cut-off (disengagement)**: one member chooses to distance themselves from one or more family member physically, emotionally, or both to manage the tension created by or pull toward enmeshment, which they have not been able to resolve.

- **Patterns of interaction/communication** arise as family members carry out various functions and fulfill various roles. Initially a pattern may be an adaptation to a demand on the family; over time, it may be repeated if the demand is the same and that adaptation worked, becoming a pattern or habit. In time, the pattern may become shorter as members become more accustomed to it. Think about a debate (or argument) about doing homework after school between a grandparent and a child. Maybe the first time this was a 15-minute conversation. Over time, it may become much shorter as both parties anticipate and assume what the other will say or do. Additionally, patterns may become so habituated that they remain even if the demands on the family change, rendering them useless, or what some might call dysfunctional.

EXERCISE 9.1: EXPLORING FAMILY ROLES, RULES, PATTERNS, AND CULTURE

We have all had the experience of going into the home of a friend or a romantic partner when their family was present. We noticed how that person's family operated similarly or differently from our own. It might have also caused us to realize something about our own family that we never saw before because we took it for granted that all families operated as ours did. This exercise asks you to apply some key family concepts to your own family and share them with others to learn the concepts and to think a bit about how they came together to create your family's culture.

Note: We all have had family experiences that were not positive, even if most of family life has been good for us. Some of us even have been harmed by our families. Negative aspects of family life are often hidden in the larger North American culture. Most of us are not posting on social media about the argument we had with our partner, sibling, or parent; we tend to put forward a "happy" face to all but those who are closest to us. It amounts to something of a cultural expectation (rule) that families *should be* supportive, loving, nurturing, and always able to provide for members' needs. The flip side to such an expectation is that we may feel shame or hide part of what occurs in our families when they do not meet the cultural norm. As you do this exercise, you can reflect on "family" as any configuration of people you choose and at any time period in your family's history. The exercise does not intend to have you explore an aspect that would trigger pain or require violation of this societal norm. However, if you are really emotionally reactive when thinking about and discussing families, you may want to do some personal work on this before you practice with families. In any area of our lives where we are reactive, there is a potential to lose our objectivity, to impose our values on others, and to be less than helpful to our clients.

Directions

- Form small groups of four to six people.

- Call to mind your current family, your family of origin (for some people these may be the same), or a time when you were living with other people.

- Thinking about that family, reflect upon and share the following:

  ○ Think about the rules in your family. Select one rule to share. Is this rule universal (common in many families, such as all members sleep in the same spot in the home every night) or is it idiosyncratic (unique to that family, such as we all watch *The Wizard of Oz* on a weekend night near Halloween).

  ○ Think about the roles in your family. What is one role you played in your family?

  ○ Think about a pattern of interaction in your family, something that occurred often. How did it come to be? What function did it play?

- For the collection of observations, discuss the following:

  ○ How did that rule, role, or pattern contribute to the family's carrying out specific functions?

  ○ How did the family decide to create that rule, that you (or others) would fill that role, or to establish those patterns? Was it an explicit decision? Did the family slide into it? Did the family repeat the patterns of earlier generations?

- Did expectations about gender, race, ethnicity, sexual orientation, national identity, or religion/spirituality shape the rules, roles, and patterns in your family?

- How did your family's unique combination of rules, roles, and patterns create your family's specific family culture?

- Come back together as a larger group and process the experience of reflecting upon and discussing family.

FAMILY DEVELOPMENT: A DOMINANT CULTURE VIEW OF THE FAMILY LIFE CYCLE

In previous chapters, ideas of normative development have been presented as a framework to understand the development of systems. Culture plays a significant role in shaping and understanding what is "normative" for the development of families. Therefore, the existence of one, normative family life cycle is a myth. There are many ways a family can develop and meet its members' needs. Despite this recognition, in much of North America there is dominant cultural expectation of a family life cycle that is promoted in the media and endorsed by public policy. In some ways, this mythology is based on a Caucasian, middle-class, post–World War II understanding of family (McGoldrick et al., 2011). Nonetheless, it can still be useful for social workers to understand it. McGoldrick et al. describe seven stages, with four additional stages that may occur.

Each stage is marked by emotional and practical demands that the family must navigate to meet members' needs. For example, when two people decide to couple by marrying and begin to live together, they face many practical choices, big and small, like where they will live, who will clean the bathroom, will they have a shared checking account, and/or how they will celebrate holidays. Emotionally, that same couple has to learn how to meet one another's needs and support one another.

According to the U.S. Census Bureau (Lewis & Kreider, 2015), in 2012, 30.7% of the U.S. population had never married, 52.3% had married once, and 17.1% had married two or more times. With nearly half the population not following the seven stages, one can easily see that family development is not simple. Moreover, some of the emotional and practical tasks of two or more stages may be occurring at the same time in a single family. For example, you might have a joined couple that is rearing adolescents and launching young adults at the same time it is assisting and supporting parents who are near the end of life.

EXERCISE 9.2: IDENTIFYING FAMILY LIFE CYCLE STAGES

Directions

- Form small groups.

- Read each vignette and identify which family life cycle or cycles are being experienced.

- Discuss some of the practical and emotional demands on a family at this stage of life.

- Reconvene as a class and discuss the vignettes.

7 Stages of Family Life Cycle	Additional Stages of Family Life Cycle
• Leaving home, the emerging young adult	• Divorce
• Joining of families through marriage or union	• Post-divorce families
• Families with young children	• Recoupling through marriage or union
• Families with teens	• Living single
• Midlife/launching children	
• Families in later middle age	
• Families at end of life	

Vignette 1

Ari (26) and Paula (28) just welcomed their first child, Kalliope, into the family. Their parents are very excited. Kalliope has been a little colicky but otherwise quite healthy, and their mothers are visiting to plan a baptismal celebration.

Vignette 2

Reece (78) and Lydia (84) have only been married for about six years. It was a first marriage for both of them. About one year ago, Lydia was diagnosed with advanced liver cancer and given a prognosis of about five to seven months. They live near two siblings and many friends.

Vignette 3

Mario (27) and Annalee (27) have been married for five years and have two children, Rodrigo (4) and Reni (3). Their relationship has never been an easy one. Mario left about six weeks ago and is staying with friends. They really do not own much, so Annalee proposed they do a simple divorce and figure out some custody arrangement in "a way that the lawyers don't get rich." They finally found something on which they could agree.

Vignette 4

Georgia (41) and Julia (38) are attending parent/teacher conferences for their four children. Julia has gone to the middle school to meet with the teachers of Rex (13), her son from her first serious relationship, and Dina (12), Georgia's daughter from her first marriage. Georgia is at the elementary school meeting with the teachers of Marta (8) and Danny (5), children from their marriage. Rex and Dina live with them and go to school in their district but spend weekends with their other parent.

Vignette 5

Chris (63) lives with one of their children, Geri (44), and two of their grandchildren, Katy (14) and Mike (10). Chris and Geri work full time. Chris leaves work midday, taking a ½ day vacation to transport Sally (85), Chris' mother, home from a rehabilitation center after a recent stroke. Sally's children (Chris's siblings) and Chris's other children (Geri's siblings) live out of town, and Sally's insistence on going home has everyone nervous. The rehab has promised that the home health agency will have everything in place today.

FAMILY ENGAGEMENT AND INTERVENTIONS

Generally, when families come or are referred for assistance, one person, sometimes more, is identified as having a problem, rather than the whole family. This leads to an expectation by many members of the family that the professional will adopt the shared family view. Working from a systems framework, however, suggests that the identified person (or persons) has simply become symptomatic for the entire family (Goldenberg & Goldenberg, 2007), indicating that the family is not able to meet the demands/needs of all its members at this time. Those demands can be external, like an economy in recession causing a job loss, or internal, such as a family member with a chronic health condition like Huntington's disease, or a combination. Therefore, when engaging families, the first task is to connect to every person and not overly align with any one member (Lukas, 1993). If one person has or is the problem, then someone or several people are to blame, leading to a lot of defensiveness and wishes for others to change. In order to change family patterns or increase insight, the social worker needs to use techniques to shift the family's perspective away from blaming one member to reduce that defensiveness and fear. A few of the more common techniques that can be used both to engage and intervene with families are as follows:

- **Normalization using family life cycle**: reframe the family's issues in the context of the life cycle to help to take the focus off the person who has become "symptomatic" for family and remove "blame."

- **Activity scheduling**: assigning family members to do certain activities together or apart to strengthen or lessen intensity in relationships.

- **Communication analysis**: breaking down communication patterns within the family so members can understand their interplay with emotion and behavior. Helping them to restructure communication.

- **Content-to-process shift**: moving away from the topic at hand to consider what people are feeling or thinking in that moment as well as the way the interaction is taking place in the moment; being attentive to the process.

- **Enactment**: process of bringing a real life issue into the helping space for the purpose of assessment or the purpose of intervening. Differs from traditional role playing as family members are being themselves.

- **Joining**: process of connecting the social worker with the family, which leads to the development of the "therapeutic system" (Minuchin & Fishman, 1981), and this system works toward positive change.

- **Manipulation of space**: rearranging the space or the people in the space to create different interpersonal connections

- **Rehearsal**: practicing a behavior, conversation, or skill in session. May take the form of a role play.

- **Ritual creation**: could be for the purpose of emotional release or shifting patterns. Identify purpose of ritual, select elements of the ritual, design it, and explore impact of carrying it out

- **Rulemaking**: negotiating rules for family functioning or communication, either in session or as homework

- **Segmentation**: working with either a subsystem or some part of the family separately from others for either part or all of an interaction

The goal of the next exercise is not for you to learn how to do family therapy; rather, its modest goal is to help you begin the process of understanding family communication patterns. All family work understands that interactions are not linear but circular in nature. How one person acts or reacts in the family sets off a reciprocal chain of interactions that impact the full family system. Recall that families (like most systems) are pulled toward homeostasis and that shifting family patterns requires energy to form a new way of interacting.

EXERCISE 9.3: ANALYZING AN INITIAL FAMILY INTERVIEW

This exercise consists of two parts. The first part involves the instructor and four student volunteers acting the beginning of an initial social work interview with a presenting family, using the script below. The scene is shown in two ways. The second part involves students analyzing the interactions to understand the dynamics of the family.

Directions

- Select four student volunteers to play the roles of the family members in front of the class. These students receive the exercise in advance, so they can review it prior to the class.

- The instructor plays the role of the practitioner.

- The practitioner and family members role play Script Take 1 and Script Take 2.

- After the role play is over, the rest of the class forms small groups of four to six people.

- The small groups review the script and use it to discuss the questions at the end of the exercise.

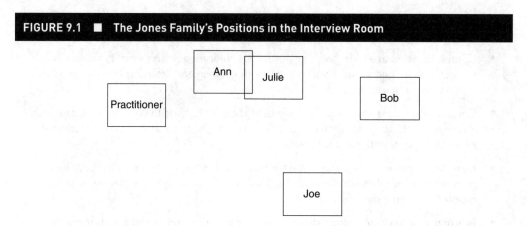

FIGURE 9.1 ■ The Jones Family's Positions in the Interview Room

Setting: The family members are mother, Ann Jones (37); father, Bob Jones (43); daughter, Julie (12); and son, Joe (16). The practitioner is a social worker employed by a family services agency. The mother called the agency one week prior to the interview asking for help in dealing with her son Joe. After discussing some of her concerns, the practitioner asked to meet with the whole family, which includes the father, mother, son, and daughter.

Stage Direction: The family comes into the interview room in the following manner: the mother comes in first holding Julie's hand and "towing" her behind, the father comes in next, and then Joe follows his father at a slight distance. Julie and her mother sit close together on the couch. The father sits in a chair some distance away, and Joe sits further away in a chair (see Figure 9.1). Joe slouches down, has one ear bud in from a personal device, and pulls a cap down over his forehead.

Script Take 1

PRACTITIONER: Hello, I'm [INSERT NAME]. I am the person who you talked to on the phone last week. Could you all please introduce yourselves to me?

MOTHER: Well, I'm Ann Jones and this is Julie. Over there is my husband and that's Joe. (*Mother sits back in her chair and folds her arms. Julie looks up at her mother anxiously.*)

PRACTITIONER: I'm very pleased to meet all of you. Now, could you tell me a little bit about what has been going on and how you would like me to help?
(*There is a short silence of a few seconds.*)

MOTHER: (*Turning to her husband*) Well, aren't you going to say something? (*Sighs in an exasperated way*) Typical. Anyway, I called because we're at the end of our rope with Joe. He won't do as he's told, just sits in his room playing that awful music, and then last week I found marijuana in his dresser drawer.

JOE: Geez, is *that* what this is all about? What are we here for? Just to pick on me again? (*Slouches down further.*)

MOTHER: (*Glares at her husband, who looks away. Then she continues.*) Well, I don't know what to do. And I don't like the idea of that kind of influence on Julie.

JULIE: Mommy, that's okay.

JOE: Oh, brother!

MOTHER: (*Glares at her husband again.*) Look, aren't you going to say something? He's your kid, too, you know.

FATHER: Oh for crying out loud, Ann, the kid's just feeling his oats. Look, I didn't want to come here to begin with. You're the one who wants a shrink.

MOTHER: (*To practitioner.*) See what I have to deal with? Julie, honey, sit up straight. (*Turns to husband*) Marijuana is a *drug*! Our son is using drugs! Don't you care about that?

FATHER:	So what do you want from me?
MOTHER:	Oh, I give up. (*Begins to cry. Julie pats her mother on the back and then turns to look at Joe.*)
JULIE:	See what you do to her.
JOE:	See, what'd *I* do? I get blamed for *everything*.
PRACTITIONER:	Mrs. Jones, could you describe exactly how you happened to find the marijuana?
MOTHER:	I found it in his room.
JOE:	See, I never have any privacy.
MOTHER:	I wouldn't be forced to look if you'd shape up and keep your room clean.
JOE:	Geez. (*Crosses his arms in front of his chest, sticks his headphone buds in his ears, and slouches down further in the chair.*)
PRACTITIONER:	Mrs. Jones, please describe exactly how you found the marijuana, that is, why you went into Joe's room and so on.
MOTHER:	Well I couldn't stand the way his room looked one minute longer, so I went in to clean it up. If he'd clean his room, I wouldn't have had to go in it. Anyways, I was simply straightening up a drawer, and I found it—under his socks.
JOE:	So you were poking into my stuff!! (*Looks at his father.*)
FATHER:	The boy's got a right to his privacy.
MOTHER:	You're a fine one to say that. What do you want him to do—ruin his brain? End up in jail? At least I care what happens to him.

Script Take 2

PRACTITIONER:	Hello, I'm [INSERT NAME]. I am a social worker [or appropriate credential] who has been trained to work with families. I am the person who you talked to on the phone last week. I am very comfortable with everyone calling me [first name], but I know some parents are not comfortable with their children using an adult's first name. Mr. and Mrs. Jones, what would you prefer your children call me? And could you all please introduce yourselves to me and tell me what you would like to be called?
MOTHER:	Well, I'm Ann Jones. You can just call me Ann. This is Julie. Over there is my husband and *that's* Joe. The children should call you [title and last name]. (*Mother sits back in her chair and folds her arms. Julie looks up at her mother anxiously.*)
PRACTITIONER:	Great, [title and last name] it is then. Mr. Jones, what is your first name, and how should I address you?
BOB:	My name is Bob, and you can use that, thanks. (*Turns head, glaring at wife.*)
PRACTITIONER:	Joe and Julie, what do you like to be called?
JOE:	Joe is fine.
JULIE:	Yes, Julie is fine.
PRACTITIONER:	Thank you. I want to hear a bit more about each of you, but before we do that, I want to let you know about a couple of things. First, I will keep what we discuss confidential. Julie, do you know that means?
JULIE:	(*Very quietly and shakes head.*) No.
PRACTITIONER:	What about you Joe?
JOE:	(*Reluctantly.*) Well . . . just that you won't tell our stuff all over the place. It will be private.

PRACTITIONER: Great, that is right. I have a duty to all my clients to keep what we say together private. I cannot control what you say, but I will keep our conversations private as well as the records of them . . . except in a couple of cases. Those are if you tell me you are going to harm yourself or that you intend to harm or abuse someone else. I am a mandated reporter, meaning I might have to tell authorities like medical professionals or protective services. The other persons I will share information with are my supervisors, so they can help me give you the best services. Any questions about that right now? We can come back to it later.

FAMILY: (*Shake heads no.*)

PRACTITIONER: Okay. Now, let's get to know one another a bit better. This may seem silly, but since I don't know you, it really may make sense. Imagine we are meeting for the first time in a restaurant. Your job is to introduce me to everyone in your family, saying one interesting thing about them, including yourself. Let me give you an example; pretend I am part of a family. It is really great to meet all of you. I am [name], and I really like to ride my bike in the park, so this was a great restaurant choice since we could bike from home. This is my daughter Carrie, and she loves eating Italian food so we came here for dinner, and this is John, my partner, who loves all the TVs in here so he can catch several baseball games at one time. Julie, would you be willing to get us started?

JULIE: Okay. (*Thinks a minute before speaking, then smiles.*) Hi, I am Julie and love painting, especially with glitter; this is Mom and she is really good a keeping things clean, so she doesn't love all my glitter; this is Dad, and he likes football a lot; and this Joe and he is really funny . . . mostly.

PRACTITIONER: Thanks. Joe, what about you?

JOE: You are right, this is silly, but (*sighs*) okay. (*Looking up fleetingly.*) This is Julie, and she likes games and, you know, is not pesty like some little sisters. This is my Dad. He is cool, kinda chill. This is Mom. (*Pause*) She's a decent cook.

PRACTITIONER: Thanks. Bob or Ann, who would like to go next?

(*Silence.*)

ANN: I guess I will go (*glares at husband*). (*Shifts to smiling.*) This is Julie; she is just a delight. She loves art and painting and playing dolls. This is Bob (*slight hesitation*), and he is a hard worker and takes care of the yard well. This is Joe, (*longer pause*) he is very smart but doesn't always apply himself.

PRACTITIONER: And . . .

ANN: Oh, and I am Ann. My family is the most important thing to me, and I put a lot of energy into caring for everyone.

BOB: I guess that leaves me. Really, is there any point to this? It seems like a waste of time. I am not even sure why we came here.

PRACTITIONER: Thanks for asking that question. I find that a little game like this one can really give me a lot of information about the family and warm everyone up to talking, since it can be a little awkward to see a social worker. The reasons you came are very important, and we will come to that. Are you willing to do the introductions first?

BOB: Okay, but just so you know, this was not my idea to come. I am Bob, and I, also, think my family is the most important thing (*turns and smiles wryly at wife*). This is Joe; he's a typical teenage boy who needs some space to grow up. This is Julie, and she is a pretty good sweeper for her soccer team. And, this is Ann (*pause*), and she makes the best pineapple upside down cake.

Questions for Discussion:

1.   What family rules can you identify from the family's communication patterns?

2.   What do you think the family role is for each family member?

3. Who does what and who comments on it?

4. What are the various family members' alignments?

5. What is the apparent family pattern of interaction?

6. Who is defined as a villain?

7. Who is defined as a victim?

8. What is the "critical incident" in this family?

9. If you were the practitioner in this scenario, what might be the next steps that you could take in engaging the family?

10. What questions for further assessment would you have if you were the practitioner in the scenario?

11. What strikes you as different in the way the practitioner engaged the family in the two scenarios?

EXERCISE 9.4: EXPLORING FAMILY PATTERNS AND STRUCTURE USING A GENOGRAM

A genogram is a pictorial tool that allows professionals and families to understand how a family is organized and structured over three or more generations. Some service providers utilize them routinely because they are effective in pulling out information that does not always arise in general conversation (McGoldrick, Gerson, & Petry, 2008). For example, some child welfare programs work with families to create genograms to identify family strengths and resources that may be helpful when doing family team conferencing. Several hospices routinely complete genograms near admission to better understand patterns of loss and grief within the family; this helps them identify possible interventions and family members who may struggle after the patient's death. The key elements of a genogram are as follows:

1. A basic family tree showing people within the same generation horizontally and different generations vertically

2. Indicators of each person's gender

3. Timeline through indicators of birth, death, coupling/marriage, separation, divorce, or other key family events (in a complex genogram, this may be separated from the family tree and shown as a traditional timeline)

4. Indicators of who is living together in a household (typically shown by circling the household members)

5. The current nature of relationships, including coupling relationships, cut-offs, and triangles (in a complex genogram, these may be pulled out to the side)

6. Indicators of patterns. This varies a great deal depending upon the family. Patterns might include a disease or condition in the family, like diabetes or addiction, faith traditions in the family, caregiving, immigration and migration, musical skills, professions, and any other topic relevant to a particular family.

7. A key that defines the symbols or demarcations used (see Figure 9.2)

Creation of a genogram with a professional can be very helpful for families. Its visual nature is better for some clients who are not as verbal or auditory, including younger children. Creation of it is an active, and often nonthreatening, way to start working together. It frequently reveals information that not all family members know (McGoldrick et al., 2008). And it enables the social worker to better understand complex relationships. Like any tool, it is not useful in all circumstances. For example, a genogram is probably not helpful if a person has come to the food pantry because her refrigerator/freezer no longer works, and she needs food until her paycheck comes so she can get a new one. It might be quite helpful if a family member's reaction to something seems out of proportion with the issue at hand.

FIGURE 9.2 ■ Genogram Symbols for Keys

Typical Genogram Symbols

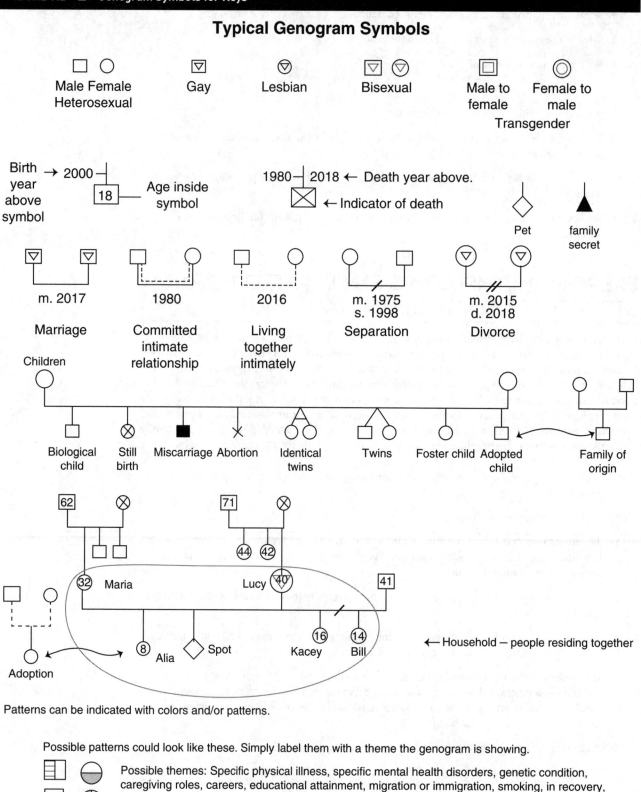

Patterns can be indicated with colors and/or patterns.

Possible patterns could look like these. Simply label them with a theme the genogram is showing.

Possible themes: Specific physical illness, specific mental health disorders, genetic condition, caregiving roles, careers, educational attainment, migration or immigration, smoking, in recovery, or any other relevant pattern in a family.

FIGURE 9.3   ■   Jones Family Genogram

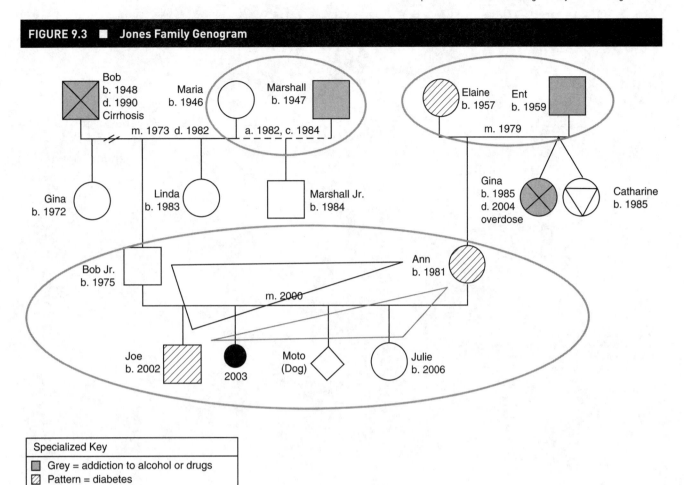

Specialized Key

■	Grey = addiction to alcohol or drugs
▨	Pattern = diabetes
◯	Grey circles = households

Directions

- Form groups of three to six students.
- Review the genogram of the Jones Family in Figure 9.3.
- Answer the questions below.
- Create your own genogram using your own family or a family from a book, a movie, or a television show.
- Share your genogram with another student and discuss it.
- Explore your reactions to the process of creating the genogram.
- Discuss how using a genogram might help you assess a family.

Note: As with any exercise in which you choose to use your own life, please only reveal that which you are comfortable revealing.

Questions

1. What new information did you learn?
2. What patterns occur in this family?
3. Can you identify on this genogram the triangles that you observed playing out in the family in Exercise 9.3?
4. How might this help you understand each family member's reactions?
5. How might this help the family understand itself?

10

WORKING WITH GROUPS

ocial work practitioners work with groups in three main ways: (1) direct work with clients, (2) collaborative work with colleagues, and (3) work with institutional or community groups. It is rare for a social worker to practice without any group involvement in one of these ways. Some social workers find themselves involved in multiple groups, both treatment and task groups, simultaneously. In some cases, a social worker will be a formal group leader (Leadership with a capital "L"), and in other cases, the social worker may be leading as a member (leadership with a lower case "l"). In some interprofessional settings, the social worker may be one of a few (or the only person) with formal group training. As such, social workers have great opportunities to be effective in shaping and leading groups. Below are some basic concepts and definitions related to working with groups, followed by exercises to build understanding of the group process and group skills.

DEFINITIONS AND GROUP TYPES

A *group* may be defined as a system of relationships between and among people. This system involves (1) interaction among members; (2) common goals, values, and norms; (3) a social structure; and (4) cohesion among members.

Groups are a mechanism to promote mutual aid—reciprocal and cooperative interaction for the benefit of all involved. Steinberg (2010) suggests,

[the] mutual-aid process is evidence of group work, or at least social work with groups in action. It is a process through which people (1) develop collaborative, supportive, and trustworthy relationships; (2) identify and use existing strengths and/or to develop new ones; and (3) work together toward individual and/or collective psychosocial goals, which reflects the very essence of social work with groups. (p. 54)

When asked about when and how they are willing to accept help or assistance, many people report that they feel most comfortable if they have a sense of contributing, not just receiving. Mutual aid provided by a group experience can maximize that reciprocity. For example, a person in a social skills treatment group receives and gives help to others at the same time. A member of a workplace task group may create policies that improve clients' experiences and their own workflow.

A number of characteristics are common to all groups:

1. A primary purpose/function

2. Simultaneous attention to tasks that facilitate the group process and tasks that lead to the realization of the group's purpose (sometimes called content)

3. Interaction among group members

4. Members who have different positions/roles/statuses within the group

5. Development of the group's own values, norms, and culture

6. An inherent tendency to maintain the status quo while at the same time evidencing an inherent tendency to grow, develop, and change

Many terms are used to describe groups and to better understand how they are similar or different in function, leadership, and resource needs. Typologies or categories are often suggested, indicating tasks and consideration for practice, yet social workers should always keep in mind that the complexity of actual groups is greater than such descriptions. One of the most important distinctions is between treatment-oriented and task-oriented groups (see Table 10.1).

Some groups may have features that fall into both categories rather than neatly fitting into one. For example, an empowerment group may begin with an individual focus of building awareness and skills but over time choose to take on a collective task. Other groups may fit neatly into one of the two broad categories and then fit more than one of the subtypes. For example, many formally led support groups have goals to build social support and to provide psychoeducation in the same group context.

It is important to note a distinction in regard to self-help groups. Self-help groups are a type of support group, but, by definition, they are peer led rather than professionally led. Alcoholics Anonymous

TABLE 10.1 ■ Treatment-Oriented Groups vs. Task-Oriented Groups	
Treatment Groups	**Task Groups**
Bring people together to harness the collective power of the group to help individuals respond to problems/challenges	Identify a particular task (or set of tasks/functions) to accomplish collectively
• Psychoeducational	• Boards
• Socialization	• Committees
	○ Advisory
	○ Policy
• Support	• Panels
○ Self-help	
• Therapy	• Treatment Teams
○ Counseling/psychotherapy	
○ Skills	

serves as a prime example: Everyone in the group is living or trying to live in recovery. In such groups, a social worker or other helping professional is not going to be the official leader.

Groups may also be further defined as natural or formed. Natural groups develop in an unplanned way in the natural course of events. Formed groups are deliberately created to deal with specific circumstances.

Natural groups are less likely to have formal social work leadership than formed groups. Sometimes, a naturally formed group will reach out for professional leadership or assistance if it finds that it lacks a skill or resource. Formed groups are more likely to have official social work or professional leadership.

GROUP LIFE CYCLE

Just as other social systems have life cycles, groups do, too. Thinking about life cycle suggests common developmental tasks that need to be addressed for a group to function. Although they are presented linearly, some groups do not experience their life cycle that way. One of the most commonly taught models of group life cycle comes from Tuckman (1965). Other group theorists have built upon it, and it has been used to explain both task (its original context) and treatment groups. It outlines the interpersonal process for small groups, not the task or content of groups. Table 10.2 suggests some of the key tasks for groups at each stage, utilizing Tuckman and Jensen's (1977) terminology.

TABLE 10.2 ■ Key Tasks for Groups	
Stage	**Key Tasks for Group**
Forming	Orientation to task/purpose, creation of ground rules, begin to establish relationships
Storming	Often marked by conflict, learning to express self in presence of others, establishing trust, testing limits, beginning to find roles and establish norms
Norming	Development of cohesion, roles and norms become established, greater expression of self
Performing	Functional activities consistent with purpose of group
Adjourning	Separation from group, solidifying what has been gained for future use

A theoretical model of the group life cycle, like the one in Table 10.2, tends to assume that all members join and leave the group at the same time—that all members work on these developmental tasks collectively together. However, not all groups have this closed format. Many groups, both task and treatment groups, have open formats, and different members join and leave the group routinely. Inpatient, outpatient, and substance use treatment groups, as well as many support and self-help groups, operate with an open membership based upon admission or discharge dates or court mandates. In organizations, members of many committees and teams participate by virtue of their positions, not due to a specific skill. The challenge is to get an ongoing group into the performing phase of the work even if not all members are at that phase. Enough members need to be able to "perform" that they can provide leadership, even if only by modeling, to new members. The leader will need to build structures into the group that account for the needs of new members (build trust, understand group norms) and longstanding members to really work on the groups' goals and purposes.

It is possible that groups will rush or skip some of the storming and norming activities, moving too quickly into performing. This occurs often in task groups; you might hear people say something like, "We are all professionals and adults here; let's get right to the work." They may have to go back to and revisit an earlier stage if the interpersonal work of an earlier stage was not done well.

EXERCISE 10.1: GROUP TYPE AND STAGE OF DEVELOPMENT

Directions

- Form small groups of three to five students.

- Read each vignette and determine what type of group it is and what stage of the group life cycle it is currently experiencing.

- Discuss the reasons for your choices and note them in the space provided.

Case Vignette 1

Tamara meets for the second time over lunch and recess with seven students at Belmar Elementary School. Group members are between 8 and 11 years old. They each have experienced loss related to community and/or family violence that seemed to a teacher or school administrator to be interfering with their school performance. The purpose is to help the students learn and employ coping skills at school as they adjust to their losses. All the children were screened to determine whether they needed more services than this group can provide. A parent or guardian gave each student permission to join the group. Because of their ages and development, Tamara decides to do an exercise to teach them about confidentiality. She has brief scripts they can read and discuss to think about how to keep the group's privacy rule. She thinks she needs to build up their trust in each other.

Type of Group: Task or Treatment (circle one)   Subtype: _____

Stage in group life cycle: _____

What are the reasons for your choices?

_____

_____

Case Vignette 2

Linda leads a long-standing monthly meeting of a group of nine people as they oversee the operation of a job training program. Each group member was selected because of expertise in a certain skill or field. Today's agenda was set during the previous meeting when they had been informed by the director that a senior administrator had embezzled funds and that oversight processes/controls were not sufficient, including their own. This led to the first open and heated disagreement for this particular group under Linda's leadership, and they discovered they had been too polite and accommodating, not daring to raise concerns even though many reportedly saw red flags. They decided that they needed to take some time to revisit how they want to do their work. They decided to ask a consultant to lead them through team building and communication exercises today.

Type of Group: Task or Treatment (circle one)   Subtype: _____

Stage in group life cycle: _____

What are the reasons for your choices?

_____

_____

Case Vignette 3

Roderigo is leading a bi-monthly group of persons recovering from strokes. The group is typically attended by the person who had the stroke and a friend or family caregiver. The purpose is to connect to others dealing with the condition, learn tips from them, and support them in their efforts. It is an open group format, so different people can come each time; however, he has a solid corps of 14 members (7 dyads) that have been coming regularly for well over a year. Today's meeting is attended by 16 people; 12 of them come regularly, 2 are there for a second time, and 2 are new. As the group begins, Roderigo invites everyone to introduce themselves. The long-time members also explain the group's rules and purposes. Then Roderigo invites everyone to help set the agenda. Joe and Judy ask if they can talk about regaining independence. They have been arguing about whether Joe is ready to stay alone. They wondered how others make such a decision. Joe thinks Judy is being too protective. Ralph and Eric want to discuss post-stroke depression and how to deal with it. All agree to these topics for the meeting.

Type of Group: Task or Treatment (circle one)   Subtype: _____

Stage in group life cycle: _____

What are the reasons for your choices?

_____

_____

Find the Answer Key on page 132 at the end of this chapter.

GROUP LEADERSHIP SKILLS AND BEHAVIORS

When social workers serve as a primary leader of a group, the capital "L" leader, they are expected to understand group process and facilitate the group in accomplishing its purposes and goals. Depending upon the nature of the group, the primary leader may need some specialized skills or knowledge. However, all group leaders rely on basic generalist skills like empathic communication, being authentic, active listening, and seeking clarity and concreteness. Even when social workers are not the formal leaders, they can provide leadership by using their group knowledge and skills to improve the overall functioning of the group. Below you can review behaviors that facilitate group functioning and those that may disrupt it. The formal leader is expected to model and promote facilitative behaviors and to intervene to prevent or address those who disrupt it.

Facilitative Group Member Behaviors

1. Expresses concern and empathy for others

2. Shows organizational or leadership ability that benefits the group

3. Expresses self clearly and openly with others

4. Cooperates and supports others

5. Assists in maintaining the group's focus and accomplishing its purpose

6. Responds openly and positively to constructive feedback

7. Gives constructive feedback to others

8. Works within the guidelines established by the group

9. Takes responsibility for his or her behavior, including errors

10. Is open to and values others' opinions

11. Is inclusive toward others in the group who may be different

12. Participates constructively in discussion with others

13. Has a good sense of humor that is not demeaning to others

Disruptive Group Member Behaviors

1. Interrupts, speaks for others, or rejects others' ideas

2. Is placating, patronizing, or condescending toward others

3. Belittles, criticizes, or expresses sarcasm toward others

4. Argues, blames, attacks, engages in name calling

5. Verbally dominates the group and monopolizes discussions in the group

6. Gives unsolicited advice prematurely and insensitively

7. Expresses disgust and disapproval nonverbally toward others

8. Talks too much or too loudly or whispers so others have difficulty hearing him or her

9. Withdraws, isolates, ignores, or shows disinterest in the group and its members

10. Talks about tangential topics or sidetracks the group in other ways

11. Manifests distracting physical movements like tapping a foot or squirming

12. Is physically aggressive or "horses around" in a disruptive manner

13. Clowns, mimics, and/or makes fun of others

14. Forms destructive subgroups within the larger group

15. Blames other group members for problems that arise and does not take responsibility

Two Basic Principles

As formal group leaders or members, social workers must recognize that each group is more than the sum of its parts (or each person); it is a unique social system. One person cannot will a group to function, and overfunctioning for a group is unlikely to result in strong products or outcomes. Social workers must keep in mind these two principles:

1. Be clear as to your role in the group.

2. Recognize that the group is the agent of change, not the practitioner/leader.

The group leader's primary responsibilities are to (1) see that the group experience is a good one for all, (2) see that the purpose of the group is constructive, and (3) be willing to disband the group if it becomes ineffectual or destructive and cannot or will not constructively change.

Three Common Categories of Group Leadership Style

Group leaders must select and utilize the correct style for the purpose and nature of the group and facilitate how power and authority are exercised within the group.

1. Democratic: decisions are made by collective group decision making

2. Autocratic: all decisions are made for the group by a higher authority

3. Laissez-faire: there are few or no controls at all and things spontaneously evolve

Although a democratic leadership style is common, and it can be tempting to suggest that it is always preferred, this may not be the case in all group situations. There are groups for which one of the other styles may be a better fit, such as a group working toward self-actualization in which a laissez-faire style might be more appropriate.

Specific Skills in Groups

In addition to the generalist skills that social workers will use in groups, they often employ other skills, either more often or in a slightly different fashion, in groups. (See Table 10.3)

Additionally, groups, especially treatment groups, utilize the here and now of the interaction in the group as a way to help members learn new information about themselves, to practice skills, and to provide help to others. In other words, such groups depend upon the process of what is happening. Therefore, group practitioners need to be skilled in switching from the *content* of the group to its *process* and back. Such switches can be simple statements:

- I would like to switch from the details of our discussion to talk about how you feel right now hearing what others are saying.

- Can we take a little time to talk about how we are doing [some part of the agenda]? Was everyone comfortable with the way we did it? Did you share all your thoughts or did you hold back?

- What was most helpful to you in that last interaction? Was it the act of telling your story, hearing another person's story, or hearing strategies others used?

TABLE 10.3 ■ Group-Specific Skills	
Blocking: Intervening to stop counterproductive behaviors in the group or to protect members	**Linking:** Promoting member-to-member interaction and promoting exploration of common themes in a group
Clarifying: Focusing on the underlying meaning and details and assisting others to get a clearer picture of what they are thinking or feeling (combines seeking concreteness and questioning techniques)	**Modeling:** Demonstrating to members desired behaviors that can be practiced both during and between group sessions
Evaluating: Appraising the ongoing group process and the individual and group dynamics	**Supporting:** Offering some form of positive reinforcement at appropriate times in such a way that it has a facilitating effect
Facilitating: Helping members to express themselves clearly and to take action in a group	**Terminating:** Creating a climate that encourages members to continue working after/between sessions

Source: Corey, Corey, and Corey (2015).

HUMAN SERVICES TEAMS AND INTERPROFESSIONAL PRACTICE

A *team* in a social or human services agency is a group composed of people who each possess particular expertise and are responsible for individual decisions and actions. Team members share a common purpose and pool their knowledge and ideas via interaction among members in order to take appropriate actions to fulfill the team's purpose. Although teams are sometimes made up of multiple people from the same profession, more often team membership consists of people from diverse professions. This leads to the need for social workers to understand interprofessional practice and communication. Several ideas are worth consideration for such teams (Gucciardi, Espin, Morganti, & Dorado, 2016; Pecukonis, Doyle, & Bliss, 2008).

- Each team is a unique group, a social system, subject to the same dynamics present in any group. Teams must build identity and cohesion, be able to mediate and resolve conflict, and adapt to changing demands and membership.

- Each profession has strengths and limitations, as well as a scope of practice and its own culture, which flows from its particular professional values and ethics. This can lead to biases (sometimes unstated), profession-centrism (favoring/valuing one's own profession above others), and miscommunication, all of which can impede working together.

- Teams tend to focus on their purpose or product, sometimes forgetting to be attentive to the process of how they work together. Groups perform better when attentive to both the process and content.

These points suggest that social workers, as members or formal leaders of such teams, can utilize their knowledge of group development and process, communication, and diversity/cultural humility to promote effective teams.

TECHNOLOGY USE WITH GROUPS AND TEAMS

Organizations are utilizing online forums, video chat technologies, and telephone/audio conference call technology to facilitate group interactions. The new technology can be beneficial; for example, it can enable a distant family caregiver to be part of the treatment conference or pull together a widespread coalition of policy advocates to collaborate. As members of task groups, social workers may find themselves meeting on telephone or computer conference calls or video chat spaces to facilitate the opportunity for people in different settings to participate without having to travel. In treatment groups, these same technologies as well as moderated private group spaces online may be utilized to promote building skills, gaining education/psychoeducation, support, or therapy. Such technologies can overcome difficulties in accessing resources from rural areas, lack of transportation, fitting groups into busy work/life schedules, and need for specialized or focused services.

Social workers who lead groups that use technology need to think about how it impacts the purpose and process of the group. As with all technology, there are both advantages and challenges. For example, participants in audio-only conferencing may say they find it difficult not to get distracted and multitask, and, thus, they are not as present to the group as they would be in a face-to-face format. And leaders of treatment groups must assess the appropriateness of and risks associated with using technology all or part of the time to meet (NASW et al., 2017). Social workers must also help clients make informed choices about whether a technology-aided group would work for them. Research on and understanding of technology and its impact with the helping professions is still at an early stage. Before beginning such groups, social workers should check to see what updated information is available about technology-assisted groups with the function/problem and population of their group. As group rules and norms are established, group leaders must be attentive to additional challenges and ethical concerns regarding privacy (NASW et al., 2017).

EXERCISE 10.2: IDENTIFYING GROUP LEADERSHIP SKILLS IN TREATMENT GROUPS

Directions

- This exercise can be done as a class (six students read the script before the entire class) or in small groups of six people.

- Arrange 10 chairs (if classroom space permits) in a circle, leaving an open space so that the audience can see the group members (see Diagram 10.1).

- The scene is performed twice. In Take 1, there are more blatant and obvious mistakes. In Take 2, there is better use of the group skills. Each class can decide whether to do the scenes back to back or on separate occasions.

- Student participants read the Take 1 script aloud, and the audience identifies the skills the group leader is using.

- Afterward, discuss whether the skills have been used well or poorly. What might have been done differently?

- Now students read Take 2, and, again, the audience identifies the skills used. Try to identify how process is used, note boundary setting, goal focus, thematic linking, and the leader's stance.

Note: Several of the names in this scenario are not gender specific and "their" and "them" are used as gender neutral, singular pronouns.

Setting: The group members are a group leader and members Chris (29), Erik (48), Jamie (34), Jason (41), and Ricki (52). The group leader is a social worker employed by a general social service agency that has a contract to help people become "re-employed" after a major business left the area. This group was established to work on social skills as several talented clients have struggled to get rehired or to maintain employment, due to their problematic interpersonal skills. The group format is somewhat open in that new people can join and others leave the group, but all clients must be recommended by one of the employment case managers. Usually the group has about nine attendees.

Stage Direction: The group leader is seated in the middle. Jamie and Chris enter having a private conversation. They sit close to one another on the right side of the circle. Erik and Jason enter separately; Erik sits to the left and Jason sits to the right, leaving a space between himself and the others. Ricki will arrive late.

DIAGRAM 10.1 ■ Treatment Group Stage Layout

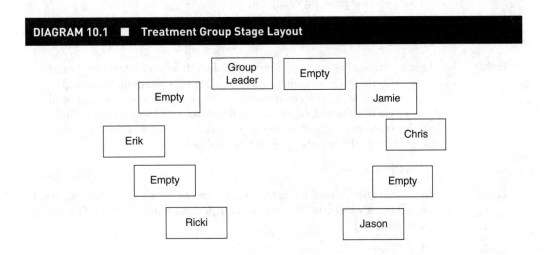

Treatment Group Scene Take 1

Leader:	(looking at clock) Hi, it is nice to see everyone today. It is the hour, so we should get started. Seems like a smaller group today. Wonder where everyone is? Hmmm. No matter, let's get started.
Erik:	(under his breath and to the side) Everyone knows why no one is here.
Leader:	Erik, did you say something?
Erik:	No, nothing.
Leader:	Okay then. Our plan for the day will be to do a check in; then we will do an exercise on listening; then we will wrap up. That sounds good to everyone, right?
Members:	(Slow murmurs, shrugging shoulders, bit of awkward silence)
Chris:	Yes. That is fine. Let's get going.
Leader:	Okay, so today's check in is recalling one way you screwed up an interaction this week.
Jamie:	(looks at Chris, rolls eyes) We did this one already. How many times do we have to do this one?
Erik:	Yeah, I agree with Chris. Let's do something new.
Jamie:	(with a slight edge) I am Jamie, not Chris.
Erik:	(not sincere) Sorry, it's only my third time here.
Jamie:	No worries.
Leader:	You know that this group is about improving your interpersonal skills. How are you going to do that if we don't talk about them?
Erik:	Fine.
Leader:	Do you want to go first, Erik or Jamie?
Jamie:	Sure. Why not? I got into an argument with the cashier at the Stop N' Shop on Main Street because she was being a total witch. I suppose you would say that I should have been polite and that maybe she was having a bad day and all that. But really, I just wanted a little respect as I was buying milk. I didn't need the lecture on the evils of sugar in my candy bar.
Leader:	I am so very proud of you for realizing that you contributed to the negative interaction. Chris or Erik?
Erik:	I got my brother-in-law good in front of his kids. It was epically funny. I wound them up so they were marching around like they were protesting some major injustice when he didn't let them watch TV while my sister was working. Well, after he got them to bed, he let me have it: told me that I would need to find another place to live ASAP because he was done with me. As soon as my sister got home, she talked him out of it. So it is all cool now.
Leader:	Is it really okay now?
Erik:	Sure. I mean, he isn't talking to me, and he won't let the kids play with me. But, I am still living with them rent free. He'll forget about it in a couple of days. Plus it was a great laugh.
Leader:	Okay. Jason?
Jason:	I didn't have any negative interactions with anyone this week.
Leader:	None?

Jason: Not one.

Ricki: (entering room noisily, looks around) Is this the social skills group my case manager said I had to come to?

Leader: Yes, you are late. That isn't very respectful.

Ricki: Well, you could put some kind of sign on the door. I mean, I have been walking around the floor trying to figure out which room for a while.

Leader: There isn't a sign on the door for privacy reasons. The group has rules about attendance and being late. This counts as one of your three violations. If you violate the rules two more times, you will be kicked out of the group.

Ricki: Fine. It wasn't my idea to come.

Leader: Are you Ricki or Jo? I was told there would be two new people today.

Ricki: I am Ricki.

Leader: Was anyone else wandering around out there lost?

Ricki: No.

Leader: Welcome, Ricki. I am [fill in name], the leader of the group. This is the group (motions around the circle). We are just doing our check in. Because everyone who comes to the group has some story about how their interaction with others interfered with getting or keeping a new job, we check in with a story of a bad interaction from the week. Jason was just doing his. (Turning toward Jason.) You were saying?

Jason: I wasn't saying much. I didn't have any bad interactions.

Chris: (looks at Jamie and rolls eyes) Of course you didn't. A perfect person doesn't need the group.

Jason: Well, I didn't. You can't have bad interactions if you hang by yourself all week, and that is what I did. You haven't shared anything yet.

Chris: (glaring) Well, for the record, I just had the same one as before. My partner and I fought about me getting a job. Same fight all the time . . . and, maybe that's why you don't have a job—you don't interact with anyone.

Leader: Thanks for sharing Chris. Jason, you have to try harder. Ricki, it is your turn.

Ricki: Yeah, ummm. Yeah. I am not sure. Can I just hang back and get sense of all of you first? This all seems really weird to me.

Jamie: I think we should give them a pass. They are new. I am, by the way, the only person who said something about someone outside the family. I mean come on—family stuff? That's not the same as getting along with people in the work place. Jason isn't trying. Erik is always telling how he messes with his brother-in-law's head. If I was him I'd kick you out.

Erik: Don't forget your friend over there who always says the same story, every time, just to not have to give anything more. Really.

Leader: Well what does everyone think? Should we give Ricki a pass since they are new?

Members: (Generally nodding their heads)

Leader: Ok, Ricki, just be prepared for next week. (looking around) Do you think you are being respectful to each other right now?

Chris: Yeah, mostly we are. So, I say let's not talk about talking respectfully.

Erik and Jason: (at the same time) I agree.

Jamie:	Uhhh. Sure.
Ricki:	(Shrugs)
Leader:	Well this isn't productive. Maybe, we should just start the exercise.

Treatment Group Scene Take 2

Leader:	(looking at clock) Hi, it is nice to see everyone today. It is the hour, so we should get started. Seems like a smaller group today. Did you see anyone outside? We are supposed to have two new members.
Erik:	Yeah, there is some clueless person wandering around out there. I used to see them at the factory before it closed. But, I never knew them or their name.
Leader:	When you saw the person, Erik, what did you think?
Erik:	I thought they might be coming here.
Leader:	Did you say something? You said you saw the person was looking lost.
Erik:	Yeah, they looked lost, but, no, I didn't say anything.
Leader:	Why not?
Erik:	I don't know. (thinks a bit) I guess that is just me; you know, I don't really help other people much. I let them figure it out on their own.
Jamie:	Erik, this seems like one of those opportunities we were talking about for you to connect better to other people. If I was walking around looking lost, saw you, and then later found you were in the group, I would think what a—
Leader:	(interrupting Jamie) —I am going to interrupt, Jamie. Is this one of those times that we talked about for you, when you say the first thing that comes to mind? Do you want to say what you were about to say?
Jamie:	Wow, yeah. (pause) Erik, you get the idea. I just wouldn't think highly of you if I were in that person's shoes. I think I will stop now.
Erik:	Yeah I do get you. And, good recovery.
Leader:	Jamie, thanks for letting me interrupt you. Seems like people's goals are front and center today. Erik, would you be willing to go see if the person is looking for us, or would you prefer I do it?
Erik:	Yes, to both. I would prefer that you do it, but Jamie is probably right that it is one of those ways I could show people I care. So (reluctantly) I will do it. I will also look to see if there is anyone else out there.
	(Erik leaves the room and brings Ricki in)
Leader:	Welcome. Please have a seat.
Ricki:	(looking nervous and unsure about being there). Thanks. I am Ricki. My case manager said I should come.
Leader:	Well, we are small group today; a couple of people are absent. Since we have someone new, why don't we start with introductions? My name is [insert name here], and I am the group leader. I have been with the group since the agency started it. I am one of the supervisors for the case managers here but don't see any of the case management clients one on one. This way, I, as the group leader, don't have two kinds of relationships with you as members of the group. Who would like to introduce themselves next? Maybe you could say a bit about how you came to be in the group. (looks around and stops on Erik)
Erik:	I am Erik, like I said in the hall. I am kind of new to the group. This is my fourth time, I think. Like you, my case manager said I should come. I used to work in

the mechanical department at the company. I have been sacked from two jobs since the factory closed for "stirring up trouble." I think I saw you around in the halls before.

Chris: Hi, I am Chris. I worked in accounts receivable before the company closed. I heard that people have been telling potential employers not to hire me because I am nosy and in other people's business. So when I get an interview, I don't seem to get an offer if they check references. I have been in the group the longest, about 10 weeks.

Jamie: I am Jamie. I have been in the group about eight weeks. I have gotten one job since the factory closed but lost it when I told it like it is. (looking at group leader) What did you call it? Oh yeah, I have no filter. So, like the others, the case manager said I should come here and work on it. Oh, and I used to work in the accounting office.

Leader: Jason?

Jason: Yeah, umm, I am Jason, and basically, I . . . . well, I just don't really like people very much. You know. I like the people I like, and that's it. I am a tech person and great with numbers and code. And, I can't interview for crap, so I am having trouble getting a job. My case manager sent me here, too.

Leader: And can you share how long you have been in the group?

Jason: I have been coming around six or seven weeks now.

Leader: Ricki, can you tell us a bit about you?

Ricki: So, I worked at the company over 30 years. I worked in a lot of departments, recently the order fulfillment center as a shift supervisor. I am a little older than all of you. And frankly, I don't get how you go interview with some kid in human services who is young enough to be your own kid. They act all entitled and like they know way more than someone with my experience. So I blew up at a few interviews. That's why I got sent here. I really don't see how a group is going to help me.

Members: (smile and nod their heads knowingly)

Leader: As you can see looking at the others, they seem to agree with you. Many of them said the same thing when they first came. I would like to come back to your point about not knowing how the group can help you in a few minutes, if you don't mind. I think it is important to share a bit about the group itself and about the rules we set for ourselves so you can decide what you want to share with us. Would someone state our purpose?

Jamie: (rolls eyes at Chris) We do this every time there is a new person.

Jason: Yeah, I agree. Ricki can pick up on this stuff.

Erik: I think we should do this. It was helpful when I came a few weeks ago. (looks at Jamie)

Jamie: Okay. Was it really?

Erik: Yes (exasperated). Maybe try to remember what it was like to be new.

Leader: Before we go over purpose, can we quickly look at what is happening here?

(little pause)

Chris: Jamie said what they thought from their point of view right away without seeming to think of anyone else. Erik actually took the other person's perspective, which was sort of different for him and nice. I can't tell what Jason seemed to do.

Erik: Yeah, I did. Wow.

Jamie: And, I screwed up again.

Leader: Was it a "screw up?"

Jamie: Yeah, sort of. I am trying to think before I speak, and I just blurted it out.

Leader: Don't you have to start by being aware? You cannot change unless you are aware, right? Are you more aware?

Jamie: I guess, yeah. I will practice my three-second count for the rest of session.

Leader: Sounds good. Erik, did you intend to be thoughtful?

Erik: Not really; it just sort of happened. Hmmm . . . I am not always unkind. What's your story, Jason?

Jason: I don't know. I just find it boring to go over the same stuff all the time. I guess that was another example of why a person might think I don't care. Thinking back to it, it was helpful that first time I came. I was pretty nervous. So, we can go over purpose. (looking at Ricki) Our purpose is to improve our interpersonal skills so we can get and keep jobs.

Leader: Jason, both your personal statement and the group's purpose are well stated. Thanks for looking at this a minute. Ricki, this was an example of how we do the work on skills. We take the here and now with each other—whatever anyone says—and then use it to think about how we interact with people in other places, like at work. Then each person sets their own goals that fit with the overall goal. This is why we took a look at what just happened and how it fit with people's goals. Three people had a chance to think about their own goals and practice skills, like Jamie's waiting three seconds to speak. Would you like to tell Ricki what your individual goals are?

Jamie: Sure. Why not? Mine is to slow down my mouth and think about what I say before I say it. That should go a long way to getting along with people better.

Chris: I am trying to slow down and think about how to talk to people so I don't seem so nosy and not tell their business all over the place if I learn it. I am also thinking about how to repair some old relationships.

Erik: I am trying to figure out how to show people I care about them. Turns out stuff I find funny is not funny to other people. My goal is not as clear as their goals since I am kind of new to all of this.

Jason: I am working on basic stuff like responding like I care and making eye contact.

Leader: So, as you get to know the group, you will be able to pick your own goal. What about the rules?

Chris: The number one rule—the one I struggled with the most—is what happens in Vegas stays in Vegas, or the group version of that. So, you can't leave here and talk about the group to anyone else, not even your live-ins if you have them. Oh, yeah, and definitely only your part of group should be shared with your case manager.

Jamie: We listen and don't talk over each other. We also use "I" statements, not "You" statements. We don't have to share anything we don't want to and certainly not deep, deep stuff.

Jason: And my least favorite but the one hardest for me—everyone has to try to contribute.

Leader: Nice recap of the rules. I want to come back to the one Chris mentioned because it makes a lot of people nervous. Groups are only as confidential as the group members make them. I will keep all your confidences, but you all have to do that, too. So, I cannot 100% promise you confidentiality. My experience is that others don't want their stuff shared, so they tend to assume you don't want yours shared and respect that. I won't tell your individual case managers what you say in group unless we agree that I should. I will discuss the group with my supervisor to make sure I am giving you the best service I can. There are a couple of instances where I might have to share information whether you want me to or not; they are the same ones you heard when you first came to the agency. If you reveal that a child or vulnerable adult is being abused or neglected, I may have to break confidentiality. Also, if you reveal that you have an intention to harm or kill yourself or someone else, I would break it. Does all of that make sense?

Ricki: Yeah it does. (looking at Chris) I was really nervous when I saw you in here. You definitely had a reputation at the company. I knew who you were even though I didn't know you. You were known as a gossip. In fact, people sometimes used you to spread information about others by telling you it. They used you. So, how do I know that I can trust you?

Chris: Well, I am kind of offended.

Leader: Do you want to respond right now? It is an opportunity since you think this is going on at your interviews.

Chris: Yeah, I want to respond. After 10 weeks, I can hear that without flipping out and respond. I am changing. You are right; I probably blabbed people's stuff way too much at the old company. I also goofed early in the group and broke the rules. I learned from the people here before me that I had to be more careful. The group took me back. If I ever break the confidentiality rule again, I will be kicked out immediately. But, ultimately, I guess you will have to decide if you can trust me. So, maybe start slow and let me prove it. Can I ask you a question? Are you always this direct and blunt when you speak to people?

Ricki: Okay, fair enough. I am still not sure about being here or trusting any of you. And, yes, I am pretty blunt. I was actually nicer now than I usually am. I suspect, I might be a bit like (looks at Jamie)—I forgot your name.

Jamie: Jamie.

Ricki: I think I might be like you.

Leader: How so?

Ricki: I tend to call it like it is, and people don't always like that.

Leader: Could that be something you want to take a look at?

Ricki: Maybe, but I am still not sure.

Leader: Everything you said strikes me as typical, and something similar has been said by these group members, especially being nervous about being in a group. It is my experience that you can find in these interactions pieces of what happens outside of group and use that to change. Are you willing to try to be with us for a few weeks to see if it will help you?

Erik: I was really doubtful, too. But, I am finding it helpful.

Jason: Yeah, and I discovered we don't talk about our childhoods and some of that non-sense you see in movies.

Ricki: Okay, I will try it a few times.

Leader: Great. If you do not find it helpful, please let us know, and we can talk about whether you should stay in the group. While it wasn't a true check in, would this suffice for our check in today?

Members: (all nod) Yes.

Leader: How about we set the agenda for today? (looking at everyone) In addition to last week's homework, what would you like to discuss today?

EXERCISE 10.3: IDENTIFYING GROUP LEADERSHIP SKILLS IN TASK GROUPS

Directions

- This exercise can be done as a class (five students read the script before the entire class) or in small groups of five people.

- Arrange five chairs around a table (see Diagrams 10.2 and 10.3).

- The scene is performed twice. In Take 1, there are more blatant and obvious mistakes. In Take 2, there is better use of group skills. Each class can decide whether to do the scenes back to back or on separate occasions.

- Student participants read the Take 1 script aloud, and the audience identifies the skills the group leader is using.

- Afterward, discuss whether the skills have been used well or poorly. What might have been done differently?

- Now students read Take 2, and, again, the audience identifies the skills used—both group-specific skills and standard communication skills. How did the leader's activities differ? How did others lead without being the named leader?

- If the class also did Exercise 10.2, they can then compare and contrast how the leadership skills are used similarly or differently in task versus treatment groups.

Note: Several of the names in this scenario are not gender specific and "their" and "them" are used as gender neutral, singular pronouns.

Setting: The committee members are (1) Ari, assistant director, (2) Jess, finance department rep, (3) Jo, clinical services rep, (4) Lee, I&R rep, and (5) Billie, quality improvement officer. The assistant director is a social worker and the group leader. The clinical services rep is also a social worker. The agency received feedback that clients and potential clients find it difficult to actually get services, with a four-week lag time between first contact and provision of services and reports that the process is really repetitive. This ad hoc task group has been charged with proposing changes to agency intake procedures to make them more consumer friendly and to improve getting and retaining clients.

Stage Direction: The meeting is in a small conference room with a table in the middle of the room. For Take 1, Ari, Jess, Jo, and Billie are seated at the table as shown in Diagram 10.2. For Take 2, they are seated as shown in Diagram 10.3. Lee arrives late.

DIAGRAM 10.2 ■ Task Group Stage Layout Take 1

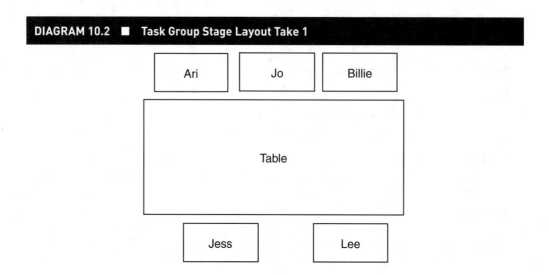

DIAGRAM 10.3 ■ Task Group Stage Layout Take 2

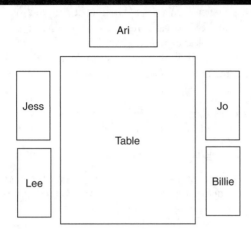

Task Group Scene Take 1

Ari: Well, three of you are here. Where's Lee?

Jo: I think stuck with a walk-in because Sylvie called off today. They are short in I & R today.

Ari: Okay, well we should get started anyway. I was looking at my notes from last time. We were going to research how other agencies handle intake. Did anyone do that?

Billie: I contacted my friends at the county and GFD Agency. I can report on that.

Jo: I spoke to my counterpart at the homeless shelter but didn't get around to chasing down the people at ZYX Company.

Jess: You know with the audit, I didn't have time to reach out to the agencies we said I would call. What about you, Ari?

Billie: (makes a dissatisfied noise and crosses arms)

Ari: I spoke to both of my contacts. Does anyone know if Lee got it done?

Others: (shaking heads) No.

Ari: So we have something on at least 5 of the 10. Billie, why don't you hand out what we have? Okay, let's go over the details.

Billie: We don't have anything. I have mine. No one sent me their information.

Ari: That's not true. I sent it to you.

Billie: Last night at 8 p.m.! I didn't have time to add it to mine before our meeting today. I had a full morning. I forwarded it to others right before I got here.

Ari: Well, just pull out your computer and add stuff as people talk now.

Billie: (rolls eyes and gets out laptop)

Jess: Let's not start this. Since Lee isn't here, maybe we should postpone. We will just have to go over them again when Lee gets here.

Billie: We have only four weeks before we owe the director a report, and we don't even have enough ideas to propose a change in process. Half of us don't follow through on assignments. We cannot postpone again. Finance said it wanted to be a part of this, but this is the third time you haven't done your part. Why are they even on this committee?

Jess:	Well, frankly, this group has misused my expertise. I should only be here to comment on the financial implications of a possible plan. I shouldn't have to find out what other agencies are doing. (Looking at Ari) You should have assigned your assistant to make these calls. Really, what a waste of resources! Jo's time is also expensive. Lee is less expensive, and this is really Billie's job. They somehow talked you (looking at Ari) into a committee to do it for them. Billie could also make these calls, make a proposal, and then we could react. You could step it up (looking at Ari and Billie).
Jo:	Jess, you know that the last time a plan was tried that didn't get input from every department in advance, it didn't work. This isn't just Billie's job.
Jess:	There you go again, making excuses for Billie's incompetence!
Billie:	Excuse me, I did my part and offered to do part for all of you by collating this. I cannot change quality alone. Now, I am wondering if part of the dissatisfaction comes from interacting with finance?
Lee:	(Rushes in) Sorry; you just never know how long it will take with a walk-in, and we are short staffed again. I wonder if part of why our time lags are so long is the way we have the front of office organized. Tif said to just put Ezra out there, but he doesn't know how to answer most of the questions and kicks everything back to me. It is so frustrating. (looks around at group and sees that all are a bit irritated) Is everything okay? What did I miss?
Jo:	Oh, the usual: Jess's being too good to do the same work we do, Billie's being exasperated that we have only four weeks left, and Ari's being too nice to say anything about the fact that half of us didn't get the information we need. Did you get yours?

Task Group Scene Take 2

Ari:	Well, four of us are here. Where's Lee?
Jo:	I think stuck with a walk-in because Sylvie called off today. They are short in I & R today.
Ari:	This is the third or fourth time this has occurred, right? Once for Jess with an audit, once for you with a client situation, and now twice for Lee.
Billie:	Actually, I think this is the third time for Lee. It is why we moved the meeting time twice.
Ari:	Right.
Jess:	The rest of us manage to get here. Lee should make this a priority.
Jo:	I'm not sure that it is fair to conclude this isn't a priority for Lee. When you are dealing with clients, you cannot always predict how long it will take. We don't always have as much control of our schedule as finance and QI. I have more control than Lee. This committee is, after all, about trying to figure out better ways to handle client intakes. Maybe Lee's not being here is simply symptomatic of the wider problem.
Jess:	The process of handling client inquiries isn't like dealing with a mental illness (looks at Jo), and we cannot work without Lee.
Jo:	I am not so sure about the process being differ—
Ari:	(interrupts)—Jo, excuse me, but I am going to interrupt here. I think you both have some good points, and we may want to come back to them later. First, I hear the frustration and feel it, too. It is frustrating to have any member of the committee missing because it slows our work. Second, the fact that Lee seems to have so little control of their schedule may be an indicator of part of the problem we were

tasked to solve. (looks at Jo then Jess) After all, a symptom is simply another word for indicator. Sometimes, I think we talk past each other in our various roles. But, before we jump into that, I want to take a look at the agenda I sent out to you two days ago.

(All look at their agendas)

Ari: Is this agenda okay with you? Is there anything we need to add?

Billie: Once Lee is here, can we add taking a look a meeting times again?

Jo: I see that item three is to revisit the factors contributing to the problem. I think the staffing issues in I & R are on that list already, but if they are not, they should be. Can we add that there?

Ari: Sounds good. Are those two changes okay with everyone?

(All nod yes or murmur yes)

Ari: Excellent. Then let's do approval of minutes and select a minute taker for this week. Thanks for doing the minutes the last time, Jo. Are there any corrections or changes?

Billie: There is one slight correction. The regulators and grant funding source want to see the intake times dropped to under 30 days. The two weeks number was our idea about a goal time.

Jo: (typing on laptop) Okay, I will note that correction.

Jess: I have a suggestion, too. The labor hours figures are much better in that table. Can you add the table?

Jo: Sure; can you send it to me? I am not going to retype it.

Jess: Yeah. (on laptop) It is sent now.

Jo: I will add it in the final after the meeting.

Ari: With those two changes, are the minutes accurate?

(All nod yes.)

Jess: I make a motion to accept and approve the amended minutes.

Billie: Second.

Ari: All in favor, say "aye."

Others: Aye.

Ari: Then the minutes are approved. Who will be our minute taker this week? It should be Lee's turn, but they're not here. That brings Jess up next on the list.

Jess: I am going to again say my thought that this is a poor use of my time. You should have one of the support staff do this.

Jo: You have your laptop with you; I don't see why you can't take some notes while we talk. The support staff is stretched, too. We aren't a corporation; we are small nonprofit.

Ari: Jess, your dissatisfaction about having to do minutes is noted. We just need something simple that helps keep us on track and keeps us accountable. Lee will have to do them next time.

Jess: Fine. I am going to save and cut and paste into Jo's file.

Ari: Next item. Research on intake from other organizations. Each of us had two organizations to explore. Billie agreed to make a master list. Billie, what do we have?

Billie: Well, we have the two I did on the chart. You sent yours late last night (at 8:00 p.m.), and I was tied up all morning. Jo, Jess, and Lee did not send anything.

Jo: I got one of two done. I have been playing telephone tag with the person at ZYX. I probably should have started calling them sooner.

Jess: With the audit, I didn't get them called.

Billie: (looking at Jess) I guess Lee isn't the only person who isn't meeting their commitments to this committee—

Ari: (interrupts)—I am going to call "time out" here. There is a real tension in the room today. Before we try to do anything, let's check in on that.

(some silence)

Jo: Speaking for myself only, this committee has been tough. I was already busy and then I have to do research and minutes. I personally feel frustrated when others don't do their parts or miss meetings because it slows us down, but I am as guilty as anyone of not getting stuff done—for example, today. Then I feel like a bad committee member. Plus, I am not sure that all this energy will result in any changes. After all, I was on the committee that was supposed to fix this problem six years ago. We did all this work, and then Board let the E.D. go and hired a new one. Those recommendations were never used.

Jess: I like the way you said that. I would have been less polite about it, but I essentially agree. I am not sure if this makes a difference. I also don't really see the point for me to be on this committee, so I don't feel bad about not doing the work. I suspect Billie thinks I am a deadbeat on this committee. I think everyone would have preferred Astral to me.

Billie: Honestly, yeah, I do think you have been a bit of a deadbeat. You have made it really clear that you don't want to do this by never following through and never wanting to take minutes. But the last initiative we tried without a finance person on the committee didn't work because there was an aspect to the work that didn't get noticed until too late. It was glaringly obvious to finance. Your boss picked you. I am not sure why, but she did.

Jess: Well, just like the notes today, it was my turn.

Ari: I am glad we got some of this into the open. It sounds as if people are concerned this is a lot of effort and may be for nothing because of past initiatives in the agency.

(Jess and Jo nod their heads)

Billie: Yeah, I agree, although maybe I am not as concerned as Jess and Jo.

Ari: Let's step back and look at the bigger picture. Do we all agree that from the point of view of quality services, client well-being, and the agency's bottom line, we need to get a better intake process?

(All heads nod yes)

Ari: Do we all agree that we need multiple departments to be a part of shaping the change, or it is likely that this will not work?

(All nod or murmur yes)

Ari: Really, you are all agreeing with me because of my role?

Jess: No, really. You are right.

Ari: So, what are we going to do about it then?

Lee: (rushes in) Sorry; you just never know how long it will take with a walk-in, and we are short-staffed again. I wonder if part of why our time lags are so long is the way we have the front of office organized. Tif said to just put Ezra out there, but he doesn't know how to answer most of the questions and kicks everything back to me. It is so frustrating. (looks around at group and sees that all are a bit irritated) Is everything okay? What did I miss?

EXERCISE 10.4: A THERAPEUTIC PROCESS GROUP IN ACTION

The goal of this exercise is to experience a simulated group therapy session in order to give you an experiential awareness of what it is like to participate in a therapeutic process group.

Directions

- Prior to the exercise, choose one or two complicated personal dilemmas that a friend or relative is currently facing. You will discuss them in your small group.

- You should not reveal the identity of the person whose problems you choose to talk about. Remember also, what is said in the group must be kept confidential, and the discussion should be limited to the friend's or relative's dilemma rather than addressing any dilemmas or difficulties you are personally experiencing.

- Form small groups of five or six.

- Appoint one person to serve as the leader.

- Take turns sharing the concerns being faced by your friend or relative.

- In the final 15 minutes of class time, reconvene as a class to discuss the "group session" and answer the following questions:

  ○ How easy or difficult was it to be the leader? To be a member?

  ○ Which skills were easiest to employ? Which were more difficult?

  ○ What other strategies or skill might have been used?

  ○ How easy or hard do you think it might be for clients to be part of a therapeutic group?

  ○ What are the benefits and shortcomings of the exercise?

  ○ Do you have any suggestions for changes to the format of the exercise?

Hints

- If the group is reluctant to start to share, the leader may initiate the process by specifically asking one of the more vocal members to begin.

- If the group continues to struggle, the leader may make a content-to-process shift and use the struggle to talk as the topic.

- When a group member is sharing, the leader should encourage the other members to probe by using verbal following skills, in order to explore the problem further.

- The leader may also encourage other members to suggest realistic and creative courses of action to resolve the problem using thematic or person-to-person linking.

- Other members can use skills to help the group process, being a leader as a member.

EXERCISE 10.5: PARTICIPATING IN A TASK GROUP

The goal of this exercise is to simulate the start of a task group. Students should call to mind the developmental tasks at the formation stage of a group and how to lead as a formal leader or as member leader.

Directions

- Form groups of six to eight students.

- Sit in a circle (this configuration is the most conducive to good interpersonal interaction).

- Select one person to observe and report on group process. This person sits slightly outside the group and does not participate.

- As a group, choose a social problem that exists in the members' current real-life community and experience (e.g., problems that students face when registering for classes). The purpose of your task group is to (1) identify and consider several alternatives for action to resolve the chosen problem, and (2) select one of the courses of action to work on as a group going forward (action steps).

- Once the action steps have been identified, have the observer report what they saw and discuss the report as a group.

- In the final 15 minutes of class time, reconvene as a class to discuss the "group session" and answer the following questions:

  ○ How easy or difficult was it to be the leader? To be a member?

  ○ Which skills were easiest to employ? Which were more difficult?

  ○ What other strategies or skills might have been used?

  ○ Did you take the time to discuss leadership and decision making, or did you move immediately into the task? Why or why not?

  ○ Were roles and tasks assigned or taken by members?

  ○ When (if) conflicts or differences arose, how did the group resolve them?

  ○ What are the benefits and shortcomings of the exercise?

  ○ Do you have any suggestions for changes to the format of the exercise?

Hints:

- What form/structure of leadership will you use?

- What type of leadership style fits this group (autocratic, democratic, or laissez-faire)?

- How will the group make decisions?

Answer Key

Case Vignette 1: Treatment type, skills subtype, forming stage

Rationale: It was only their second meeting; they are learning about confidentiality.

Case Vignette 2: Task type, board subtype, returning to storming and/or norming from performing stage

Rationale: They failed to do needed work, they did not trust one another fully, and they did not know how to challenge one another or clarify their roles.

Case Vignette 3: Treatment type, support subtype, performing stage

Rationale: The members set the agenda, oriented the new members, and showed cohesion and ownership of the group.

WORKING WITH ORGANIZATIONS

LEARNING OBJECTIVES

1. Apply concepts about organizations to the startup phase of organizational development (Exercise 11.1)

2. Identify which basic communication skills can apply to communication in organizational interactions (Exercise 11.3)

3. Gain familiarity with an organizational assessment tool that can be used at several phases of organizational development, particularly at maturity, decline/crisis, and turnaround (Exercise 11.2)

4. Apply concepts about effective interprofessional practice and barriers to interprofessional practice to past experiences and explore social work skills that can be utilized to promote effective interprofessional behavior (Exercise 11.4)

5. Explore interprofessional practice, social justice, and ethics in organizational practice (Exercise 11.5)

CHAPTER OUTLINE

• Key Concepts for Working with and in Organizations

• Exercise 11.1: Design an Organization

• Domain and Task Environment as a Basis for Organizational Assessment

• Exercise 11.2: SWOT Analysis

• Exercise 11.3: Employing Basic Communication and Advocacy Skills in an Organization

• Interprofessional Practice

• Exercise 11.4: Social Work's Role on the Interprofessional Team

• Exercise 11.5: Clinical Director Opening at New Hope Human Services

Most social workers begin their careers, and some spend their entire careers, working within an organization or multiple organizations. Some social workers specialize in or focus their practice on administration of organizations and the services that they provide; they work predominantly at this system level. The policies of service organizations affect their clients, the social workers who work for them, and the communities they serve. Generalist helping skills apply to the organizational context, too. So regardless of the system level at which students plan to use their social work skills, they will need to understand how to apply their communication, group, and advocacy skills at the organizational level. This chapter explores how to assess and interact within organizations to promote change along with healthy organizational functioning and advocate for individuals and families. After going over key concepts about organizations, these exercises let you explore how to assess and interact in an organizational context.

KEY CONCEPTS FOR WORKING WITH AND IN ORGANIZATIONS

An **organization** can be defined as "a group whose members work together for a shared purpose in a continuing way" (Cambridge Dictionary) or as "any structures with staff, policies, and procedures, whose purpose in operating is to attain certain goals" (Kirst-Ashman & Hull, 2015, p. 131). A **human services organization** is an "organization whose primary function is to define or alter the person's behavior, attributes, and social status in order to maintain or enhance his well-being" (Hasenfeld & English, 1977, p. 1), fulfilling three functions of socialization, social control, and social integration. A **community organization** is a "collective human effort centered on mobilization, planning, and advocating/negotiating for resources to address community-identified issues" (Murphy & Cunningham, 2003).

The very definition of an organization immediately points to the fact that an organization is a social system made up of *people* who have a shared reason to act together. According to Warren (1983), "Most formal organizations appear to function as quasi-political systems balancing the needs and interests of policymakers, constituencies, functionaries, and clientele" (p. 27). Therefore, the basic communication skills social workers learn to use with individual and family clients become a necessary part of their practice with social work peers and colleagues from all professions in organizations. The ease or challenge of that communication varies by setting and is influenced by the organization's shared purpose. Each organization develops a mission, a structure, and a culture and experiences a life cycle; consequently, social workers fulfill many different roles in those organizations (see Figure 11.1). These are concepts that you learned about other system levels that may be applied to the organizational system level, too.

Every organization has a purpose, which is set out in its **organizational mission statement.** The mission statement articulates the shared purpose and guides the activities of the organization. It drives decisions about who to serve, how to serve, and the appropriate organization type to help people. Below are the most common types of organizations that provide social and human services.

The type of organization providing services is important for many reasons, including service provision and legal and financial considerations.

- Governmental: a government entity authorized by public policy

  ○ Example: adult protective services provided by a county government

- Nonprofit: an organization authorized by policy or by organizational mission that is not trying to generate a profit for shareholders or owners

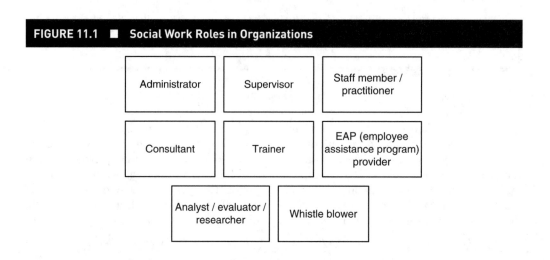

FIGURE 11.1 ■ Social Work Roles in Organizations

Administrator

Supervisor

Staff member / practitioner

Consultant

Trainer

EAP (employee assistance program) provider

Analyst / evaluator / researcher

Whistle blower

- Sectarian: a nonprofit affiliated with a religious/spiritual tradition and with a mission consistent with the beliefs of that tradition

  ○ Example: refugee resettlement services provided by Jewish Family and Community Services

- Nonsectarian: A nonprofit without any connection to religious/spiritual traditions

  ○ Example: affordable housing provided by a CDC (a community development corporation)

- For-profit: an organization authorized by policy or by organizational mission that wants to generate a profit for shareholders or owners

  ○ Publicly traded (on the stock market)

    - Example: mental health services for prisoners provided by a private company

  ○ Private (owned by one or several people)

    - Example: family therapy offered by a social worker in private practice

Another way to distinguish organizations is whether they are predominantly social service organizations or other types of organizations assisting people and communities. Students may encounter these two terms:

- Social service organization/agency: an agency that primarily delivers social services and is likely to be led by social workers and have policies aligned with social work ethics.

- Host setting: an organization that delivers assistance to people but is led or dominated by other professions, and those professions and their codes of ethics are more likely to guide organizational policy. For example, a hospital is a setting where physicians and medicine are the dominant profession and field. A school is a setting where educators/teachers are the dominant profession.

Organizational Structure: The simplicity or complexity and formality of organizations varies a great deal, from a highly structured and complex system like the U.S. government to a neighborhood group that uses text messages to communicate and cleans up and beautifies the shared medians and sidewalks once a year. Students will tend to encounter two common structures or an organization trying to create a hybrid of both:

- Hierarchical (vertical): Activity and leadership are organized with a chain of command, typically leading to an executive who is overseen by a board of directors

  ○ Makes great sense for linear work with very defined products (yes, a therapy session can be thought of as a product)

- Flat (horizontal): Activity is self-generated by workers and collectively organized; tends to have no job titles and emphasizes worker autonomy

  ○ Makes sense when the mission requires creativity and less defined products

- Flatter (hybrid): This model seeks to reduce hierarchy and bureaucracy and open up communication and collaboration among workers without entirely eliminating hierarchy, and it is dependent upon technology to enable it

  ○ Makes sense when the product requires flexibility, critical thinking, and deployment of skill sets

Organizational culture: A set of shared assumptions, values, and beliefs that guides how people behave inside the organization. Just as any family or group develops its own identity and way of doing things, so do organizations. The people within the organization come together to create the culture, for good or not. There is great risk in organizations that wider societal structures and patterns of injustice will be unintentionally repeated in organizational culture, thus disadvantaging already oppressed groups. With social work's attention to social justice, social workers may play a critical role in sharing the value of social justice and helping it to be integrated into the organizations in which they work.

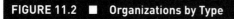

FIGURE 11.2 ■ Organizations by Type

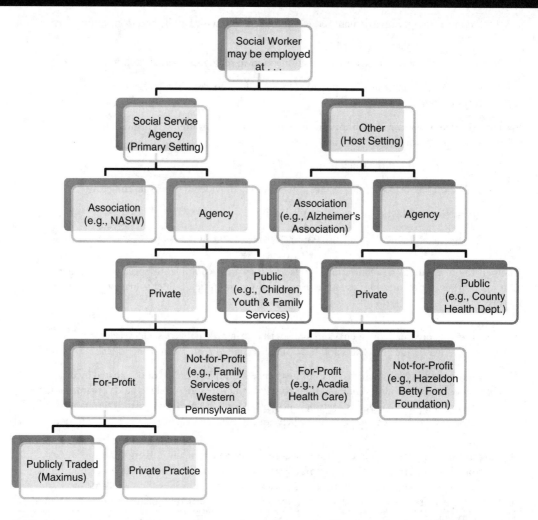

FIGURE 11.3 ■ Sectarian vs. Nonsectarian Organizations

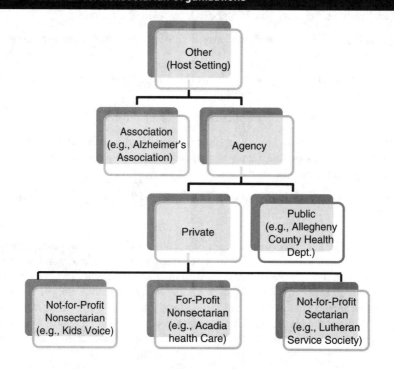

TABLE 11.1 ■ The Organizational Life Cycle	
Life Cycle Stage	**Activities**
Birth/New/Startup	Establishing mission, gathering resources, determining structure, initiating organizational activities, beginning service
Adolescence/Building the Infrastructure/ Expansion and Growth	Refining programs and service delivery, modifying structure, clarifying values, building infrastructure, securing resources
Midlife or Maturity/Impact Expansion	Expanding the impact and effectiveness of programs and assuring the sustainability of the resources
Decline/Crisis	Responding to internal and/or external demands that reduce the effectiveness of the organization
Turnaround/Restructuring/ Closing/End	Assessing and determining whether the organization should continue with a turnaround or restructuring plan or with a plan to close, activities to carry out one or other

Organizational life cycle: As organizations are social systems, ideas about the development of social systems, such as the life cycle, can be used to understand them. Organizational life cycles have been discussed by many authors (Brother & Sherman, 2011; Anheier, 2014; Worth, 2009; Carlson & Donohoe, 2010), and multiple typologies or terminologies have been used. All of them suggest that there are predictable activities that must be carried out by organizations at each stage of development, which help with transition and functioning (see Table 11.1). There is considerable overlap in the ideas of various writers regarding both nonprofit and for-profit organizations. Note how the language mirrors language for individual development, yet it is not a perfect fit, as not all organizations come to an end.

Because the focus and activities of an organization shift as it develops and responds to its environment, transitions typically produce stress for employees (and sometimes clients/consumers) and necessitate process management, resource development and/or resource management, and possible reexamination of mission and structure. Social workers' ability to understand what the organization is experiencing may give them perspective to adapt to transitions, but it does not protect them from the stress related to it. Therefore, social workers in organizations often benefit from using the broad range of generalist skills to problem solve and cope through transitions.

Organizational type and structure often combine to create advantages or disadvantages in communities, with different populations, at various times. Therefore, organizations must regularly review how well their structure and type fits their mission and developmental needs. For example, a small group of practitioners who have been working for a county government has ideas about integrating video technology into service coordination in a rural area. They share their ideas with a manager who says that they are interesting but that the public budget does not have the funds to develop the idea. They decide to begin by forming a private organization with a flat structure to foster flexibility and creativity and to be able to generate some venture capital to work on their ideas. Several years later, after trying several versions of video technology and getting contracts to pilot their ideas, they have developed software that is effective for client outcomes and from a cost standpoint. They want to scale the business to sell their package of technology and technical assistance to service organizations. They are aware of the limited budgets of the organizations to which they want to sell and recognize that their investors expect return. They weigh the pros and cons of how to grow. They decide that they are transitioning from being a startup to the expansion and growth stage for an organization. They realize they need more hierarchy in their structure, as it is no longer practical for all of them to be involved in decisions. They move to a flatter structure and decide to remain a private for-profit organization.

EXERCISE 11.1: DESIGN AN ORGANIZATION

Directions

- Form small groups of four to six students.

- Brainstorm the startup phase of an organization that seeks to address employment issues for veterans in a small community that does not have a VA facility.

- Use the following questions to guide your discussion:

  ○ What is the organization's mission?

- ○ What is the best setting for it?

- ○ How will it be funded?

- ○ How will it be staffed?

- ○ What type of structure would be best?

- ○ How will it interface with other agencies?

- ○ How will it reach its intended population?

- Reconvening as a full class, have a spokesperson for each group briefly relay to class what the group chose to do and why.

- After each presentation, give the group feedback on their plan.

  - ○ How similar or different are the ideas?

  - ○ What other information would you want?

  - ○ Are there other stakeholders you would like to involve?

DOMAIN AND TASK ENVIRONMENT AS A BASIS FOR ORGANIZATIONAL ASSESSMENT

Various frames of reference can be used to analyze an organization. Six components emerge as key factors for analysis (Soska, 2017). Gathering information about each of these areas is an important aspect of organizational analysis.

1. Mandate: charter, articles, bylaws, sanction (those who authorize the work). All of these frame the legal and regulatory domain and task environment of the organization.

2. Mission (also known as Vision): reason/purpose for the organization and what impact it sees itself having in the community

3. Goals: beliefs and values and operational guidelines to advance the mission of the organization

4. Territory/Turf: problem, population, service, and geographic area that define the service area or service targets

5. Task Environment: to whom the human service organization must relate in order to meet its mission. This includes consideration of monetary and nonmonetary resources, consumers, competitors, and collaborators.

6. Organizational Power: control over resources others need

Other areas for assessment include the following:

- Organizational structure, including size and organizational chart

- Budget: funding sources, allocation of resources, and process

- Organizational history: the story of how the organization arrived at this point

- Organizational policies: both the formal (written) and informal ways it operates

EXERCISE 11.2: SWOT ANALYSIS

Organizations use a variety of assessment tools; a SWOT (Strengths, Weaknesses, Opportunities, and Threats) analysis is one of them. This exercise will familiarize you with a tool to assess organizational change and enhancement. It can be particularly helpful when an organization is in decline or crisis (Brother & Sherman, 2011).

Directions

- Form a small group of four to six people.

- Imagine you are social workers hired by Wal-Mart or Amazon (or a similar large organization from your community that has had bad press in regard to employees or the community) as an organizational consultant to provide recommendations for how the organization can improve its employee and community relations. You have been asked to deliver a SWOT analysis to the CEO and senior executives of the organization.

- First, assess your group's familiarity with this organization and educate any members who are not familiar with it on its basic operations, mission, purpose, and controversies. You may need to examine the organization's website to see what information it shares with the public; in addition, search for news stories about the organization.

- Use Table 11.2 as a guide to conduct a SWOT analysis to inform organizational change that will improve employee and/or community relations with this organization.

- Try to identify at least three items for each category (there may be more than three).

Ideas to Guide the Discussion

Internal Assessment

- Strengths (areas to build)

  ○ What does the organization already do well for its employees? For the community?

  ○ How does the organization serve its employees and the community?

  ○ What needs or gaps does the organization fill nicely in the community?

  ○ What metrics/data does the organization have to indicate the areas where it is performing well?

- Weaknesses (areas for improvement)

  ○ What have the complaints or criticisms been about this organization? By employees? By community members?

  ○ What losses or consequences have occurred because of poor community relations? Poor employee relations?

  ○ What metrics/data does the organization have to indicate the areas where it is not performing well?

TABLE 11.2 ■ SWOT Analysis

Internal	
Strengths	Weaknesses
_____	_____
_____	_____
_____	_____
Opportunities	Threats
_____	_____
_____	_____
_____	_____
External	

External Assessment

- Opportunities (What gaps or opportunities exist for the organization to fill?):
  - Address compelling issues or conditions?
  - Fill a gap in its area of service or fill a community need?
  - Meet the interests of potential partners/allies or funders?
  - Be a leader, to set a new standard of performance?
  - Which of the opportunities above are most promising? Why?

- Threats (Does the organization face current or pending challenges?):
  - Changing demographics of current and potential consumer group(s)?
  - Evolving community issues and conditions that the organization might address?
  - Relevant cultural or social trends?
  - Trends in the economy or funding environment?
  - Politics, legislation, or regulation that affects the organization and those it serves?
  - Competition (existing/new/potential)?
  - Which of the challenges above are the most significant? Why?

- Cross-sectional view of strengths weaknesses, opportunities, and threats (Soska, 2017):
  - How do you leverage strengths to benefit from opportunities?
  - How do you ensure that weaknesses do not stop you from using opportunities?
  - How do you use your strengths to minimize the impact of threats?
  - How will you fix weaknesses that can cause threats to have a real impact?

EXERCISE 11.3: EMPLOYING BASIC COMMUNICATION AND ADVOCACY SKILLS IN AN ORGANIZATION

During the term or in earlier classes you learned a number of basic communication and advocacy skills. These skills include active listening (verbal and nonverbal), minimal prompts, clarifying, seeking concreteness, empathic communication, and summarizing.

Directions

- Form pairs or groups of three.

- One person can be the social worker, one person the other party, and a third person (if present) as be an observer who provides feedback and alternative approaches to the situation.

- Role play the vignettes below, illustrating how to use communication skills in an organizational setting.

- Reconvene as a class to discuss the vignettes and role plays.
  - Which skills did you employ?
  - How was it similar or different from communicating with clients?

○ Are you able to be as assertive in your communication in these circumstances as with clients? Why or why not?

○ What are the additional concerns and issues associated with communication to peers, other professionals, and agency staff?

Vignette 1

The social worker has a client (Janis) with limited means who has completed substance use treatment, began a job two weeks earlier, and secured an apartment, but she is in need of furniture immediately to regain custody of her children (as part of the court order). A local nonprofit provides furniture to families at low or no cost if the client gets a referral verifying the situation. The social worker is providing that referral.

Starter line:

Rep of Furniture Program:	You know, we got a lot of people who say they need furniture. Most of them are okay, but some are just running a con. We are just trying to be good stewards of the donations we get here. Are you sure your client isn't putting one over on you?

Vignette 2

The social worker was walking down the hall with a client when they overheard two of the maintenance staff making negative remarks about people who practice Islam. After discussing it with the client, the social worker follows up with the staff members.

Starter lines:

Social Worker:	Earlier this afternoon, I overheard your conversation as you were repairing the window in Cynthia's office—the one where you called people who practice Islam "terrorists."
Maintenance Staff Member:	Yeah. Well what? Looking at your face, I guess you don't agree. I suppose you are going to make some big deal about this. I know we are supposed to be inclusive and all that, but really we have to stay safe.

Vignette 3

Two social workers (Alex and Harper) are cross-trained and cover one another's clients when off. Alex has been covering a lot for Harper over the last five months because Harper's mother died. It has not improved, and Alex is tired of it. Alex has serious concerns that Harper's grief has become an impairment because referrals for clients are forgotten, paperwork is poor quality, and there are many rescheduled appointments. All of this would have been unusual prior to the death.

Starter line:

Alex:	Hey, Harper, thanks for talking today. I wanted to check in on how you are doing with the grief related to your mom's death. It seems like you haven't been able to get back to your full workload.

INTERPROFESSIONAL PRACTICE

Most social workers are employed in host settings—settings where the dominant discipline or perspective is not social work, such as medical settings, education, or corrections. This necessitates that social workers must be skilled in interprofessional practice, communication, and decision making. Some students experience both classroom preparation and field preparation in interprofessional practice; other do not. There has been some study of social workers as part of interprofessional teams, particularly in health care. Some of the barriers to social workers' being fully effective on such teams are common to all team members, and others are unique for social workers (see Table 11.3).

TABLE 11.3 ■ Common Barriers to Interprofessional Practice	
Barriers for All Team Members	**Barriers for Social Workers**
• Incomplete understanding of others' scope of practice • Underutilization or inappropriate utilization of team members • Poor team communication • Lack of stability of team membership • "Profession-centrism" blocking the ability to hear/respect other professions • Poor decision making processes/lack of mechanism to resolve conflicts	• Perceived lack of control • Subjective norms (perceived pressure to perform in a particular way in shared decision making) • Perceived lack of respect for social work practice and ideology • Limited upward mobility within a host setting

Source: Glaser and Suter (2016); Gucciardi et al. (2016); Smith-Carrier and Neysmith (2014); Légaré et al. (2013); Pecukonis et al. (2008).

So, how do students, who are being socialized into the values and perspectives of their various professions, learn to see their professional lenses as carrying both strengths and weaknesses and as yet another feature of culture about which to be humble and sensitive (Pecukonis et al., 2008)? Social work students are well equipped to do this because of their training in cultural sensitivity and humility. One approach is to view non–social work coworkers as human beings with both personal and professional strengths and vulnerabilities (Pecukonis et al., 2008). Smith-Carrier and Neysmith (2014) suggest that effective interprofessional teams in health care are marked by (1) shared vision/goals, (2) processes for ongoing communication, (3) effective leadership, and (4) mechanisms to resolve conflict. These ideas can be applied more generally to interprofessional teams in other settings, too. They are very consistent with social work. Gucciardi et al. (2016) would add role clarification to that list. One of the best ways to learn about interprofessional practice is to learn it through training with other disciplines and mentorship (O'Carroll, McSwiggan, & Campbell, 2016; Pecukonis et al., 2008). However, since that is typically not available in a social work class, the following exercise asks you to consider interprofessional practice based on your personal experiences.

EXERCISE 11.4: SOCIAL WORK'S ROLE ON THE INTERPROFESSIONAL TEAM

Note to Instructor: This exercise is most useful for students who are already in field placements, have done a field placement or internship, or are working in some capacity in human services. Instructors may not find it helpful for students who are not at this point in their education.

Directions

- Form small groups of four to six students.

- Take a minute to call to mind an interprofessional team, work group, or experience you have seen in field or past work (if you have no prior experience in the helping professions, you may be able to apply these ideas to another professional work team or setting).

- Thinking about the particular team you chose, discuss the following:

  o To what degree did the team members share a vision or goal for the work?

    • Were the goals/vision presumed, assumed, or explicitly explored?

  o Did team members seem to understand the roles and scope of practice of all members?

    • Did respect flow from that? Why or why not?

    • Were people utilized to their full capacity? Why or why not?

- Did the team explicitly discuss roles, where they overlapped and blurred, and where they were distinct?

  ○ How effective was the communication?

    - What mechanisms or practices promoted or discouraged communication?

    - Did professional identities interfere with communication?

    - Did structures promote or interfere with communication?

  ○ What type or style of leadership occurred with the team?

    - Who were the leaders—those officially titled and designated and those who led from a membership position?

    - Were leaders chosen based on skill or based on assumptions about professions, status, or perceived power?

    - Was leadership flexible or fixed over time?

    - Did the leadership promote hearing the diversity of perspectives that come from interprofessional practice?

  ○ How did the team resolve conflict?

    - How did professional identity play into the approach team members took to conflict?

    - How did specific professional values impact the approach to conflict?

    - Was there space on the team for social work perspectives?

  ○ Based on the answers to the questions, what is one idea for how that particular team might improve its interprofessional functioning?

  ○ What social work skill (communication or group) could you apply to working on an interprofessional team?

- Returning to the large group, each small group should present to the class two take-home points or reflections on interprofessional practice and social work.

EXERCISE 11.5: CLINICAL DIRECTOR OPENING AT NEW HOPE HUMAN SERVICES

Social workers are valuable leaders/employees in all aspects of community organizations. It is essential for the social work profession to promote its unique person-in-environment perspective, commitment to social justice, and broad educational knowledge and skills.

Directions

- Form small groups of four to six.

- After reading the case vignette, try to answer the questions that follow based on the given information.

- Be prepared to report your answers to the class.

Case Vignette

Judy is retiring in six months after working for the New Hope Human Services agency for 20 years. As the clinical director of the child welfare department, she is the only female and only social worker in an administrative position. Other professional disciplines administer the adult and geriatric divisions of the agency. She is hoping that a social worker will fill her position. Judy is responsible for supervising eight individuals in her department. Two of her supervisees are female, licensed clinical social workers (LCSW). Both have the experience to be the next clinical director of the child welfare department, if they choose to apply. Fortunately for Judy, she is on the selection committee and will have the opportunity to interview potential candidates. The committee consists of the agency's CEO, the clinical directors from the adult and geriatric departments, and Judy. Interviews for the position are scheduled to begin within two weeks. Judy is concerned because the CEO has only been at the agency for one year, and he has met with her only once.

She received five resumes of potential candidates from the agency's CEO. Much to her surprise, no female or social work candidates are in the applicant pool. It is disturbing to her that three of the candidates have less experience than her LCSW staff. Judy is aware that one internal LCSW staff member and two outside female social work candidates applied for the clinical director position.

Questions

1. How should Judy handle her concerns with the selection committee?

2. Should Judy request a meeting with the CEO before interviewing the potential candidates? What is your rationale?

3. Should Judy share information about the applicants with the internal LCSW staff who also submitted a resume for the position?

4. Are there ethical concerns for Judy due to this recruitment and hiring situation?

5. What factors might have played a role in choosing this applicant pool?

6. From a social work perspective, what values or ideas should be considered to guide the processes for hiring?

12

MACRO PRACTICE: COMMUNITY DEVELOPMENT AND ORGANIZING

LEARNING OBJECTIVES

1. Understand what community organizing involves and compare/contrast the various roles assumed by community organizers in their work (Exercises 12.2 and 12.3).

2. Apply knowledge about community organizing work to client case vignettes to evaluate the circumstances under which a social worker would shift from taking a micro approach to helping a client to a macro approach for meeting clients' needs (Exercise 12.2).

3. Engage in critical thinking by addressing a social problem, discussing its parameters and manifestations, and then formulating a plan for moving from a micro response to a macro response (Exercises 12.3 and 12.4).

CHAPTER OUTLINE

- Key Concepts and Definitions
  - ¢ Community Organizing vs. Community Development
  - ¢ Social Justice
  - ¢ Activities of Community Organizers
  - ¢ Roles of Community Organizers
  - ¢ Models of Community Practice
  - ¢ Organizer Guiding Questions
- Exercise 12.1: A Fence or an Ambulance
- Exercise 12.2: When Do Private Problems Become Public Issues?
- Exercise 12.3: Alternative Use of the Cases
- Exercise 12.4: Moving From Micro to Macro Practice

Almost all practicing social workers occasionally become involved in activities related to community organizing and/or community development or enhancement, particularly if they work in public services. Thus, the view that every social worker is only a direct services social worker or only an administrator or only a community organizer is not true; rather, most social workers take on all three roles, depending on what needs to be done for their clients, agency, and community.

Direct practice social workers are most likely to engage in community organizing when they identify gaps in services that must be filled to meet client needs. For example, let's say you work for the public welfare department in the area of providing services for single-parent families. You may decide to become involved in efforts to develop a program of childcare and job referral information if an effective program does not already exist and if the demand for such a program becomes evident. You may then work toward garnering community support and funding for developing such a program. This is an example of community organizing in action!

KEY CONCEPTS AND DEFINITIONS

Community Organizing vs. Community Development

Although community organizing and community development are related and often co-exist in community change endeavors, they are not the same. **Community organizing** involves collaborative activity among all stakeholders in a community, to capitalize on existing resources, and fostering reciprocal connections between community agencies and outside resources to enhance the quality of community life for all citizens. Social workers who are community organizers, take action based on the principles of social justice, which are the basis for the social work profession's value system (also see Chapters 2 and 4). Social workers must also always be cognizant of the importance of organizations in community practice and any social work effort. We often say, "Organizers organize organizations," in that our work builds organizations that maintain the systems of locality development, social planning and service development, and social action. **Community development**, on the other hand, focuses on building social, economic, and political infrastructures to support the work of the community organizers and ensure sustainable community health and well-being (Borgman & Yates, 2018).

As an example, we can use the old proverb "Give someone a fish, and they eat for a day. Teach someone to fish, and they can eat for the rest of their life" to differentiate some of the community terms (Borgman & Yates, 2018):

- **Community service** is giving fish to those who are hungry.

- **Community advocacy** is telling others that some don't have fish and should be provided with fish.

- **Community transformation** is developing a taste for fish (instead of junk food) and empowering citizens to agree to fish cooperatively and productively.

- **Community development** is teaching people how to fish and how to build a fishing rod, net, and boat.

- **Community organizing** is rallying people together to get access to the lake where the fish are and can be caught.

Social Justice

According to the NASW (n.d.),

Social justice is the view that everyone deserves equal economic, political and social rights and opportunities. Social workers aim to open the doors of access and opportunity for everyone, particularly those in greatest need. . . . Social workers also apply social-justice principles to structural problems in the social service agencies in which they work. Armed with the long-term goal of empowering their clients, they use knowledge of existing legal principles and organizational structure to suggest changes to protect their clients, who are often powerless and underserved. . . . Often, social workers bring social justice concepts into the wider social and political arena.

Activities of Community Organizers

1. Encouraging and stimulating citizens to organize around one or more issues or problem areas facing their community

2. Assisting citizens in specifying the nature of the citizen or neighborhood problem

3. Developing coordination of efforts between groups

4. Reducing friction between group members

5. Engaging in fact finding

6. Formulating realizable goals collaboratively

7. Engaging in public relations and public education

8. Conducting community-based participatory research collaboratively with the community stakeholders

9. Engaging in community and neighborhood planning

10. Identifying financial resources

11. Educating members of the community on how to accomplish certain tasks

12. Serving as a resource person

Roles of Community Organizers

Enabler: enhances the capacity of community members to come together to resolve issues.

- Focus is on developing constructive relationships with community residents

- Objective is to help people organize to help themselves

- Skills used are primarily group work skills

- Functions of the Enabler:

  ○ Helps to awaken and focus discontent about particular community conditions

  ○ Encourages organization and overcomes apathy and passivity

  ○ Nourishes good interpersonal relations

  ○ Facilitates effective planning

Broker: links individuals and groups who need help and who do not know where help is available with community services

Expert: provides information and gives advice

Social Planner: carries out sequential tasks

- Gathers facts about a social problem

- Analyzes the facts to arrive at a rational course of action

- Develops a program and seeks funding

- Strives to secure consensus among diverse interest groups

- Facilitates implementation of the program plan

Advocate: steps in when a client or citizens' group is in need of help and existing institutions are uninterested in, or even openly negative and hostile to, providing services. As an advocate, one is in a partisan role, acting on behalf of one's client.

Activist: seeks basic institutional change, typically with the objective of influencing a shift in power and resources to a disadvantaged group. The first goal of an Activist is to inspire a disadvantaged group to organize to take action against the existing power structure, which is viewed as being the oppressor. Activists' tactics often involve conflict, confrontation, and negotiation, and their role is partisan.

Additional community organizing roles: mediator, negotiator, initiator, spokesperson, consultant, and fundraiser. Although these additional roles can be subsumed within the other major categories, they should be noted.

Models of Community Practice

The **Locality Development** model asserts that community change can best be brought about through broad participation of a wide spectrum of people at the local community level by means of

1. democratic procedures

2. a consensus approach

3. voluntary cooperation

4. development of indigenous leadership

5. self-help

Community intervention through Locality Development involves collaborative work between social worker(s) and local citizens to revitalize some aspect of their community. The revitalization efforts can be directed toward improving public spaces, vacant lots, and housing (renovation and new) and commercial or business regeneration for economic development. However, always critical to social work community practice and, in particular, Locality Development is collaboration between the social worker(s) and the people who live in the community and will benefit from the change efforts. Key to this is engaging and involving local constituents in leading the vision for change and redevelopment. Well-known examples of Locality Development efforts include the Peace Corps (www.peacecorp.gov) and Habitat for Humanity (www.habitat.org).

The **Social Planning** model asserts that community change in a complex industrial environment requires highly trained and highly skilled planners to effectively guide the complex process of change. However, in today's social work macro/community practice, these skilled planners must assure that the community and service constituents are engaged through democratic, participatory processes in the change and program or service development process. Social Planning often involves needs assessments that look at community service gaps and issues; however, as in any generalist helping process, social workers must ensure a focus on identifying and building from assets and strengths of individuals and the community. This asset-based community development model is essential to both Locality Development and Social Planning. Planning is not a process that is done "to" or "for" a community; it is a process done "with" the community or those being served.

The **Social Action** model employs advocacy and activism to bring about community change. Not only is Social Action a process for engaging and activating community constituents to advocate for a cause or on behalf of their community, it is also a process of fostering recognition of how factors in the external environment—policies and decisions—as well as human rights and social, economic, and environmental justice impact individuals, families, and their communities. The social work *Code of Ethics* provides both principles and ethical guidelines relative to our professional commitment in this regard to help guide our Social Action.

Organizer Guiding Questions

- Is what I am doing going to be constructive or destructive in achieving the desired outcome?

- Is there an even better way to achieve the desired outcome?

EXERCISE 12.1: A FENCE OR AN AMBULANCE

The public health model of prevention aims to reduce three things:

- The *incidence* or rate of new cases of the problem

- The *duration* of many of the problems that do occur

- The *degree of impairment* that results

There are two models of prevention that are typically utilized: (1) Leavell and Clark's (1958) model of primary, secondary, and tertiary prevention and (2) Gordon's (1983) model of universal, selected, and indicated prevention. Leavell and Clark's model has been applied in public health and community contexts for many years and assumes the presence of a problem within a population. Gordon's model assumes an absence of disease or problem. Table 12.1 compares the two models.

Therefore, Gordon's (1983) model is really a further breakdown of Leavell and Clark's (1958) primary prevention. For Gordon, the activities of secondary and tertiary prevention are more like intervention after identifying a problem.

TABLE 12.1 ■ Models of Prevention	
Models of Prevention	
Leavell & Clark's (1958) Model	**Gordon's (1983) Model**
Primary Prevention: Efforts seek to prevent a problem before it occurs	Universal Prevention: Efforts target a broad group of people without regard for their risk for the problem
Secondary Prevention: Activities are used to identify an issue in its earliest stages and to resolve it or prevent it from becoming a full-blown problem	Selected Prevention: Activities are centered on a subgroup of a population who have characteristics or factors that place them at higher risk for developing the problem
Tertiary Prevention: Responds once a problem or condition occurs with an intention of halting it at that point and restoring wellness	Indicated Prevention: Targets people who have specific risk factors or behaviors that increase the likelihood of their having a problem

Directions

- Read the poem "A Fence or an Ambulance" aloud, perhaps asking different students to read each stanza.

- As a class, discuss social work practice and prevention, and answer the following questions:

  ○ What does the poem illustrate that is relevant to social work?

  ○ What would be an analogy to a current issue in society today?

  ○ How does the poem illustrate the public health model of prevention?

A Fence or an Ambulance
Joseph Malins (1895)

'Twas a dangerous cliff, as they freely confessed,
Though to walk near its crest was so pleasant;
But over its terrible edge there had slipped
A duke and full many a peasant.
So the people said something would have to be done,
But their projects did not at all tally;
Some said, "Put a fence 'round the edge of the cliff,"
Some, "An ambulance down in the valley."

But the cry for the ambulance carried the day,
For it spread through the neighboring city;
A fence may be useful or not, it is true,
But each heart became full of pity
For those who slipped over the dangerous cliff;
And the dwellers in highway and alley
Gave pounds and gave pence, not to put up a fence,
But an ambulance down in the valley.

"For the cliff is all right, if your careful," they said,
"And, if folks even slip and are dropping,
It isn't the slipping that hurts them so much
As the shock down below when they're stopping."
So day after day, as these mishaps occurred,
Quick forth would those rescuers sally
To pick up the victims who fell off the cliff,
With their ambulance down in the valley.

Then an old sage remarked: "It's a marvel to me
That people give far more attention
To repairing results than to stopping the cause,
When they'd much better aim at prevention.
Let us stop at its source all this mischief," cried he,
"Come, neighbors and friends, let us rally;
If the cliff we will fence, we might almost dispense
With the ambulance down in the valley."

"Oh he's a fanatic," the others rejoined,
"Dispense with the ambulance? Never!
He'd dispense with all charities, too, if he could;
No! No! We'll support them forever.
Aren't we picking up folks just as fast as they fall?
And shall this man dictate to us? Shall he?
Why should people of sense stop to put up a fence,
While the ambulance works in the valley?"

But the sensible few, who are practical too,
Will not bear with such nonsense much longer;
They believe that prevention is better than cure,
And their party will soon be the stronger.
Encourage them then, with your purse, voice, and pen,
And while other philanthropists dally,
They will scorn all pretense, and put up a stout fence
On the cliff that hangs over the valley.

Better guide well the young than reclaim them when old,
For the voice of true wisdom is calling.
"To rescue the fallen is good, but 'tis best

To prevent other people from falling."
Better close up the source of temptation and crime
Than deliver from dungeon or galley;
Better put a strong fence 'round the top of the cliff
Than an ambulance down in the valley.

EXERCISE 12.2: WHEN DO PRIVATE PROBLEMS BECOME PUBLIC ISSUES?

When do you move from micro to macro practice? It is not unusual for a direct practice social worker to "put on the hat" of a community organizer when he or she encounters a client problem that requires action on a broader level. This exercise challenges you to think about when and how you would move from employing a micro practice solution to a problem to employing a macro practice solution.

Directions

- Form groups of four to six.

- Choose one of the two cases described below and discuss each of the questions listed below the case.

- Pick a spokesperson to take notes on the discussion.

- After 30–45 minutes, reconvene the class so the spokespeople can share with the class the ideas generated by their group.

Case Vignette 1: Elder Abuse

You are a direct practice social worker who works with individuals and families at a family service agency in a large urban area. One day, at the referral of a concerned neighbor, you make a home visit to see a frail older woman who reveals that she has been verbally and physically abused by her family. You intervene by providing family therapy and, fortunately, the family is wealthy enough to afford private in-home care, which relieves the burden on the abuser (the client's daughter). One month later, you see another older adult client victimized by a family caregiver. This time, the family is poor, and there are no low-cost public home health resources available in your county. With difficulty, you manage to utilize family therapy effectively enough to stop the abuse, but the situation remains marginal. As time goes on, you see more and more older adult clients who report experiencing abuse or neglect.

1. At what point do you conclude that elder abuse is a serious social service/public health issue? What criteria might you use to determine this?

2. When does the problem of elder abuse get to the point that it would best be viewed as a "macro" community issue rather than simply a "micro" or direct practice issue?

3. As you plan how you would make the shift from micro intervention to macro intervention, discuss which of the various roles or approaches to community intervention or organizing you would utilize in intervening with this issue. What would be the *first three steps* you would take to respond to the issue of elder abuse? Be sure the steps are realistic and feasible, and remember, *this is only the beginning;* you are not expected to completely resolve the issue in three steps.

4. What other services, helping professionals, stakeholders, and agencies could or should be involved as collaborators in your work to address the issue?

Case Vignette 2: Intimate Partner Violence (IPV)

You are a direct practice social worker who works in a nonprofit human services agency in a small town of 5,000 people. One day, you see a young woman with two preschool children who comes in to your agency asking for help because she is depressed. After exploring and assessing her situation, you find out that she is being physically and psychologically abused by her husband. The night before, her husband even threatened her two children. You intervene by providing supportive therapy for her and manage to locate a friend to take the woman and her children in for a while. Eventually, the husband agrees to counseling, and the family is reunited. One month later, you see another woman who says she is being abused by her live-in boyfriend. This time, the woman cannot identify any friends or other family willing or able to take her in, and there are no shelter resources locally. With effort, you manage to get money for a bus ticket so she can travel to the nearest city for shelter. As time goes on, you see more and more clients who are victims of IPV.

1. At what point do you see enough abused clients to conclude that IPV is a serious social service/public health issue? What criteria might you use to determine this?

2. When does the problem of IPV get to the point that it would best be viewed as a "macro" community issue rather than simply a micro or direct practice issue?

3. As you plan how you would make the shift from micro intervention to macro intervention, discuss which of the various roles or approaches to community intervention/organizing you would utilize in addressing the issue of IPV.

4. What would be the *first three steps* you would take to respond to the issue? Be sure the steps are realistic and feasible, and remember, *this is only the beginning;* you are not expected to completely resolve the issue in these three steps.

5. What other services, professionals, or agencies could or should be involved as collaborators in your work to address the issue?

EXERCISE 12.3: ALTERNATIVE USE OF THE CASES

The cases in Exercise 12.2 can be used to pull together the themes of this class, which include the following:

- People must be understood in the context of their environments (PIE).

- Generalist social workers are skilled to intervene at multiple levels of practice—micro (primarily individuals, couples, and families), mezzo (primarily therapeutic groups and some task groups), and macro (primarily organizations and communities).

- Interventions can be targeted at one level alone or multiple levels simultaneously.

- Goals at all levels should reflect a client-centered strengths orientation.

- Interventions should be chosen based upon critical thinking, including use of evidence and consideration of the impact of diversity.

- The steps in the helping process are the same, no matter which system level is targeted, although the tools may change.

Directions

- Form groups of four and review the cases in Exercise 12.2.

- Select one of the clients from each case and review the cases from a micro-level perspective. Answer the following questions, and justify your answers:

  ○ What assessment tools might be good to use?

  ○ What else do you need to know?

  ○ What might a goal be in this circumstance, and which interventions that we discussed might apply?

- Next, review the cases from a mezzo-level perspective. Answer the following questions, and justify your answers:

  ○ What type of group might be useful (using the typology you learned), and, what are some of the considerations for forming that type of group?

- ○ What would be a good group goal?

- ○ Are only treatment or task groups possible in this circumstance?

- Finally, discuss how you shift from micro to macro practice. Answer the following questions, and justify your answers:

  - ○ Who are the stakeholders you need to engage?

  - ○ What additional information would you need?

  - ○ What assessment tools might you use?

  - ○ Based upon the information you potentially collect, what macro-level interventions might you use?

EXERCISE 12.4: MOVING FROM MICRO TO MACRO PRACTICE

This exercise should be done after you have completed Exercise 12.2. The goal of this exercise is to challenge you and your classmates to engage in critical thinking by addressing a social problem, discussing its parameters and manifestations, and then tackling the same questions with regard to moving from a micro response to a macro response.

Directions

- Form small groups of four to six.

- Choose one of the social problems listed—or make up your own —and then discuss each of the seven questions below.

- Pick a spokesperson to take notes on your group's discussion.

- After 30–45 minutes, reconvene the class so the spokespeople for each group can share with the class what their group discussed.

Social Problems

Adolescent suicide

Child abuse and neglect

Economic inequality and social injustice

Gender discrimination and oppression

Hate crimes

HIV and AIDS

Homelessness

Inadequate or poorly maintained housing

LGBTQIA prejudice and discrimination

Long-term unemployment

Neighborhood crime (muggings, burglaries, etc.)

Racial and ethnic discrimination and oppression

Racial disparities in the criminal justice system, including mass incarceration of people of color and disproportionate police killings of unarmed black citizens

Runaway and truant children and adolescents

Substance abuse

Undocumented immigration and exploitation of undocumented workers

Questions

1. When does this social problem get to the point that it becomes a "macro" issue?

2. What criteria could you use to determine this?

3. When should a social worker move from a micro response to an individual, family, or small group who is affected by the problem to a macro response involving a community practice role?

4. Which community practice or community organizing role(s) would be most appropriate for addressing the social problem?

5. What would be the first steps you or your agency should take to address the social problem?

6. What other services, professionals, or agencies could or should be involved?

7. Who might serve with you on a task force formed to address the social problem?

13

MANAGING BARRIERS TO CHANGE AND THE CLIENT–SOCIAL WORKER RELATIONSHIP

LEARNING OBJECTIVES

1. Recognize when threats to the relationship between the social worker and the client occur.

2. Understand the nature of threats to the client–social worker relationship and other barriers to change.

3. Constructively manage and overcome a range of interpersonal barriers to change, as demonstrated in a series of in-class role plays (Exercise 13.1).

4. Demonstrate beginning competence in engaging involuntary clients by using authenticity, genuineness, and communication skills to empathize with the client's feelings, establish rapport, and manage resistance to change (Exercise 13.2).

5. Analyze client case vignettes illustrating organizational barriers to change and formulate a plan to overcome the barriers presented in the vignettes (Exercise 13.3).

6. Recognize how personal issues could impact social work practice (Exercise 13.4).

CHAPTER OUTLINE

- Threats to the Relationship Between the Social Worker and the Client
- Exercise 13.1: Responding to Relationship Barriers
- Working With Involuntary Clients
- Exercise 13.2: Engaging the Involuntary Client
- The Role of Advocacy and Facilitating Client Empowerment
- Exercise 13.3: Overcoming Organizational Barriers
- Social Workers at Their Best: Self-Care Promotes Competent Care
- Exercise 13.4: Exploring Self-Care

Barriers to change and progress can arise when working with clients due to a number of different kinds of obstacles, including problems that occur in the relationship between the client and social worker; resistance from individuals, families, and other interpersonal systems in the client's life; and oppositional responses by organizations that can prevent access to needed resources to address clients' challenges and help resolve their problems. The critical practice issue in this regard is learning how to manage or overcome these barriers to change so progress can occur.

The relationship between you and your client is the central vehicle for supporting the helping process, and the nature and quality of this relationship has a significant impact on the outcome of your intervention efforts. Social workers must have the ability to cultivate positive relationships with clients and to keep the client-practitioner relationship healthy and productive. To accomplish this, you must be alert to difficulties that may threaten the quality of your relationship with the client and be skilled in appropriately managing such threats.

THREATS TO THE RELATIONSHIP BETWEEN THE SOCIAL WORKER AND THE CLIENT

1. Here and now reactions occurring during interactions between social worker and client

2. Practitioner incompetence or impairment

3. Racial/cultural/class barriers between social worker and client

4. Difficulties in establishing trust in the helping relationship

5. Transference and countertransference reactions

6. Romantic or sexual attraction of social worker toward the client and client toward the social worker.

Hepworth et al., 2017

Here and now reactions refers to the immediate emotional reactions between the client and the practitioner as they are interacting with each other. Such reactions may begin as a small difficulty in communication but, if ignored, can evolve into a major obstacle. Here and now reactions generally involve either mistakes by practitioners or misperceptions by clients. *Pathological or inept practitioners* refers to practitioners who repeatedly make mistakes in practice, causing irreparable damage to relationships and psychological harm to their clients. Besides harming their clients, the incompetence of such practitioners can harm their agencies and the social work profession. *Racial and transcultural barriers* can result from a social worker's lack of cultural competence and cultural humility (see Chapter 3) when working with culturally different clients, which can undermine the development of a therapeutic alliance, thereby preventing clients from getting the help they need. *Difficulties in trusting* relates to how clients vary widely in their capacity to trust the practitioner, which is essential to establishing a positive therapeutic alliance. Practitioners must possess skills for engaging and facilitating trust with clients who may be hesitant to trust. *Transference reactions* refers to clients' emotional reactions toward the practitioner that derive from their emotional attachments to early important relationships with others, such as their parents. Transference can evolve into an obstacle if such emotional reactions prevent the client from working well with the practitioner. *Countertransference reactions* involve the emotional reactions by the practitioner toward the client, both positive and negative. Countertransference can be an obstacle if it interferes with the helping relationship and reaching the goals that have been set with the client. Finally, *sexual attraction toward clients* can be an obstacle because such feelings, if left unchecked, can lead to behaving in a way that constitutes sexual misconduct. Sexual involvement with clients is explicitly prohibited in the *Code of Ethics* because it harms both clients and practitioners (NASW, 2017a). Sexual misconduct harms clients because they can suffer confusion and guilt and then have difficulty trusting other helping professionals, and it harms practitioners because they can be faced with professional and personal disgrace, loss of their license, and expulsion from their profession.

EXERCISE 13.1: RESPONDING TO RELATIONSHIP BARRIERS

Directions

- With a partner, read each client–social worker exchange.

- In exchanges in which the client says the last response, role play as if you were the client's social worker, and respond to the client.

- In exchanges in which the social worker provides the last and problematic response, role play with your partner how you would respond differently than the social worker in the exchange responded.

- Compare your responses with the modeled responses below.

- Reverse roles and role play again, employing what you learned from the modeled responses.

Client–Social Worker Exchanges

1. Here and now reactions

    SW:　　(at the beginning of the first session with client) "Hello, Mr. Smith, my name is Jane Doe, and I am pleased to meet you. Can you tell me a little about why you came into the clinic today?"

    Client:　"Why do you think I'm here? The stupid court sent me!" (glares at the social worker)

2. Practitioner incompetence

    Client:　"I don't know what to do. My life is falling apart."

    SW:　　"Whatever . . . the first thing I want to know is how you're going to pay your bill."

3. Racial, cultural, or class barriers

    Client:　(25-year-old Asian American male) "I really don't like studying medicine. I would rather do something different with my life, maybe study music or art. I know you suggested that I talk with a career counselor, but I must wait until my parents visit so I can talk with them first."

    SW:　　"You're 25 years old! You're an adult now. You shouldn't have to get your parents' permission to change careers!"

4. Difficulties in establishing trust

    SW:　　"Hello, Mr. Diaz. My name is Harold Jones, and I am a social worker here at the Alcohol Treatment Center. I understand that the court is requiring you to attend treatment here, but I'm more interested in what you would like us to help you with. Can you tell me how we can be helpful to you at this time?"

    Client:　"What's the point? You people just see me as a bum. Why should I bother telling you anything? Just do what you have to do and let me get out of here."

5. Transference and countertransference

    SW:　　(irritably) "Why don't you just go to group? It isn't the end of the world." (thinks: This client acts like my 13-year-old son!)

    Client:　"You can't tell me what to do!" (thinks: This social worker acts just like my mother! To heck with him!)

6. Romantic or sexual attraction

Male SW: (to female client) "You have worked really hard these past couple months, and it sounds like things are going well for you now. As you know, this is our last session, and I would like to conclude our work together by going over what we have accomplished."

Client: "Mr. Wong, I want to thank you from the bottom of my heart for everything you have done for me. You really care about me; I mean *really* care, and I've never had that before with *anyone*. Now that we won't be patient-therapist anymore, I hope we can be friends—maybe, more than friends? Could I make dinner for you this weekend? I'd like to really show you how much I care, too, and I just don't want to say goodbye forever."

Modeled Responses

1. Here and now reaction

SW: "You sound pretty upset. It would help me to help you better if you could fill me in on what has gone on with the court. Would you mind telling me a little about that?"

2. Practitioner incompetence

SW: "I'm glad you came in to see me today. It sounds like things are pretty difficult right now. Can you tell me more about what is going on and in what way you feel your life is falling apart?"

3. Racial, cultural, or class barriers

SW: "Of course—I understand. This is an important decision. How do you think your parents will feel about this?"

4. Difficulties in establishing trust

SW: "I imagine it is tough to be told to do something you don't want to do and have to be some place where you don't want to be. I also get the sense that you may have had some less than perfect experiences with treatment before. Am I on the right track here?"

5. Transference and countertransference

SW: (realizes she has made a mistake) "You're right. I can't tell you what to do. Whether you go to group or not is your decision; however, decisions usually have consequences of one kind or another. Let's talk about the advantages and disadvantages of attending the group, and then you can weigh things and decide what you want to do."

6. Romantic or sexual attraction

SW: "I appreciate your dinner offer, but I must decline. Let me explain why. We have done some excellent work in our therapy together, and I am very pleased to see you doing so well. But these accomplishments are due to your hard work, and, although you hold warm feelings about our work and toward me, these feelings are really about what we have accomplished in therapy. Although we won't be working together anymore, it would be unethical for me to have a friendship with you outside of therapy. I care about you as my client, but that is not the same as friendship. (empathically) Do you understand what I mean?"

WORKING WITH INVOLUNTARY CLIENTS

Today, social workers serve many clients who may be categorized as "involuntary clients." An involuntary client is a client who does not seek help from a social worker and who receives treatment due to pressure by legal authorities or fear of consequences for failure to participate (Rooney, 2009).

Social workers who practice in child welfare, substance abuse services, inpatient and emergency mental health services, and forensic/criminal justice–related services commonly work with clients who are court ordered to access services, rather than seeking services on their own.

Another type of involuntary client is not under legal mandate but, rather, is under social pressure to see you. This is the so-called socially involuntary client. An example of this would be a client who comes in for counseling because a spouse is threatening divorce, saying, "If you don't get counseling, I'm taking the kids and leaving you." Sometimes, employers or schools may require services as a condition to remain with the organization. Again, these are not clients who are freely choosing to seek services; rather, they are under pressure to do so. Additionally, almost no children can be considered voluntary because it is usually an adult (parent, teacher, pediatrician) who thinks they should receive help (Lukas, 1993). In such cases, because the choice not to participate in services is legally available, it can be helpful to clarify the personal advantages and disadvantages of engaging in services voluntarily by presenting two sides to the situation and emphasizing the client's choices and what the consequences of those choices are. Engaging a client who does not want the services you offer can be challenging; however, with the right approach, work with involuntary clients can be successful.

Exercise 13.2 presents six different client situations illustrating clients who are involuntary. Three scenarios depict legally involuntary clients, and one depicts a socially involuntary client.

EXERCISE 13.2: ENGAGING THE INVOLUNTARY CLIENT

Directions

- Find a partner and decide who will play the role of the client and who will play the role of the practitioner. Switch roles with each case vignette.

- The goal of the role play is to engage the involuntary client and help the client move toward accepting services from the social worker.

  ○ First, identify who you are and what your role is at the agency.

  ○ Using expression of authenticity, genuineness, and communication skills, establish rapport with the client and empathize with the client's position of being legally or socially involuntary.

  ○ Identify nonnegotiable requirements for legally involuntary clients; identify advantages and disadvantages to seeking services for socially involuntary clients.

  ○ Monitor your own feelings.

  ○ Establish a tentative intervention plan.

- If you have learned motivational interviewing techniques as part of your course work, you may want to consider employing some of them with this exercise. There is evidence for their effectiveness with people who may not yet be ready or committed to making a change (Miller & Rollnick, 2013).

Case Vignette 1

The client is a white male, age 18, on probation for motor vehicle theft and reckless driving. His probation officer has sent him for counseling because the P.O. is concerned about the client's inability to control his temper; thus, counseling has been made a condition of probation. Failure to comply will result in jail time. The client has a dual diagnosis of a personality disorder and substance use disorder.

"Look, man, I don't need no social worker. I've got to find me a job and a place to crash—the courts have messed me over enough already. I don't have nothing to talk about."

Case Vignette 2

The client is a Hispanic male, age 36, who had been ordered to counseling by the court because he was convicted of a second DUI. Failure to comply will result in jail time. He looks angry, slouches in his chair, and glares at the social worker.

"I don't know why I have to talk to you. So I had a couple of beers one night. So what? I don't have a drinking problem. I can stop anytime I want to. My only problem is having to see you."

Case Vignette 3

The client is a white female, age 21, ordered to counseling by the court and Child Protective Services after she left her two children, aged 5 months and 6 years, home alone for two days. The court claims she was out looking for and ingesting drugs with her boyfriend; she also has a history of bipolar disorder. To get her children back, she must comply with treatment. She sits sullenly in the chair, digs out a crumpled yellow paper from her purse, and throws it at the social worker.

"Here's the damn court paper. Do what you have to do and let me get out of here. I've got stuff to do."

Case Vignette 4

The client is an African American female, age 45, who was told to get counseling by her husband after she admitted to him that she had an affair with her boss. The husband told her that if she doesn't "get her head straight," he is going to file for divorce and demand custody of their two children, ages 6 and 8.

"My husband told me to come here. I had an affair with my boss, okay? It just happened. It's over. I don't see why I have to see a counselor."

Case Vignette 5

The client is a 14-year-old transgender girl who has attention deficit/hyperactivity disorder, inattentive type, and whose grades dropped off as she transitioned from middle school to high school. Her guidance counselor suggested that her mom seek out treatment on her behalf.

"Listen, I know that I have ADHD and that this switch to high school hasn't been very smooth. There is a lot going on; wouldn't anybody's grades drop? You know, my mom and guidance counselor are just way overreacting to everything. I'll get it sorted out. I am not crazy; I don't need to see you."

Case Vignette 6

The client is the DEF Company. It was sued for gender discrimination, and as part of its settlement agreement with the plaintiffs, the company (reluctantly) agreed to conduct an organizational analysis and implement strategies to eliminate barriers to hiring and promotion of women and gender nonconforming individuals. A meeting of DEF Company managers is convened to discuss how to approach the organizational analysis.

One of the managers opens the meeting by saying, "Look, I know we all have better things to do than deal with something like this. The problem is out-of-control political correctness. We want to hire the best people, not hire someone because they're a woman or gay."

THE ROLE OF ADVOCACY AND FACILITATING CLIENT EMPOWERMENT

Resources provided by organizations, institutions, agencies, and services are often required for clients to successfully achieve their goals. Sometimes clients run into barriers that prevent them from accessing needed resources, and you, as your client's social worker, must step in either directly or in a facilitative role. Our actions often involve advocacy and are designed to develop and enhance client empowerment. *Empowerment* may be defined, generally, as enhanced feelings of competence resulting from a client's self-directed activity to achieve their goals. Social workers often facilitate the development of empowerment via their commitment to advocacy:

1. working on behalf of clients

2. linking clients with resources

3. monitoring clients' treatment plans

4. mediating solutions to problems

5. reducing institutional barriers

Good access to needed resources means that services should be located near residences and places of work, near public transportation, available on evenings and weekends, affordable or subsidized so all people in need can access services, and matched to the population served, that is, culturally and gender sensitive and tailored to individual needs. Sometimes, however, this is not the case. Organizational barriers that can impede access include institutional racism, prejudice and discrimination, language barriers, and logistical problems such as lack of transportation. Exercise 13.3 illustrates various organizational barriers to accessing needed services.

EXERCISE 13.3: OVERCOMING ORGANIZATIONAL BARRIERS

Directions

- Form small groups of four to six.

- Imagine that you are the social worker depicted in the case vignettes below. Develop an advocacy plan to overcome the organizational barriers presented in the client's situation so that the client can access the resources he or she needs.

- The group can record their ideas and turn a paper in to the instructor, present the ideas to the class, or just discuss their advocacy plan within their group.

Case Vignette 1

Carmen is a 27-year-old African American woman who has recurrent major depression. Carmen has been seeing her social worker, Tamika, for several months for cognitive-behavioral therapy, and she takes the antidepressant Zoloft. Together, the medication and counseling have successfully relieved Carmen's depressive symptoms. However, Carmen also struggles with an addiction to crack cocaine. She says she originally began smoking crack to relieve her feelings of depression, and although her depression is under control, she still craves crack. Tamika refers Carmen to the local substance use counseling center, but Carmen only kept one appointment and refused to go back. When Tamika asked why, Carmen said, "I used to take my cousin to that drug counseling clinic, and, at that time, they had several black counselors on staff, and they helped my cousin really well. When I went this last time for myself, I found out that all the black counselors had been let go and were replaced with only white counselors. I think that's racist. How can they understand my situation? Being black, mentally ill, and an addict is different from being a white, mentally ill addict. What do I do now?"

What are some of the things the social worker could do in the role of advocate to assist Carmen in overcoming the barriers she faces?

Case Vignette 2

Alfonso is an undocumented farm laborer whose back was injured in a work-related accident. He has been suffering a lot of lower back pain as a result, and so his wife urged him to seek help at the local emergency room. Because of his immigration status, Alfonso has no medical insurance and is very scared that if he seeks help, he might be reported to immigration and customs enforcement (ICE) officials. However, the pain became so severe that he finally went to the hospital. When he was seen by the triage nurse and revealed his status, she "became very mean" to him and told him if he wanted help, he should go back to Mexico. The emergency room social worker overhears the conversation, steps in, and asks to speak with Alfonso. Wary that he might encounter another hostile interaction, Alfonso hesitates, but then is willing to sit down with the social worker to talk.

What are some of the things the social worker could do to assist Alfonso in overcoming the barriers he is facing and facilitate his empowerment?

Case Vignette 3

Hoa Pham, 13 years old, immigrated legally from Vietnam with her family six months ago. Hoa lives with cerebral palsy, and her family was told by the Catholic Charities' social worker that her disability makes Hoa eligible for a variety of services and financial supports. Hoa's family has poor fluency in English, and when they attempted to seek services at the medical clinic, the receptionist seemed friendly. However, because they could not communicate, the family was unable to get help. The family is desperate and does not know what to do to get help for Hoa. You are the school social worker at the school where Hoa's 16-year-old brother, Anh Dung, is a student in the 11th grade. Anh Dung speaks English fairly well and meets with you because he is very concerned about his sister's situation. He does not know what can be done to help her and his family.

What are some of the things you could do in the role of the school's social worker to advocate and overcome the barriers Hoa and Anh Dung's family is facing?

SOCIAL WORKERS AT THEIR BEST: SELF-CARE PROMOTES COMPETENT CARE

Because the use of self is a key ingredient to engagement and intervention with clients, we need to be our best selves to assist people. We are not immune, however, from the problems and challenges of daily life. Like our clients, we experience losses, stresses, disappointments, illnesses, and other challenges. Additionally, the work we do can be stressful, producing reactions in us that may interfere with our ability to meet clients' needs, such as countertransference, triggering, compassion fatigue, vicarious trauma (sometimes called secondary trauma), or burnout (Boyd-Franklin, Cleek, Wofsy, & Mundy, 2013). Boyd-Franklin et al. indicate that there are signs that social workers are experiencing a negative response to our work with trauma:

Physical symptoms	Emotional responses
Headaches	Numbing
Sleep disturbance	Feelings of guilt
Aches	Fear
Upset stomach	Rage
	Anxiety
Cognitive responses	**Behavioral responses**
Confusion	Jumpy
Slow thinking	Anger/lashing out
Difficulty making choices	Crying
Flashbacks	Nervous energy
Intrusive thoughts	Avoidance
	Withdrawal
	Arguing with others

Given our lives and professional experiences, our ability to interact with clients and co-workers can be diminished or impaired; therefore, self-care is an ethical obligation for competent social work practice. NASW Standards 4.01 and 4.05 let us know that we need to remain competent, and part of doing that is to "not allow [our] own personal problems, psychosocial distress, legal problems, substance abuse, or mental health difficulties to interfere with [our] professional judgment and performance or to jeopardize the best interests of people for whom [we] have a professional responsibility" (NASW, 2017a p. 25).

As with the challenges our clients face, prevention is a better path than remedy. Therefore, students can begin to try various strategies to set professional boundaries, promote health and wellness, and determine which tools will work best for them. Fink-Samnick and Powell (2012) discuss the idea of professional resilience, defined as "commitment to achieve balance amid occupational stressors and life challenges while fostering professional values and career sustainability" (p. 150). This effort is something that a social worker will need to explore and revisit across a career as demands change. The list below contains many strategies that can help in this endeavor.

- Value your profession
- Present with presence
- Have positive contact with colleagues and peers
- Achieve validation
- Use the power of professional networking
- Take breaks
- Use creative visualization
- Take control & shift activities
- Laugh at least once a day!
- Stop. Take a long, deep breath
- Develop a grounding list
- Exercise
- Release frustration
- Re-vision honestly and regularly
- Process experiences with colleagues
- Don't make rash decisions regarding personal or professional life
- Have fun and don't feel guilty about it
- Pay attention to needing "time outs"
- Pamper yourself from time to time to revitalize
- "Reframe" the power of your frustration into advocacy for your position
- Schedule self-care
- Don't work harder than your clients

(Fink-Samnick et al., 2012; Boyd-Franklin et al., 2013)

EXERCISE 13.4: EXPLORING SELF-CARE

Directions

- In small groups (four to six people), read each vignette.
- Identify the type of scenario from the following options:
  - An unhealthy work environment
  - An example of countertransference
  - A situation triggering unresolved past issues
  - A transition in personal life impacting professional life

- Identify current signs of stress, compassion fatigue, vicarious trauma, or countertransference, if present.

- Identify current or past strategies used to create/manage personal-professional boundaries.

- Identify potential concerns.

- Discuss possible strategies the social worker can use to take care of self and build professional resilience.

- Regroup as a class to discuss your responses.

Vignette 1

Kari (age 29) and Zia (age 42) enjoy packed lunches for about 20 minutes in the park across the street from the adult day health center where they work. They job share the social work position three days per week each, overlapping on Wednesdays. It has been their tradition to "step out" for lunch one day per week for the past two years. Kari is just back from 10 weeks of parental leave after the birth of her first child. Zia covered that leave and is back to her part-time schedule. As they speak, Zia remarks how good it feels to get back to her old routine, as she had put off doing things for her family and the work/life balance was all off. She is noticing a drop in tension now that she has more time to focus on her children and partner. Kari is in an opposite place and comments, "I am glad for you, but I do not know how I am going to do this. I am so tired (large sigh and headshake). I used to have such a great routine. I got home from work around 4:45. I would get a cup of tea and watch my comedy program for about half an hour. Then I would walk the dog and do a bit of housework. By the end of that, I had turned off my work brain and all my worries about the fact that Mr. Tolle was upset that day or Gerde was still grieving the loss of her sister, and I could enjoy the evening. We then split the cooking duties and ate a latish dinner together. Now, I pick up the baby from daycare, get home ½ hour later, and immediately have to tend to her. Don't get me wrong; I enjoy it. But, there is so much more to do. I can't take that 45 minutes for myself. She needs me. Our whole night centers on her. Then I find myself in bed, replaying the day including all the client stuff. I just don't know. How do you do it? You have children."

Vignette 2

Isaac has worked for eight years doing child protective work. He really loves his work and is passionate about it. He has had opportunities for other jobs but remains committed to this field. It is stressful. During the first year of his career, he almost left social work. He took his work home all the time. As the year went on, his then-girlfriend complained that he was irritable and emotionally unavailable. After his girlfriend broke up with him and he ended up complaining to his PCP that he was not sleeping enough and had some stomach problems, he realized that maybe the job was the problem. He started looking around and confided in his supervisor. His supervisor, Dawna, was great. They started really working on promoting good personal-professional boundaries. He learned to use morning exercise and a meditative letting go transition ritual in the car involving his favorite music and absolutely no news. Dawna held weekly supervision meetings with the team where they could process not only the specific issues for the families they helped but also their own reactions, including some humor and mutual support. He met another person, fell in love, and had a child without difficulty in the following years. Last year Dawna retired. Her replacement, Erica, was promoted from within and never liked Dawna's approach. Immediately, she decided that the weekly group supervision was a waste of time and stopped it. They should know how to do their jobs and get them done; they do not need all the "hand holding nonsense that Dawna did." During individual supervision and when she calls a team meeting, she lectures at them and drops little digs at him and a coworker, both of whom applied for her job and did not get it. Three team members have taken jobs elsewhere; now they have to train new people. His wife complains that he is "not himself lately that he has a short fuse with their son." When he was at his PCP for stomach problems, it occurred to him that work might be the problem once again.

Vignette 3*

Mo (age 56) has been working in hospice for 17 years. They love the work, its spiritual nature, the honor of being with a person at the moment of death, helping families to stay connected through death, and promoting healing after a loss. Many people, including other social workers, have said, "Oh, I could never do what you do—working with people who are dying." They acknowledge that it is hard but have a lot of personal practices to help, including gardening, hiking and snowshoeing, and playing poker with friends. About six months ago, Mo's father was diagnosed with lung cancer and metastasis, and he was given about three to six months to live. Mo has not been enjoying work or life nearly as much since then. They are short and snapping with coworkers, impatient with the students training in the hospice, and dreading going to work every day. The other day at a patient's home, they found they were suddenly tearful and popped quickly into the bathroom. Two weeks earlier, they totally forgot to do a depression screening, a routine part of the assessment. A month ago, they got totally lost going to a patient's home. After work every day, Mo goes to their parents' home to help their mother. They have not had time to plant their garden this year and only get outside to hike about once a week.

*This vignette employs gender-neutral pronouns.

Vignette 4

Jay, a Marine veteran of Operation Enduring Freedom/Operation Iraqi Freedom, discharged honorably, has been recovering from injuries related to a car bomb explosion. His physical recovery has been excellent, and he reports he never had any psychological problems beyond a little despair immediately after the injury. "I am a can-do guy and turned that around after a short pity party." After about four years back in the community, Jay returned to school on the GI bill to get a MSW. His long-term goal is to work with veterans. While working with faculty to find his second field placement, he expressed an interest in the VA. His advisor asked him if he was ready or if he thought such a placement would be triggering or problematic because "sometimes we are too close to something to work with it." He said that was not the case with him, interviewed, and began the field placement. About mid-semester, his advisor got calls from a couple of his instructors. Jay had failed to submit some assignments and was late with others. The quality of the work was poor. This was odd, as Jay maintained a 3.7 GPA. The advisor called the field site. The reviews were glowing. Jay was really empathetic; his engagement was outstanding. The other veterans were really opening up to him. He was moving from shadowing to splitting the assessment duties. From the VA's perspective, all was good. The advisor scheduled a meeting to see what was happening. After the advisor asked some questions, Jay said, "I don't know. This semester has been so much harder than the first two. I really like working with the veterans. I am there for them. It takes a lot of energy, you know. And the stories . . . . well, they aren't surprising exactly. I mean, I know what happened. It's just . . . (trails off). Well, it's just that it's really hard to leave them at the door. I get home, and I think about them. It's like I'm all keyed up. I get distracted while trying to read and study. I cannot put it all together easily. Then I get irritated that I am not doing the work as well as I could. Then I cannot sleep. Plus my sleep has been poor. I even have had some dreams about my time in country. I have been using energy drinks to get through the day sometimes. Then I crash. I don't know; this semester is kicking my butt."

14

TERMINATION, CONSOLIDATING GAINS, AND FOLLOW-UP

LEARNING OBJECTIVES

1. Identify and break down the tasks embodied in the termination phase of the helping process/planned change.

2. Define the five types of termination and the circumstances under which they occur.

3. Analyze client case vignettes to identify the type of termination illustrated in the vignette and the underlying issues depicted by the scenario (Exercise 14.1).

4. Apply the skills used in successful client-practitioner termination for resolving termination dilemmas, using realistic case vignettes (Exercise 14.2).

5. Recognize how cultural differences can impact the termination process (Exercises 14.3 and 14.4).

6. Manage and apply skill strategies for consolidating gains and planning change maintenance (Exercise 14.2).

7. Communicate that termination can produce a variety of emotions in both the client and social worker (Exercise 14.5).

8. Apply the skill strategies of termination with a family (Exercise 14.7).

9. Recognize follow-up as an extension of the termination process and the impact it has on both the client and social worker (Exercise 14.6).

CHAPTER OUTLINE

- Tasks Embodied in Termination
- Five Types of Termination
- Consolidating Gains, Planning Maintenance Strategies, and Follow-Up
- Evaluation of Practice
- Exercise 14.1: Managing Termination
- Exercise 14.2: Ms. W's Last Appointment
- Exercise 14.3: Judy's Decision—A Nine-Month Relationship
- Exercise 14.4: Kevin—An Unexpected Termination
- Exercise 14.5: Ralph—An Unexpected Termination
- Exercise 14.6: Managing Follow-Up With Mrs. Wilson
- Exercise 14.7: Revisiting the Jones Family for Termination of Treatment

Although it is generally given less attention in the literature, the final phase of the helping process is critical because it strongly influences whether clients consolidate gains, maintain progress, and continue to grow; thus, termination must be handled skillfully and sensitively. Inherent in termination is separation from the practitioner, and it usually involves mixed and ambivalent feelings, primarily a sense of loss coupled, in most cases, with joy and the satisfaction of achieving goals. The intensity of the feelings of loss varies according to a number of factors, including the degree of success achieved by the client and practitioner, the intensity of the practitioner-client attachment, the type of termination, and the previous experiences of the client and practitioner with separation from significant others. The process of termination occurs across micro, mezzo, and macro levels of social work practice.

Successful termination involves certain tasks that assist in making the transition from being a client to becoming independent. These tasks include determining when to implement termination, mutually resolving emotional reactions commonly experienced during the process of separation, evaluating the service provided and the extent to which goals were accomplished, and, finally, engaging in planning to maintain the gains achieved and to ensure continued growth.

Follow-up is also a component of the helping process during this phase. It involves contacting the client to see how they have progressed since the final visit. In many instances, the way that follow-up is conducted will be determined by the policies of the agency. If there are no guidelines, the social worker must decide when and how to contact the client. Communication can occur by mail, telephone, or by using secure electronic devices such as smartphones and tablets. From a therapeutic perspective, follow-up shows respect, caring, and concern for the client. Clinical judgement must be used in deciding the best way to communicate with the client or, in some instances, deciding whether follow-up is necessary or not (Okun & Kantrowitz, 2015).

TASKS EMBODIED IN TERMINATION

At each stage of the helping process, the social worker and client engage in tasks that assist in accomplishing what is necessary as they move their work together toward termination. The list below outlines some of the common tasks associated with termination.

- Determine when to implement termination as a collaborative task with the client

- Mutually resolve emotional reactions on the part of both client and practitioner

- Collaboratively evaluate the services provided and the extent to which goals were accomplished

- Collaboratively plan to maintain gains achieved and to ensure continued growth by

  o Reviewing the client's problems and the steps used in resolving them

  o Helping the client understand how these skills can be applied to future problems in life

Now, the significance of each task and the extent to which each is accomplished depends on the type of termination, particularly whether the termination is planned or unplanned, and the extent to which the termination outcome is successful or unsuccessful.

FIVE TYPES OF TERMINATION

1. Premature or early unplanned terminations by clients (as expressed by failing to appear for appointments, offering perfunctory reasons for termination, or refusing to return to discuss matters further)

2. Planned termination determined by agency time constraints (some agencies offer services within strict time parameters due to shrinking resources, managed care, and the increasing reliance on brief treatment modalities)

3. Planned termination associated with interventions that are time limited (again, brief treatment modalities are often emphasized these days and may be equally as effective as longer-term approaches for some problems)

4. Planned termination involving open-ended modalities (the general recommendation is to introduce termination when a client has reached the point of diminishing returns, i.e., when gains are minor in significance, and the client says things are going well)

5. Termination precipitated by the departure of a practitioner (reassignment, change of employment, retirement, maternity leave, end of field placement or internship, etc.)

CONSOLIDATING GAINS, PLANNING MAINTENANCE STRATEGIES, AND FOLLOW-UP

Social workers and clients typically want to maintain the progress made during their work together. To ensure this, it is necessary to anticipate future challenges and barriers that may arise that can undo what has been accomplished. The following strategies for consolidating gains, planning maintenance strategies, and employing follow-up actions are helpful.

- Together, review the client's problems and the steps used in resolving them.

- Help the client understand how these skills can be applied to future problems in living.

- Progress can be maintained and extended by

  ○ Planning and connecting with natural or arranged social support systems;

  ○ Employing booster interviews or follow-up interviews; and

  ○ Making referrals to other appropriate services and following up to make sure the referral worked out.

- Make appropriate follow-up referrals by

  ○ Ascertaining the client's readiness for a referral;

  ○ Determining together which resources best match the client's needs;

  ○ Offering recommendations for appropriate referral resources; and

  ○ Avoiding making false promises or unrealistic reassurances.

EVALUATION OF PRACTICE

When social workers think about evaluation of practice, they consider *outcome evaluation* (did the client or program accomplish the intended goals?) and *process evaluation* (how effective and efficient was the helping process or the way the work was conducted?). In Chapter 8, we explored how writing measurable goals contributes to outcome evaluation for a particular client system. In students' research classes, they learn ways to evaluate practice and programs by pulling together all of the outcome data from many clients. Process evaluation can occur individually with clients by routinely checking with them throughout the relationship about which activities are most and least helpful. Social workers may also want to evaluate their practice across many clients. Looking at outcomes and processes with an analytical eye can (1) help you to hone your social work skills, (2) assist in reevaluating choices in intervention techniques, and (3) help you identify your personal skill strengths and deficits.

EXERCISE 14.1: MANAGING TERMINATION

The following vignettes describe situations related to termination commonly encountered in practice.

Directions

- Form groups of three.

- Two of you will participate in the role play (one plays the role of the practitioner and the other plays the role of the client), and the third person will act as an observer.

- After each role play, the observer shares what he or she observed in terms of verbal and nonverbal interactions and the effective use of social work skills.

- Switch roles for each vignette, so you each have a chance to play all the roles. Keep in mind there is no single correct response.

Case Vignette 1

You and Mr. Smith have spent your allotted 10 sessions working on his temper problem that has plagued him all of his adult life. He has faithfully attended all appointments and has made earnest attempts to modify his emotions and subsequent behaviors. Although his behavior has marginally improved, he continues to have problems getting along with people at work and in his personal relationships. How do you manage this situation?

Case Vignette 2

Jose, 18 years old and on court-ordered probation, has nearly completed the court-required 18-session group program you facilitate. He left the gang that caused his legal problems and has worked successfully at a job he secured doing drywall work for a construction company. Over the past several weeks, he has been late to work several times and has been in contact with members of his former gang. What do you believe is going on, and how might you handle this?

Case Vignette 3

You are in the last month of your field placement at the university counseling center and have begun the process of termination with the three clients with whom you have been working. One of your clients, Samirah, is close to your age, is also a graduate student, and has been working with you on strategies to help her become less shy with other people. Samirah knew from the beginning that you would only be able to work with her for 10 sessions because of the ending of your field placement. When you bring up the fact that this is the next to the last session with you, Samirah becomes upset and says, "No, this can't be ending yet. You are so helpful to me. You are the only African American counselor here, and you understand what it is like for me as a woman of color and trying to meet men and all . . . (begins to get teary-eyed). I don't know what to do now." How would you respond to Samirah's distress?

EXERCISE 14.2: MS. W'S LAST APPOINTMENT

Ms. W has had intensive outpatient treatment for drug addiction for the past eight weeks. She has been meeting with her social worker twice a week. Today is her last day of treatment, and she is being discharged from the intensive outpatient program.

Directions

- Choose two students to role play the Take 1 and Take 2 scenarios in front of the class.

- In a class discussion, compare and contrast the two planned termination scenarios and answer the following questions:

- What are the similarities between the two scenarios?

- What are the differences?

- Is one more appropriate than the other?

- Are Ms. W's concerns addressed in both scenarios?

- What would you have done differently in each scenario?

- Is follow-up needed in either scenario?

Take 1: Ms. W's Last Appointment

SW: Today is the last day of your intensive outpatient treatment. I want to summarize how far you have come since we first met. You have really worked hard and have made significant progress. We completed all of the goals established at the beginning of our relationship. Keep in mind, living with addiction requires hard work and strong support systems.

Ms. W: I feel good. Our meetings have been a source of support for me. I do feel ready to transition to a traditional outpatient program.

SW: I am confident you are ready. You have come a long way since we first met. Do you remember how angry and resistant you were at first? I have made an appointment for you in the outpatient program three weeks from today. The program is located on the north side of town. Tell me, how are you going to continue your recovery until the next appointment?

Ms. W: I was resistant and angry in the first couple of weeks. I am learning to respect myself again. Thank you for helping me. I am going to take advantage of the many support programs available to me. I'm going to attend the NA meetings we talked about last week.

SW: Remember your triggers and how important it is to surround yourself with supportive and positive individuals.

Ms. W: I know—people, places, and things. Can I keep in touch with you until I meet my new therapist?

SW: What I would like for you to do is start attending the NA meetings. I believe you will find the meetings to be supportive. Attending one or two meetings per week will be helpful for you. If there is a crisis situation, you can call me for support. You have signed the release of information forms, which allows me to send information to your new therapist.

Ms. W: Thank you. I will do my best to keep moving forward.

SW: You will do well! Take care.

Take 2: Ms. W's Last Appointment

SW: Today is the last day of your intensive outpatient treatment. I want to summarize how far you have come since we first met. You have really worked hard and have made significant progress. I think we completed all of the goals we established at the beginning of our relationship. Keep in mind, living with addiction requires hard work and strong support systems.

Ms. W: Thank you, but I am feeling nervous. I have so many concerns, but I guess that is to be expected.

SW: You will be fine. Just remember what you have learned. You started with much anger, denial, and resistance. Look at you now. I feel you are ready.

Ms. W:	Yes, we have talked about all aspects of my life. I do appreciate your help these past eight weeks. Are you sure I can't continue my treatment with you? Starting a new relationship with another therapist is something I am not excited about.
SW:	You are welcome. I have made an appointment for you with your new therapist in the traditional outpatient program located on the north side of town. You have an appointment in three weeks. Make sure you keep it.
Ms. W:	What should I do until my appointment? Three weeks is a long time. I am not sure if I can make it until the next appointment. We have talked about support systems I can use. Maybe I should contact them over the next week or two?
SW:	Well, continue to work on what you have learned. We have covered the importance of staying engaged with support systems, being mindful of relapse triggers, and surrounding yourself with positive people, places, and things.
Ms. W:	I know we have covered a lot of information, but I am nervous. Can I call you if I am at risk of relapsing? It would mean so much to me. It would be helpful if I could call you once a week.
SW:	What I would like for you to do is use the tools we have discussed. I can't hold your hand at every turn. You will be fine. I am confident you will stay strong and make positive decisions. Good luck, and remember all you have learned over the past eight weeks.

EXERCISE 14.3: JUDY'S DECISION—A NINE-MONTH RELATIONSHIP

Judy is a second-year student in the master of social work program. She has been working with Roberto, a 12-year-old Latino male referred to the agency due to anger outbursts. Judy started working with Roberto nine months ago at the beginning of her second-year concentration internship. She speaks English and Spanish. This enables her to communicate with Roberto and his mother, who speaks very little English. Judy feels her relationship with Roberto is strong and trusting. Roberto's mother has talked about the positive change she has seen in her son over the past nine months. She credits Judy for this change. She has expressed concerns about what will happen once Judy's internship ends because Roberto has had multiple losses in his life. She is fearful of how he will respond to Judy's leaving him. Judy has expressed concern as well but assures Roberto's mother she is working to minimize the impact of her leaving. The plan was to introduce Roberto to the social worker who will take Judy's cases once she leaves. The new social worker sat in on several sessions with Judy, Roberto, and his mother. This provided time for everyone to get acquainted, start building a relationship, and review goals for Roberto. After several meetings the past two months, the time has come for Judy to leave the agency.

Directions

- Form groups of three or five.
- Read the scenario. The last response for Judy is left blank. Discuss how you would respond if you were Judy.
- Keep in mind the impact Judy's response will have on Roberto and his mother after working with them for nine months.
- Identify any cross-cultural issues.
- The responses to these tasks may be written down individually or collectively or the responses can be presented orally in the class.

Scenario

Judy:	It has been a pleasure working with you Roberto; I think we have had some great conversations and certainly played a lot of games together.
Roberto:	I beat you at most of them.
Judy:	You realize why we played so many games, right? Plus, I got to see your beautiful smile and even learned some new things about sports.
Roberto:	I helped you improve your Spanish, so give me credit for that. I also learned how to control my anger much better. It has been four months since I had an anger outburst at school.
Judy:	Yes, you helped me with my Spanish. I am proud of the progress you have made over the past four months. You are beginning to understand there are other ways to resolve conflict than getting angry and becoming aggressive. I know your mother is pleased with your progress, and so am I.
Roberto:	Thank you. Where are you going to live after you leave? Will I see you again? Are you on Facebook or Instagram? I want to keep in touch.
Judy:	I am not sure where I will be living next, probably in another state. We may see each other again one day. I am not on Facebook or Instagram. Bob will be your social worker starting next week. He has sat in on several of our meetings over the past two months. I know you feel comfortable talking with him, and that's good.
Roberto:	He is a nice man. Can I bring my mother in now? She has some gifts for you.
Judy:	Some gifts? Yes, bring her in.
Mother:	We want to give you a couple of gifts to show how much we appreciate all you have done to help Roberto and our family. Please accept this necklace and bracelet that Roberto picked out for you. I made you two dozen of our favorite cookies. We hope you like them.
Judy:	_____

EXERCISE 14.4: KEVIN—AN UNEXPECTED TERMINATION

Kevin decided to keep his second appointment with Mr. Frazier, his assigned social worker. He was referred to Mr. Frazier by Arvin, his close friend; Arvin felt that Kevin could relate to and benefit from working with an African American male social worker. Mr. Frazier was excited to continue working with Kevin.

Directions

- As a whole-class exercise, the instructor plays the role of Kevin. Students play the role of Mr. Frazier and share what their responses would be to Kevin. Keep in mind this is an unexpected termination for Mr. Frazier.

- Alternatively, students form groups of three.

  ○ One student plays the role of Mr. Frazier, the second plays the role of Kevin, and the third person acts as an observer.

  ○ Observers share what they observed in terms of verbal response and the effective use of social work skills. Keep in mind there is no single correct response.

Scenario

Mr. Frazier:	Hi Kevin! It's good to see you again.
Kevin:	Mr. Frazier, I won't waste your time. I came to tell you that I will not be working with you anymore.
Mr. Frazier:	_____
Kevin:	I don't think you will be able to relate to me. We are from different generations. What do you know about what I am dealing with in the real world?
Mr. Frazier:	_____
Kevin:	Listen, I am sure you are a good man. I see your college degrees on the wall, but it's not going to work out! It's important that I feel comfortable sharing my personal issues with the right person, a younger person.
Mr. Frazier:	_____
Kevin:	Thank you for your time. I will find another social worker. Are there any papers I need to sign before I leave?
Mr. Frazier:	_____
Kevin:	Ok, thanks. Goodbye.

EXERCISE 14.5: RALPH—AN UNEXPECTED TERMINATION

Ralph was 40 years old when he first met his social worker, Bill, who was assigned to work in homeless shelters throughout the city. Now 42, Ralph is still homeless despite efforts to improve his situation. Ralph enjoys meeting with Bill. They meet twice a month at the City Shelter during dinner time. They have formed a close relationship over the past two years. Bill recently placed Ralph's name on the waiting list for the new supportive apartment program scheduled to open in five months. Ralph is number 10 on the list. While reviewing Ralph's six-month service plan, Bill informed Ralph about the new supportive living program. Ralph was excited and said he was getting tired of living on the streets. During this meeting, Bill could not help but notice the cough Ralph had. Ralph was seen by the nurse practitioner at the shelter and immediately sent to the hospital emergency room. He was admitted and diagnosed with stage IV small cell lung cancer, a particularly aggressive subtype of the disease. Bill was saddened to hear this news and visited Ralph frequently. He also attempted to locate family members but was unsuccessful. On what would be Bill's final visit, Ralph was able to speak, but he was struggling to breathe.

Directions

- Read the scenario and write down how you feel after reading it.
- Answer the following questions:
  - Is this a strong therapeutic relationship?
  - Do you think this relationship was rewarding for both the social worker and the client?
  - What are some emotions that Bill could be experiencing after this unexpected termination?
- Discuss your responses with the class.

Scenario

Ralph:	Thanks for coming to see me again. You have been the only visitor I have had other than hospital staff.
Bill:	We have known each other for two years. Do you remember when we first met at the old shelter? The first thing you asked me was to give you five dollars. What did I do? Do you remember?
Ralph:	You gave me a dollar and your business card. I knew you were a good guy at that instant. I want to thank you for all of your help. I have been quite stubborn over the past two years, but you never gave up on me.
Bill:	How could I give up on you? You were not just stubborn but very stubborn. I do wish there was someone to contact for you. I reviewed my old notes in hope of locating a family member but was unsuccessful. I have enjoyed our many conversations. Is there anything I can do for you before I leave today?
Ralph:	Don't worry about it; everything will be all right.
Bill:	I admire how well you are handling this situation. But then again, I shouldn't be surprised. You have always known what you want. I want you to know that I will never forget you.
Ralph:	Thank you. That means a lot to me.

(Two days after this visit, Bill was informed of Ralph's death.)

EXERCISE 14.6: MANAGING FOLLOW-UP WITH MRS. WILSON

Mrs. Wilson met with her social worker, Mrs. Gonzales, for three sessions. Mrs. Wilson was excited to continue the relationship, but due to her husband's changing jobs, his insurance would not cover therapy with Mrs. Gonzales. She was given the opportunity to continue with Mrs. Gonzales on a sliding pay scale, but she simply could not afford the cost. As a result, Mrs. Wilson was referred to a program that took their insurance. The earliest appointment she could schedule was six weeks away. During their last session, Mrs. Gonzales scheduled a video follow-up with Mrs. Wilson in two weeks.

Directions

- Read the scenario and the options listed at the end.
- Imagine you are Mrs. Gonzales. Which option would you choose? You can pick more than one option, or pick an option that is not on the list.
- Be prepared to justify your choice in a class discussion.

Scenario

Mrs. Gonzales:	Hi, Mrs. Wilson! Thanks for agreeing to do this video follow-up. I hope this is a good time. Can you see and hear me ok?
Mrs. Wilson:	Yes, this is a good time, and I can see and hear you. I have been looking forward to this conversation. Things haven't been going so well.
Mrs. Gonzales:	What has been happening since I saw you two weeks ago? I must say, you look really sad.
Mrs. Wilson:	I haven't been sleeping. I don't have much energy or interest to do anything. I lost my part-time job the other day. Yeah, things are not good right now.

Mrs. Gonzales:	I am so sorry you lost your job. You had been working at the Center for a long time. Can you tell me what happened? Did anything else happen since we last met? Your appointment with your new social worker is four weeks away.
Mrs. Wilson:	I don't want to talk about the job right now. I don't know why I am feeling this way. I really enjoyed coming to meet with you, though. Hopefully I can hold on until my appointment with the new social worker. Talking about my concerns does help me.
Mrs. Gonzales:	I can see that you're tearing up. What are your plans until your next appointment in four weeks?
Mrs. Wilson:	I don't have any plans.

Which of the following options would you choose if you were Mrs. Gonzales?

A.   Make an appointment to see Mrs. Wilson, regardless of the insurance coverage

B.   Suggest to Mrs. Wilson that she go to the hospital emergency room for an evaluation

C.   Contact the new program and request an earlier appointment

D.   Speak with Mrs. Wilson's husband about your concerns

E.   All of the above

EXERCISE 14.7: REVISITING THE JONES FAMILY FOR TERMINATION OF TREATMENT

The Jones family (introduced in Chapter 9, Exercise 9.3) has now completed 13 family therapy sessions, and things have improved significantly over the weeks. The family's insurance sets a limit of 15 sessions, so the family has two sessions left, the current session and a final session next week.

Throughout the course of therapy, Ann and Bob have become more unified in their approach to handling the issues surrounding their son, Joe. Joe eventually disclosed that he is depressed and had been using marijuana in an attempt to self-medicate his symptoms. Both parents supported the decision to refer Joe to a psychiatrist specializing in adolescent depression, and the combination of antidepressant medication, individual counseling, and group therapy have succeeded in helping Joe to feel better. The communication between Ann and Joe has improved. Ann has realized that, as an adolescent, Joe does need to have his privacy, and Bob is supportive of Ann's efforts to respect that. Bob has made efforts to engage daughter Julie in doing some activities with him, such as playing chess, which she loves, as well as encouraging her to get involved in more peer activities at school. Bob and Ann have also committed to enjoying a "date night" every two weeks when they go out as a couple to do something enjoyable, such as having a nice dinner or seeing a movie. As Bob and Ann's relationship has improved, Julie has been relieved of feeling responsible for her mother's emotional health. It is now the penultimate family therapy session and the subject of termination must be addressed.

Directions

- Form groups of five to role play the Jones family therapy session.

- Review Exercise 9.3, "Analyzing an Initial Family Interview," in Chapter 9.

- Choose four group members to play the four Jones family members and one to play the practitioner. Arrange seating as shown in Diagram 14.1.

- The practitioner introduces the topic of termination and addresses the issues and questions below with the family (Treacher, 1989; Epstein & Bishop, 1981). The remaining students respond, using the information provided about the Jones family.

DIAGRAM 14.1 ■ Jones Family's Seating Positions During the Session

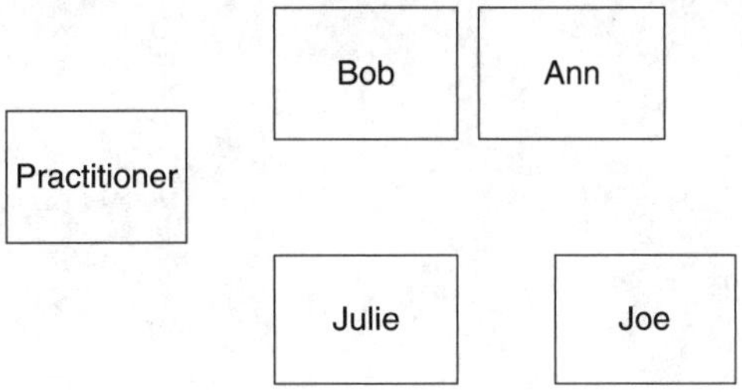

```
              [Bob]   [Ann]
[Practitioner]
              [Julie]  [Joe]
```

- The practitioner asks the family members to summarize what has happened over the course of treatment and what they have gained. The practitioner responds by confirming perceptions and adding his or her perceptions.

- Have the family's expectations of therapy (as a family and as individuals) been met or not? In real life, if you were actually working with this family, whether the family sees expectations as being met would be based on the goals laid out in the original treatment contract negotiated at the beginning of therapy.

- Is the family ready to test their newly developed problem-solving skills, or should therapy continue?

- What are the family's long-term goals? If problems occur, how will they cope?

- Does the family want to participate in a follow-up session for monitoring (not additional treatment)?

15

DOCUMENTATION

LEARNING OBJECTIVES

1. Identify the elements of well and poorly written assessments, plans, notes, e-mails, and business letters (Exercise 15.1).

2. Select information obtained during assessment and draft documents that present hypotheses for the nature and causes of the client's presenting challenges, identify client strengths, and describe progress toward goals (Exercise 15.2).

3. Draft a professional e-mail and/or a business letter (Exercise 15.2).

CHAPTER OUTLINE

- Elements of Documentation
  - o Types of Documents
  - o Audiences and Purposes
  - o Tone and Style
  - o Ethics
- Exercise 15.1: Better Expression
- Exercise 15.2: Draft a Document
- Answer Key for Exercise 15.1: Document Commentary and Revisions

This chapter explores how social workers communicate in writing. All social workers, whether in micro, mezzo, or macro practice, need to communicate ideas using the written word. Whether it is an e-mail, a basic note about a client interaction, a complex assessment, or a business letter, some people will form opinions of your professionalism and capability based upon the way you express yourself in writing. In interprofessional settings, some team members will interact more with your written discussion of clients than with you face to face. The ability to accurately and *succinctly* convey information is as important for competent practice as being able to engage a client system. Will your colleagues read through lengthy notes to find needed information, will they come look for you to clarify a nebulous word, or will they ignore your notes because they do not have time to wade through something that is poorly written? Documentation can provide a roadmap for the client system and you to reach desired outcomes and measure progress.

Some social work programs teach documentation skills in a stand-alone course, while others infuse documentation into many classes, such as the class you are taking right now. Because there are textbooks on professional writing—and because there is not a single definitive way to write professionally—this chapter will focus on broad guidance and skill exercises for five of the most common types of documentation, with an eye to building and practicing skills. Many generalist field placements will expect these types of documentation:

- Assessments
- Plans
- Interaction documentation (a.k.a. session/progress notes)
- Professional e-mail correspondence
- Business letters

Note: This chapter does not contain exercises on writing SMART goals because they were included in Chapter 8. Please refer to that chapter for goal-writing exercises.

ELEMENTS OF DOCUMENTATION

Types of Documents

Assessments are written summations of information gathered from getting to know a client system and exploring the reasons for service. Depending upon the practice setting and the client system, the needed information and format will vary. A student working with an individual might conduct a bio-psycho-social-spiritual assessment while a student in an organization may conduct a SWOT analysis. Some assessments take the form of very structured tools, while others may be in a narrative format. Today, many students report that the agencies where they intern have computer-based assessment programs that combine questions with text boxes to insert more detail and explanation, thus having elements of both structured and narrative assessments.

Plans, like assessments, take many forms depending upon the practice setting and the client type. A couple might develop a treatment plan with a therapist while a community might create a strategic plan. The best plans serve as a flexible roadmap that can guide the work that is being done and are not simply created for regulatory compliance. They also state how the client (and you) will know that the plan or goal has been met, in other words, how you will measure accomplishment. The SMART acronym (Specific, Measurable, Attainable, Realistic, and Timely) can assist in creating plans that are developed and revised in a client centered manner (Doran, 1981).

Interaction documentation has many names. Session note is one of them; other names might be progress note, interaction note, update, log, or contact note. These notes convey what has occurred with and on behalf of the client system. At a minimum, they say who did what, when, where, and how; they also connect that activity to the goal or plan. In most modern documentation systems, you might have to identify key elements through structured questions and then write a more open note about the specifics of that interaction.

Professional **e-mail** correspondence is one of the most common ways you communicate with clients and with others about clients. Some students have only used e-mail as an informal type of communication. However, in professional settings, more formality is expected. Additionally, because many in our society view e-mail casually, we may have to be very thoughtful about how we use e-mail to practice ethically, including paying attention to security and encryption, as explained in the NASW *Code of Ethics* (2017a) and the *NASW, ASWB, CSWE, & CSWA Standards for Technology in Social Work Practice* (NASW et al., 2017).

Business letters are a formal type of communication with various stakeholders (other organizations, clients, funders, or regulators). Today, e-mail has replaced many business letters, but not all. Students may find they need to draft a business letter to solicit support for a policy change, to recommend a client to a program, or to confirm in writing something that was communicated verbally.

Audiences and Purposes

The documents social workers create have multiple audiences, each with its own reasons for reading them. As you write, keep your potential audience in mind:

- **Self**. You are the primary audience for some documents, particularly items like assessments, plans, and session notes. The act of pulling information together for the written assessment enables you to review it, contemplate it, and pursue practice thoughtfully. Writing about an interaction enables you to keep track of what occurred. You will find that you may be too busy to keep track of every detail of your work; notes enable you to keep each client system's information separate.

- **Colleagues**. Many of you will work in interprofessional settings where it will be important to understand what others are doing with a client and for them to understand what you are doing. As a student, you will probably not be at the field agency the entire time; your supervisor or another employee of the agency may need to step in when you are not there. Also, you will take vacations. Your coworkers will need your documents to understand what to do so that services are delivered well in your absence.

- **Supervisors**. Your supervisor will use your notes as a way to monitor your work, client outcomes, and possibly program outcomes. Notes assist supervisors in assuring and promoting competent practice and holding social workers accountable.

- **Regulators and/or insurers**. Depending upon the type of service, your program or agency may be subject to regulatory oversight, building in accountability. That oversight may take the form of reviewing documentation to ensure that the program is delivering the services in a capable way consistent with expectations (e.g., as specified by statute, regulation, or grant condition). The documents may also be necessary for reimbursement.

- **Clients**. In almost every state and in many service sectors, clients are entitled to see their records. If clients were to see what you have written about them, how would they react? Would it sound fair? Would they understand it?

- **Courts and other providers**. Many social workers do not interact with courts; others, such as those in child welfare and forensic settings, may commonly interact with courts. Most social workers interact with other providers and parties involved with clients. It can be quite difficult to write a document that meets the specific needs of outside stakeholders. Sometimes, social workers share original documents; sometimes, they create summary documents that meet a specific purpose for an outside audience.

Tone and Style

- **Perspective**: Professional documents are often written from a third-person perspective; however, that is not universal. For example, you may write a session note in the third person but then follow up in an e-mail or business letter in the first person. The audience dictates the perspective of the document. This can be somewhat odd for students doing clinical writing where it is the convention to refer to oneself in the third person. For example, you would not write, "I met with Ms. Halstan in my office," even though you would think about it that way. Instead, you would write something like, "Social worker met with Ms. Halstan in office."

- **Tone**: As much as possible, you want to use a neutral tone. The easiest way to do this is to clearly report on what you know and the source of the information (a colleague's report, an observation, the client told you, results from an assessment tool) without adding your ideas about it. Then you can pull together all the "data" you have gathered and utilize critical thinking skills to make sense of it. Clearly label your conclusions, formulations, hypotheses, or thoughts on "what is really occurring" in a given situation. The reader should be able to see the information on which you based your point of view.

- **Organization**: Most professional writing must be succinct. You need to make your points and move on. Repetitiveness, lengthy transitions, and flowery language are better left to other writing styles because they lose professional readers. Use of headings to organize information and ease the reader's ability to find it is important. It is also helpful to understand the preferred organization style of the setting where you are interning or working. If everyone organizes information similarly, communication is easier.

- **Grammar**: Like it or not, grammar matters. People tend to discount or discredit a poorly expressed idea. Readers may pass judgment on your intelligence or critical thinking skills if they have to struggle through the way the ideas are written. If grammar is not a strength for you, seek out assistance while you are in school. Ask for feedback from instructors and utilize it. Most campuses have writing centers to help students improve grammar. With that said, there is big caveat to grammar guidance. Some clinical writing will drop subjects as a means to reach the brevity mentioned above and get around the use of the first person. For example, a professional might write, "Met with the Garcia family in their home. Discussed challenges around managing Marc's medical appointments and Angela's work schedule." The pronouns have been dropped. They could be first or third person and still make sense.

- **Abbreviations, Terminology, and Acronyms**: Avoid abbreviations and unclear terminology unless they appear in approved agency policy, and be sure to spell out acronyms. Two programs may use the same acronym, or the same terminology might be understood two ways. For example, does "dual diagnosis" mean a person with a mental health disorder and a substance use disorder or a person with a mental health disorder and a developmental disability?

- **Person-Centered Language and Strengths**: Documentation, like interactions, should convey dignity and respect. Professionals strive to use person-first language and minimize the use of professional jargon. People are not their problems or their diagnoses. Therefore, the note would say, "Mr. Jones has alcohol use disorder" rather than "Mr. Jones is an alcoholic." The note would also use the pronouns that are preferred by the client; for example, "ze does not identify on a gender binary." For adults, use of title and last names conveys respect, particularly if records end up in court. Such language links to recognizing people's strengths. Strengths go beyond recognition of resources and include noting what options clients have at that time, the possibilities they have not tried, information about when "the problem" is not requiring their attention, and their past solutions to problems, or what Graybeal (2001) characterizes as ROPES (Resources, Options, Possibilities, Exceptions, Solutions). Such strengths can be infused throughout the note. They do not need to be segregated into a section unto themselves.

Ethics

As in all facets of practice, we need to be ethical when we document. The NASW *Code of Ethics* (2017a) speaks to documentation in several places. Additionally, there are regulatory standards that can apply to documentation, along with whatever policies are in place within organizations. NASW et al. (2017) have issued *Technology in Social Work Practice* guidance that also contains important information about collection, storage, and use of documentation in digital formats. Students must familiarize themselves with this, too.

NASW *Code of Ethics*

Standard 3.04 Client Records speaks to the need to be accurate, timely, and protective of clients' privacy, "includ[ing] only information that is directly relevant to the delivery of services" (NASW, 2017a, p. 22). It also suggests that documentation should promote continuity of care and be maintained for the length of time mandated by state, regulatory, or contractual requirements.

Standard 1.08 Client Access to Records discusses that access to records should be reasonable and guidance and/or support should be provided if there are concerns about the client's misunderstanding or reacting badly to his or her records.

Standard 1.07(l) Privacy and Confidentiality suggests that measures need to be in place to assure the confidential and private storage of records, paper or electronic, and that access be limited to only those who have authorization to see them.

Statutory/Regulatory Requirements

The Health Insurance Portability and Accountability Act (HIPAA) is a lengthy piece of legislation passed in 1996. Part of its function is to protect the privacy of medical information. It outlines which pieces of information are "protected" and what settings are "covered entities," thus making all their employees responsible for carrying out the law. It also establishes rights for those receiving medical services. Some field agencies will require you to complete HIPAA training if they are a covered entity.

State regulations on privacy vary widely. In many states, certain types of information may be treated differently from other types of information. For example, some states may limit who can share an HIV diagnosis with a patient or how much mental health information can be released to courts. It is important to understand the laws governing your specific state and service.

Mandated Reporting and Duty to Warn

Most social work students have learned that the collective public interest is placed ahead of our duty of confidentiality if we become aware that a vulnerable person protected under state law (most often children, older adults, or other vulnerable adults) is experiencing abuse or neglect. The specifics of this vary from state to state; however, it is generally referred to as *mandated reporting*. In addition, most states have some degree of a *duty to warn* when a person threatens to harm others and a *duty to protect* when a person threatens to harm himself or herself. This means that we may have to make reasonable efforts to alert those who are threatened or alert appropriate authorities (such as police or school officials) to protect the client or others. Section 1.07(c) in the *Code of Ethics* speaks to a social worker's duties in such circumstances (NASW, 2017a). These circumstances—duty to warn, duty to protect, or mandated reporting—often create ethical challenges because professionals must break confidentiality and provide information that a client may wish to hold private. In some states, social workers can provide the information verbally and then document what was done for their employer. Other states have online reporting platforms, which are a written form of documentation. Guidance from Standard 1.07(c) on only releasing "directly relevant" information would apply.

EXERCISE 15.1: BETTER EXPRESSION

Directions

- Individually or in small groups, read the five sample documents below, identify the problems with the way they are written, and decide how you would revise them.

- Discuss your revisions with the entire class or submit them to your instructor.

- After you have shared your proposed revisions, read the section at the end of this chapter headed "Exercise 15.1 Documents: Commentary and Revisions."

Brief Assessment (Narrative Form)
TOPAZ MULTISERVICE CENTER

Date: May 05, 2017   **Service(s)**: Food Pantry

Client Name: Belton/Agiana Family   **No. of People in Household**: 6

Allergies/Special Dietary Needs: 4-year-old lactose intolerant

Presenting Request: I met with Sophia Belton who came to the food pantry because her live-in boyfriend was laid off and they can't pay bills. He used to work as a mechanic.

Family Background: Sophia (33) and her partner Jose (31), who is a mechanic, reside in the Thousand Oaks neighborhood. They reside with 3 children and Sophia's mother, Regina Palicetti (62). All three children are in good health. The older children attend the local public schools. Two of the children have visitation with their other parent two weekends a month. Mrs. Palicetti a diagnosis of breast cancer with metastasis to the brain and now requires supervision most of the time. Both have siblings who cannot help.

Work/Finances: Jose was a repair guy for a high-end car dealer and the dealership got merged with another and he was tolt there would be work but they laid him off two weeks ago anyway, probably because he was the least skilled and a minority. He applied for unemployment. He looking for work as a mechanic now. Ms. Belton is a nurse who works with old people so she is good at taking care of her mom. She made a bad choice to quite working 7 months ago because she didn't want her mom to live in a nursing home because the cost of in home care was too high, and they exhausted all savings. She made a good choice to drop her four year old's day car to save $. They are behind on the EB and GB by one month. They were just "scraping by" before the layoff. They have credit card debt (another bad choice), and expenses exceed their income by $1500 a month (see budget worksheet). For someone who works in aging Sophia doesn;t seem to know much about community services and never applied for Food Stamps or Waiver.

Impressions and Plan: Sophia doesn't seem to know a lot about services but agreed to learn more. Provided food at the time of visit, normalized what's going on. They can come back to the pantry a couple of weeks until they apply for other stuff. I will make a home visit in 3 days.

Elyse, (electronic signature)   05/05

Client Service Plan

As you read this plan and look for problems with it, consider a couple of other ideas. Is this plan SMART? Plans are the most person-centered when the client system stars in them and when they are understandable documents that can be used to guide the work. That means the language should be understandable to the clients, without a lot of professional jargon, and everyone's roles should be clear. Services appear in the plan as a support to what the client will accomplish.

Topaz Multiservice Center

CS PLAN

Client Name: Belton/Agiana Family

Service(s): Service Coord./Employment/Pantry

Start Date: 05/08/17

Target Date:

Goal: Will not need the FP and UB to cover expenses		
Objectives	**Task (A, A, TF)**	**Progress/ Update**
Family will use agency supports to spread spending and apply for other temporary services to fill gap until re-employed.	Family will use FP services to reduce food costs.	
	Will apply for F/RC lunches as school by end of week.	
Find employment and begin within 8 weeks.	Follow through on the unemployment application while continuing to apply for jobs.	
	Employment specialist will review resume, edit it, and give feedback.	
	Jose will do a PI within two weeks.	
	Meet or talk every couple of weeks to problem solve or alter plan.	
Select CB program(s) to help Mrs. Palicetti live at home and to reduce OOP costs to family.	Ms. Belton will rehearse with SW the kinds of questions to ask when calling these agencies within 2 weeks.	
	Family will talk over information they collected and follow through to apply to at least one, but may be more, program and/or support weeks 3 to 5.	
	Social worker explaining various programs to the ladies so they can pick some.	
	Monitor the status of applications and advocate for Regina if needed.	
Family will explore if Sophia will go back to work.	SW will talk over the pros and cons of going back to work by week 2 and begin to problem solve issues and concerns.	
	Contact her old employer to see if they could re-hire her on a casual basis.	
	Contact two medical agencies to see what policies and whether temp work would fit.	
	Ms. Belton will contact people to see if any of them are willing to help by week 3.	
	Family will use the new information to make a decision in 4 weeks.	

Signatures: *Sophia Belton, Client*   Date: 5/ /17

Jose

Elyse Hillmer, MSW

Interaction Note

Read the note and identify the challenges associated with it as well as how it might be improved. Notice that it is not a transcript of what occurred. Instead, it is organized according to the Plan. In some settings, the electronic record might have check boxes for various items. The electronic records might actually have progress notes or updates that populate the Plan itself. Some settings may have specific note formats; for example, a medical setting might have all professionals use a SOAP (Subjective, Objective, Assessment, Plan) note format. This is more of an open, narrative format. If you can develop a narrative format, you will be able to determine how to populate the fields in electronic records.

Topaz Multiservice Center

Date: June 15, 2017   **Service**: Service Coord./Employment/Pantry

Met with family. Reviewed and updated plan. Both presented as hopeful and expressed optimism because as Sophia said "maybe some of this effort is going to pay off."

Objective A: Family reports continuing pantry use, the older children are still getting free school brakefast and lunch, and Mrs. Palicetti is getting MOW. SVDP greed to a one-time payment. Unemployment benefits started a week ago. Children are now on CHIP for insurance, but Ms. Belton and her husband have let their insurance lapse for lack of payment. That is a worry; agreed to add this to plan and work on this issue.

Objective B: Jose is on a 2nd interview at a car dealership.

Objective C: Applied for the waiver for dual eligibles. The AAA started Mow immediately. They also toured ADHC. She thinks it is great. But mom states she "can live with it" a few days a week if it makes it easier, lets her daughter work at least part time, and keeps her out of a nursing home. The care plan that has been proposed includes going to the ADHC three days a week, having a home health aide come in two days a week for two hours, meals on wheels the days she is home, and a one-time home modification to make the bathroom more accessible.

Objective D: Rehired by her previous employer on the 3-11 shift three times a week. She has been back at work. Others are "taking shifts" to stay with Mr. Palicetti. "So far so good."

Impressions and next steps: Each and every family member will continue their efforts to be self-sufficient. Moreover, decided to add to Objective A to try to find insurance resources for Sophia Belton and Jose Agiana. Social worker will send information on options to them via agency's secure website which they can then read over and discsuss. Everyone can, then, have a phone conversation before next meeting in 2 weeks. Plus, social worker will call the Area Agency on Aging to find out how long typical eligibility is taking. Next meeting will be at office on pantry day with either Ms. Belton or Mr. Agiana. Family will decide closer to date based upon interviews and work schedules a that time. Family may reach its goal by the 8 week target date.

Elyse Hillmer, MSW (electronic signature) 06/15/17

Professional E-mail

E-mail is less formal than business letters, but in business circumstances, it should not be as informal as it might be with friends. Note that e-mail communications with clients should be done through secure systems with appropriate encryption and security to ensure confidentiality (NASW et al., 2017). This example does not fully address that aspect of e-mail with clients. Moreover, if there is confidential information in a document that is distributed, it should have some type of disclaimer or legal statement. Internships or work settings should have a means to address these communication needs and have policies on e-mail communication. As with other types of documentation and because cybersecurity is a concern, be mindful of the information placed in an e-mail.

Subject: Insurance

June 15, 2017

To: Sophia Belton (sbelton555@gmail.com)

From: EH – Elyse Hillmer (hillygirl@gmail.com)

Hey Sophia,

Per our meeting and information on income ($1000 a month from your job and $1500 a month unemployment), Medicaid is a nogo. Check out the ACA Marketplace. You guys are eligible for a Special Enrollment Period. See https://www.healthcare.gov/have-job-based-coverage/if-you-lose-job-based-co.

I am attaching a state ACA brochure. So have docs ready when you go online. If you want help Insurance Help on pantry day. Just call Cassandra at the front desk to schedule.

Elyse

Business Letter

Business letters typically include agency letterhead; name, title, and address of addressee; a line indicating the subject of the letter; body of the letter; a closing, signature, sender's name/credentials, and sender's title; and indicators of enclosures and/or copies for others. In this example, which elements are missing? What other aspects of professional writing are not well illustrated?

In this scenario, a client received a notice of ineligibility related to some type of processing issue, which appears not to have been the client's fault. The social worker made a telephone inquiry to the appropriate agency and learned that there is an appeal process and that it typically moves more quickly with a letter from an organization within the community. The social worker was advised to send verification with the letter.

1111 Main Street Everytown, XX 12345

555-555-5000 info@topazmsc.org

June 23, 2017

Waiver Program

Everytown, XX 12345

Dear Toby:

RE: Aging Waiver Services

As discussed, Mrs. Palicetti needs expedited eligibility for the waiver. Mrs. Palicetti and her family received a denial claiming that they had not submitted stuff. Like I told you, they had. This family is brooke taking care of her and should be totally eligible, maybe fore even six or more months. Her son-in-law got laid off, and if they don't get relief, they will have to place in her an SNF. They have waited long enough with all this red tape. Shout me an e-mail or call if you want to talk it over more. I enclosed some documents, they can help you see I am right.

Sincerely,

Elyse

Elyse Hillmer, MSW

EXERCISE 15.2: DRAFT A DOCUMENT

Directions

- Independently or with a partner, read the following dialogue.

- Draft an Interaction Note based on the dialogue (this can be done in class or assigned as homework).

- With a small group of peers, compare what you each have drafted to create the "best" Interaction Note, critiquing one another using the guidelines in this chapter.

- If the classroom has technology, project and revise as a group.

- Write an e-mail or a business letter to the home health agency discussed. For the sake of the exercise, the contact information is A. Smith, Scheduling Supervisor, CDE Home Health Agency, 123 Elm Street, Everytown, US, 12345, A.Smith@CDEHH.com.

- Individually or collectively, discuss and revise.

Setting: Alvin Assan, a 25-year-old single man, is recovering from serious injuries suffered in a motorcycle accident. You are his social worker and you have arrived at his apartment today for a follow-up visit.

Alvin's mother: (opening door) Hi, it is nice to see you again. Alvin told me that one of his people was supposed to come today. We were just looking for the calendar to figure out who it would be. You know, it is so hard to keep all these appointments straight. Thanks for coming by.

Social Worker: Hello, it is nice to see you again, too, Mrs. Assan. I didn't realize you were here. Just as a reminder, since we only met the two times, I am [insert your name] from the Community Center.

Mrs. Assan: I recognize the face but like that you didn't assume I remembered everything. I do get people and what they do confused. What services does your agency provide again?

Social Worker: Our agency has been helping Alvin with food and transportation mostly.

Mrs. Assan: Right, I recall now.

Social Worker: Is Alvin here?

Mrs. Assan: Oh, yes, he is. Sorry, please come in. He is around the corner in his bedroom. The aide from the agency called off again, and I cannot get him out of bed by myself. (directs SW to bedroom)

Social Worker: (knocking on bedroom door even though it is open) Hi Alvin, it is [insert name] from the Community Center. Are you still okay with a visit? Is it okay for me to come into your bedroom?

Alvin: Hi. Yeah, why not? At least someone shows up when they say they will.

Social Worker: You sound frustrated. You really have been having some reliability problems with the home health agency, haven't you?

Alvin: You don't know the half of it. I don't even know why I bother. I work to set up a plan, and then something else goes wrong with my health or my helpers. I am so sick of being dependent on people. My mom is here again, burning vacation days because of all these people who "no show" me. I bet your drivers reported me for "no showing" them. Isn't there a policy if I "no show" three times I lose the service? "There he goes again—totally unreliable."

Social Worker: Wow, that was a lot of information. Can we break that down a bit?

Alvin:	Sure. Why not?
Social Worker:	Where should we start? How you are feeling and what are you thinking about your recovery and getting help from people like me and your mom? Or, the policy for our transportation services? Or, the fact that some of your services are not reliable? Or, something else I don't know about?
Alvin:	I don't want to talk about how I am feeling. Can we leave that alone?
Social Worker:	Sure.
Alvin:	Let's talk about the screwed up services and the transportation. They kind of go together. They are the reason I "no showed" the drivers. They told you about that, right?
Social Worker:	Right. That is part of what I wanted to talk about today.
Alvin:	The doc cleared it and wants me to start coming down to your Center, right? You even arranged for the personal trainer to meet me and the PT there a week ago. It went great. I thought everything was set because the PT is going to have dial back soon. You know, I am supposed to start lifting and doing exercises there at the Center, but . . . then I am not out of bed for the drivers. So then I miss the appointment with the personal trainer, and people start thinking I am a screw up. But it's not me, I swear. That agency messes up like two or three times a week.
Social Worker:	Okay, so let's go with this topic. I have reports of three missed transportation appointments, one with a call too close for the cancellation and two without a call—yesterday, and last Wednesday and Friday. Does that sound right to you?
Alvin:	Yeah. (some irritation in his voice)
Social Worker:	So, are you saying that your aide did not come on Wednesday, Friday, or yesterday?
Alvin:	Yeah . . . well, not exactly. The aide didn't come at all on Friday. I was stuck in bed all day. The aide came both yesterday and Wednesday, but it was a different person each time. And they came later, after it was too late to get to the Center Wednesday and yesterday.
Social Worker:	Did you miss anything on Friday?
Alvin:	Yeah, a doc appointment.
Social Worker:	So, on which day did you call the cancellation?
Alvin:	I called it on Friday. I called both the Center about the ride and the doc's office about 20 minutes before the appointment.
Social Worker:	Why did you think to call the center on Friday but not on the other days?
Alvin:	Honestly, the nurse at the MD office reminded me, so I called right away. Does it help that I called even though it was too close to the time allowed in the policy?

For the next 15 minutes, Alvin and the social worker discussed specific details about what he missed, who he told, when he told them, and why he made those choices. Then once that information was gathered, they began problem solving to figure out how he could address this issue, including how to handle the issue of the current agency's being unreliable.

Social Worker:	Thanks for taking the time to dig into that more deeply. It seems like we have a couple of action steps. Should we get started?
Alvin:	Yeah, let me grab my phone. Okay, (fumbles with the phone) let me put the Center's number in here [SW gives it to him]. And, I am putting the visits to the Community Center to work with the personal trainer in here and alarmed them for 1 hour in advance. If the aide isn't here by then, I will phone.

Social Worker:	Excellent, those are two of the new steps needed to reach your goal of transitioning from physical therapy to a community space to exercise. Now we need to see if they work. As I said before, sometimes making a change in routine will have a few stumbles, and our strategies may need some tweaks. Let's review the other steps we agreed to try.
Alvin:	I will keep a very accurate calendar of who comes from the agency and when. I will use my phone calendar for that, too. We already wrote on paper a pretty accurate account of the past week.
Social Worker:	Do you want to add a reminder to your calendar to prompt you to enter the info or not?
Alvin:	Yeah, I can do that.
Social Worker:	We also agreed that I would call the home health agency rather than you this time and follow up with either a business letter or e-mail, so there is a record in writing. I will explain how their lack of consistency is impacting your other appointments and recovery. I will ask for a definite window of arrival, like one hour. We will give them a chance to improve their service. If this agency doesn't improve, there are others out there. You can reach out to your insurer to select another one if they don't turn it around. How much longer should I indicate you will give them to become more reliable?
Alvin:	Let's say two weeks.
Social Worker:	Ok. Anything else?
Alvin:	That about covers it.
Social Worker:	Do you want to go back to the feelings that you said no to discussing earlier?
Alvin:	No, I really do not want to get into it. (whispers and motions) Mom is probably listening to all of this.
Social Worker:	Okay, before I go, any feedback for me about how we did the work today? What was helpful? What was not?
Alvin:	Well, I appreciated that you slowed me down to think stuff through. I need to do more of that rather than getting angry and discouraged. So breaking it all down, step by step, was helpful. Nothing really stands out as a problem.
Social Worker:	Would you tell me if I did something you didn't like? You are hesitant to tell the agency sending the aides.
Alvin:	Yeah, I think I would. You proved that you won't just jump to judgments like some other people do.
Social Worker:	Okay, I really hope you will. When and where should we meet again?
Alvin:	What do you mean where?
Social Worker:	Well if you are coming to the Center, we could meet there.
Alvin:	I didn't think of that, like if I wasn't so disabled. An office visit instead of a home visit. . . yeah . . . yeah! I think that I would like that. So, next Tuesday are you there in the morning?
Social Worker:	(looks at calendar on phone) Yes I am. What time will be you be finished with the trainer?
Alvin:	I am thinking about 11:00.
Social Worker:	Okay, how about 11:15? My office is on the third floor. There is an elevator in the back corner by the gym. See you next week.
Alvin:	See you then. [Yells] Mom, can you let [name of social worker] out?
Social Worker:	Bye.
Alvin:	Bye.

ANSWER KEY FOR EXERCISE 15.1: DOCUMENT COMMENTARY AND REVISIONS

Each document from the exercise is here in two forms. The first has commentary pointing out issues with the document. The second is a possible revision of it.

Commentary on Brief Assessment (Narrative Form)

Topaz Multiservice Center

Date: May 05, 2017   **Service**: Food Pantry

Client Name: Belton/Agiana Family   **No. of People in Household**: 6

Allergies/Special Dietary Needs: 4-year-old lactose intolerant

Presenting Request: I met with Sophia Belton who came to the food pantry because her live-in boyfriend was laid off and they can't pay bills. He used to work as a mechanic.

> Comment: Use of first person
>
> Comment: Seems out of place and was repeated elsewhere

Family Background: Sophia (33) and her partner Jose (31), who is a mechanic, reside in the Thousand Oaks neighborhood. They reside with 3 children and Sophia's mother, Regina Palicetti (62). All three children are in good health. The older children attend the local public schools. Two of the children have visitation with their other parent two weekends a month. Mrs. Palicetti a diagnosis of breast cancer with metastasis to the brain and now requires supervision most of the time. Both have siblings who cannot help.

> Comment: Information related to the children is not complete, so this makes partial sense.
>
> Comment: Word missing, poor grammar. There are multiple other instances of poor grammar.

Work/Finances: Jose was a repair guy for a high-end car dealer and the dealership got merged with another and he was tolt there would be work but they laid him off two weeks ago anyway, probably because he was the least skilled and a minority. He applied for unemployment. He looking for work as a mechanic now. Ms. Belton is a nurse who works with old people so she is good at taking care of her mom. She made a bad choice to quite working 7 months ago because she didn't want her mom to live in a nursing home because the cost of in home care was too high, and they exhausted all savings. She made a good choice to drop her four year old's day car to save $. They are behind on the EB and GB by one month. They were just "scraping by" before the layoff. They have credit card debt (another bad choice), and expenses exceed their income by $1500 a month (see budget worksheet). For someone who works in aging Sophia doesn;t seem to know much about community services and never applied for Food Stamps or Waiver.

> Comment: This is a judgment and possibly a personal opinion. Is it your idea that she made a bad choice or hers? It is not neutral; it draws a conclusion without full facts to support it.
>
> Comment: Would you know this meant electric bill or gas bill? Avoid abbreviations.
>
> Comment: Overall the whole note is not very strengths focused.

Impressions and Plan: Sophia doesn't seem to know a lot about services but agreed to learn more. Provided food at the time of visit, normalized what's going on. They can come back to the pantry a couple of weeks until they apply for other stuff. I will make a home visit in 3 days.

Elyse, (electronic signature)   05/05

> Comment: Why did the social worker normalize? There is no context for that choice.
>
> Comment: Vague and imprecise.
>
> Comment: Last name missing
>
> Comment: Year missing

Revised Brief Assessment (Narrative Form)

Topaz MultiService Center

Date: May 05, 2017

Service: Food Pantry

Client Name: Belton/Agiana Family

No. of People in Household: 6

Allergies/Special Dietary Needs: 4-year-old lactose intolerant

Presenting Request: Ms. Sophia Belton requested food pantry assistance for her family due to her partner's recent job loss and her not working due to her mother's care needs. She came to the pantry with her daughter Mariana, reporting the following information.

Family Background: Sophia Belton (33) and her partner of six years Jose Agiana (31) reside in the Thousand Oaks neighborhood. They live with three children—Kara Welston (13) from her previous marriage, Javier Agiana (8) from his previous marriage, and Mariana Agiana (4) from their current relationship—and Sophia's mother Regina Palicetti (62). All three children are in good health. The older children attend the local public schools. They both have visitation with their other parent two weekends a month. Mrs. Palicetti has a diagnosis of breast cancer with metastasis to the brain and now requires supervision most of the time. Both have siblings in the area but indicate that they have gotten as much financial and physical help as they can from them.

Work/Finances: Mr. Agiana worked as a mechanic for a high-end car dealer; the dealership was purchased and merged with another. Initially, he was told there would be work to accommodate all the mechanics. However, he was let go two weeks ago with only one week's notice. He applied for unemployment and has been told he should hear about a determination in the next two weeks. He also has put applications into three other dealerships and four garages. Ms. Belton is an LPN who had worked in long-term care since she was a teenager. She has the skills to take care of her mom. Initially, they were paying for in-home care for her mom, so she could continue to work. However, the cost of in home care was too high, and they exhausted all savings (Mrs. Palicetti's and theirs). Ms. Belton stopped working seven months ago to be her full-time caregiver and took Mariana out of childcare to save money. They are behind on electricity and gas bills by one month. They were just "scraping by" before the layoff. They have credit card debt, and expenses exceed their income by $1,500 a month (see budget worksheet). When asked about other types of income support services and community-based elder care services, Ms. Agiana stated she did not think they would qualify for Food Stamps and thought Medicaid would only pay for her mother to stay at a nursing home. She was interested to hear more about services to support older adults in the community.

Impressions and Plan: Ms. Belton appears to be a hardworking, genuinely caring person, and characterizes her husband similarly. They reached out for support informally and through services and seem to be able to follow through when they have accurate information. She also seems to be feeling some shame about asking for help, as she looked down frequently and dropped her voice to a barely audible level several times. Provided food at the time of visit, normalized her family's struggles in the current economy, and offered food support for a month until family hears about the unemployment compensation. As her mother would have to be part of any care decision, Ms. Belton requested a home visit. Agreed that this service coordinator will make a home visit in three days to meet with Ms. Belton, Mrs. Palicetti, and Mr. Agiana, if he is available, to discuss public welfare benefits and community care options for Mrs. Palicetti, including family caregiver and Medicaid Wavier programs.

Elyse Hillmer, MSW (electronic signature) 05/05/17

Commentary on Client Service Plan

Comment: What is the target date? By when will they accomplish this? When we set dates, we create accountability, promote hope, and suggest that problems can be solved.

Comment: Not strengths focused. What do they hope to accomplish? This is what they hope to stop. You can add the "who" will do it. In this case the family. It lets them know they have to do work to accomplish their goals. They are not passive in the process.

Comment: Who will do this? Is this the entire family or a certain person? In this case, different family members may have different objectives.

Comment: While it is fine for the service provider to appear in the plan, when possible have the client star; services providers should be supporting players. The client must accomplish the goal. The way we write notes can communicate that. How would you flip this to shift the employment specialist into a support role?

Comment: Again, who will do this?

Comment: The order is wrong for this set of tasks.

Comment: There is a grammatical error. There are a few others.

Comment: Reference to the client informally.

Comment: The social worker can help, but the adult members of the family need to make this decision.

Comment: By when. Not all of these are 8 weeks out. Some of them must be done sooner.

Topaz Multiservice Center
CLIENT SERVICE PLAN

Client Name: Belton/Agiana Family Employment/Pantry.

Service(s): Service Coord./

Start date: 05/08/17

Target date:

Goal: Will not need the food pantry and unemployment benefits to cover expenses

Objectives	Task (Activities, actors, time frames)	Progress/ Update
Family will use agency supports to spread spending and apply for other temporary services to fill gap until re-employed.	Family will use pantry services to reduce food costs.	
	Will apply for free/reduced cost lunches as school by end of week.	
Find employment and begin within eight weeks.	Follow through on the unemployment application while continuing to apply for jobs.	
	Employment specialist will review resume, edit it, and give feedback.	
	Jose will do a practice interview within two weeks.	
	Meet or talk every couple of weeks to problem solve or alter plan.	
Select community-based program(s) to help Mrs. Palicetti live at home and to reduce out-of-pocket costs to family.	Ms. Belton will rehearse with social worker the kinds of questions to ask when calling these agencies within two weeks.	
	Family will talk over information they collected and follow through to apply to at least one, but may be more, program and/or support weeks three to five.	
	Social worker explaining various programs to the ladies so they can pick some.	
	Monitor the status of applications and advocate for Regina if needed.	
Family will explore if Sophia will go back to work.	Social worker will talk over the pros and cons of going back to work by week two and begin to problem solve issues and concerns.	
	Contact her old employer to see if they could re-hire her on a casual basis.	
	Contact too medical agencees to see what policies and whether temp work would fit.	
	Ms. Belton will contact people to see if any of them are willing to help by week three.	
	Family will use the new information to make a decision in four weeks.	

Signatures: *Sophia Belton, Client* Date: 5/ /17

Jose

Elyse Hillmer, MSW

Comment: is really br What type help? Who people? Fa members? staff?

Comment: incomplete

Comment: is incomple

Revised Client Service Plan

Topaz Multiservice Center
CLIENT SERVICE PLAN

Client Name: Belton/Agiana Family

Service(s): Service Coord./Employment/Pantry.

Start date: 05/08/17

Target date: 07/05/17

Goal: The Belton/Agiana family will have enough income and caregiving support to live independently (they define this as not needing the food pantry and unemployment benefits to cover expenses) in eight weeks.

Objectives	Task (Activities, actors, time frames)	Progress/ Update
Family will utilize agency supports to spread spending and apply for other temporary services to fill gap until employment is gained.	Family will use pantry services to reduce food costs through eight weeks.	
	Family will apply for free/reduced cost lunches at school by end of week.	
Mr. Agiana will find employment and begin within 8 weeks.	Mr. Agiana will follow through on the unemployment benefits application while continuing to apply for jobs.	
	Mr. Agiana will see the employment specialist at Topaz in one week to review his resume, edit it, and better understand how to fit the information into the online applications he is completing.	
	Mr. Agiana will do a practice interview with the employment specialist within two weeks.	
	Employment specialist and Mr. Agiana will meet or talk every couple of weeks to problem solve or alter plan weeks three on.	
Ms. Belton and Mrs. Palicetti will explore and select community-based program(s) to help Mrs. Palicetti live at home and to reduce out-of-pocket costs to family.	After social worker explains various programs, Ms. Belton and Mrs. Palicetti will pick three to explore in more depth within one week.	
	Ms. Belton will rehearse with social worker the kinds of questions to ask when calling these agencies within two weeks.	
	Family will talk over information they collected and follow through to apply to at least one, but may be more, program and/ or support weeks three to five.	
	Ms. Belton and social worker will monitor the status of applications and advocate for Mrs. Palicetti if needed week three on.	
Family will explore and decide if Ms. Belton will go back to work.	Adults in the family will talk over with social worker the pros and cons of Ms. Belton's going back to work by week two and begin to three problem solve issues and concerns.	
	Ms. Belton will contact her old employer to see if they could re-hire her on a casual basis since they are often hiring by week two.	
	Ms. Belton will contact two medical staffing agencies to see what policies are and whether temp work would fit well by week two.	
	Ms. Belton will contact her siblings and older nieces and nephews, as well as an aunt, to see if any of them are willing to help provide supervision for her mother at their house by week three.	
	Consulting with social worker if necessary about program requirements, adults in family will use the new information to make a decision in four weeks.	

Signatures: *Sophia Belton, Client*   Date: 5/08/17

Jose Agiana, Client

Elyse Hillmer, MSW

Commentary on Interaction Note

Topaz MultiService Center

Comment: Where is the meeting? Since this agency does office and home-based work, the setting should be clear. Were all family members present?

Comment: Which two people are both?

Comment: Informal reference.

Comment: Grammar concerns.

Comment: Payment for what?

Comment: He is her partner.

Comment: Which woman?

Comment: Wordy with unnecessary language.

Date: June 15, 2017   **Service**: Service Coord./Employment/Pantry

Met with family. Reviewed and updated plan. Both presented as hopeful and expressed optimism because as Sophia said "maybe some of this effort is going to pay off."

Objective A: Family reports continuing pantry use, the older children are still getting free school breakfast and lunch, and Mrs. Palicetti is getting MOW. SVDP greed to a one-time payment. Unemployment benefits started a week ago. Children are now on CHIP for insurance, but Ms. Belton and her husband have let their insurance lapse for lack of payment. That is a worry; agreed to add this to plan and work on this issue.

Objective B: Jose is on a 2nd interview at a car dealership.

Objective C: Applied for the waiver for dual eligibles. The AAA started Mow immediately. They also toured ADHC. She thinks it is great. But mom states she "can live with it" a few days a week if it makes it easier, lets her daughter work at least part time, and keeps her out of a nursing home. The care plan that has been proposed includes going to the ADHC three days a week, having a home health aide come in two days a week for two hours, meals on wheels the days she is home, and a one-time home modification to make the bathroom more accessible.

Objective D: Rehired by her previous employer on the 3-11 shift three times a week. She has been back at work. Others are "taking shifts" to stay with Mr. Palicetti. "So far so good."

Impressions and next steps: Each and every family member will continue their efforts to be self-sufficient. Moreover, decided to add to Objective A to try to find insurance resources for Sophia Belton and Jose Agiana. Social worker will send information on options to them via agency's secure website which they can then read over and discsuss. Everyone can, then, have a phone conversation before next meeting in two weeks. Plus, social worker will call the Area Agency on Aging to find out how long typical eligibility is taking. Next meeting will be at office on pantry day with either Ms. Belton or Mr. Agiana. Family will decide closer to date based upon interviews and work schedules a that time. Family may reach its goal by the eight week target date.

Elyse Hillmer, MSW (electronic signature) 06/15/17

Comment these app acronyms everyone what they

Comment Is there a additiona informatic applicatic interview or work w employm specialist

Comment This is jar professio may unde it, but wou court or c if they rea note?

Comment women ar moms.

Revised Interaction Note

Topaz MultiService Center

Date: June 15, 2017   **Service**: Service Coord./ Employment/Pantry

Met with Ms. Belton and Mrs. Palicetti at home for 35 minutes. Mr. Agiana had an interview. Reviewed and updated plan. Both women presented as hopeful and expressed optimism because, as Ms. Belton said, "maybe some of this effort is going to pay off."

Objective A: Family reports continuing pantry use, the older children are still getting free school breakfast and lunch, and Mrs. Palicetti is getting meals on wheels. St. Vincent de Paul Society agreed to a one-time mortgage payment. Unemployment benefits started a week ago. Children are now on CHIP for insurance, but Ms. Belton and her partner have let their insurance lapse for lack of payment. That is a worry; agreed to add this to plan and work on this issue.

Objective B: Mr. Agiana is on a 2nd interview at a car dealership. He had an interview the previous week at a local garage but didn't get the job. Ms. Belton reports that the benefits and pay would be "better at the dealership anyway so keeping fingers crossed."

Objective C: Mrs. Palicetti has applied for the aging waiver program for people who are Medicaid and Medicare eligible. They met with the nurse assessor and submitted all the financial paperwork. Awaiting the determination. The Area Agency on Aging (AAA) started meals on wheels immediately. They also toured an adult day health center (ADHC). Ms. Belton thinks it is great. Ms. Palicetti states she "can live with it" a few days a week if it makes it easier for her daughter, lets her daughter work at least part-time, and keeps her out of a nursing home. The proposed care plan includes going to the ADHC three days a week, having a home health aide come in two days a week for two hours, meals on wheels the days she is home, and a one-time home modification to make the bathroom more accessible. They are unsure how long until approval.

Objective D: Ms. Belton was rehired by her previous employer on the 3-11 shift three times a week. She has been back at work 1 ½ weeks. Her siblings, two older nieces, and Mr. Agiana are "taking shifts" to stay with Mr. Palicetti. "So far so good."

Impressions and next steps: Family continuing efforts. Added to Objective A to find insurance resources. Social worker will send insurance information via agency's secure website and can talk by phone before next meeting. Will check with AAA on average wait time for eligibility. Next meeting in two weeks at office with either Ms. Belton or Mr. Agiana; family will decide closer to date. Family on track to meet goal by target date if Mr. Agiana gets a job offer.

Elyse Hillmer, MSW (electronic signature) 05/05/17

Commentary on Professional E-mail

Subject: Insurance

June 15, 2017

Sophia Belton (sbelton555@gmail.com)

EH – Elyse Hillmer (hillygirl@gmail.com)

Hey Sophia,

Per our meeting and information on income ($1000 a month from your job and $1500 a month unemployment), Medicaid is a nogo. Check out the ACA Marketplace. You guys are eligible for a Special Enrollment Period. See https://www.healthcare.gov/have-job-based-coverage/if-you-lose-job-based-co .

I am attaching a state ACA brochure. So have docs ready when you go online. If you want help Insurance Help on pantry day. Just call Cassandra at the front desk to schedule.

Elyse

Comment: Personal email address rather than the agency's. This crosses professional boundary lines and probably compromises security, privacy, and confidentiality.

Comment: Unnecessary private information that you both already know. It doesn't need to be in the e-mail in case it was ever compromised.

Comment: Will she know what the ACA is, as most people call it Obama Care?

Comment: Does this provide enough support and explanation for the client to do this on her own?

Comment: "check ou "nogo," ar "docs," th sets a rea informal t which sou more like are talkin friend tha a professi

Comment Missing a disclaime confidenti statement

Comment Missing official ag informatio well as so worker co informatio

Revised Professional E-mail

Subject: Insurance Options for Adults

June 15, 2017

Sophia Belton (sbelton555@gmail.com)

EH – Elyse Hillmer (ehillmer@topazmsc.org)

Hello Sophia,

Per our meeting and information on income, it appears that Medicaid is not an option. This means you may want to go through the ACA (Affordable Care Act) Marketplace (state insurance exchange). I confirmed what we discussed. The loss of your husband's job, which caused loss of insurance, has made you both eligible for a Special Enrollment Period that is outside the Open Enrollment Period. For an explanation, go to https://www.healthcare.gov/have-job-based-coverage/if-you-lose-job-based-co.

I am attaching a brochure explaining how the ACA works in our state. Please go to the state website on the brochure to explore your options. You will want to have the financial documents listed in the brochure available before you log into the Marketplace. If you would prefer to have assistance when doing this, our agency partners with Insurance Help, a local nonprofit. They send in a representative on pantry days. Our clients can make an appointment to meet with them. If you want an appointment, e-mail or call the main desk (information below) to schedule with Cassandra, who you have met.

If you would like to talk this over, please feel free to call before we meet again.

Thanks,

Elyse

Elyse Hillmer, MSW

Service Coordinator

Address: Topaz MultiService Center ✿ 1111 Main Street ✿ Everytown, XX 12345

Main Phone: 555-555-5000, Personal Extension 555

E-mail: ehillmer@topazmsc.org ✿ scheduling@topazmsc.org

LEGAL DISCLAIMER

Confidentiality Notice: This e-mail message, including any attachments, is for the sole use of the intended recipient(s) and may contain confidential and privileged information. Any unauthorized review, use, disclosure, forwarding, or distribution is prohibited. If you are not the intended recipient, please contact the sender by reply e-mail and destroy all copies of the original message.

Commentary on Business Letter

1111 Main Street Everytown, XX 12345

555-555-5000 INFO@TOPAZMSC.ORG

June 23, 2017

Comment: Address incomplete.

Waiver Program

Everytown, XX 12345

Dear Toby:

Comment: True but not fully descriptive.

RE: Aging Waiver Services

As discussed, Mrs. Palicetti needs expedited eligibility for the waiver. Mrs. Palicetti and her family received a denial claiming that they had not submitted stuff. Like I told you, they had. This family is brooke taking care of her and should be totally eligible, maybe fore even six or more months. Her son-in-law got laid off, and if they don't get relief, they will have to place in her an SNF. They have waited long enough with all this red tape. Shoout me an e-mail or call if you want to talk it over more. I enclosed some documents, they can help you see I am right.

Sincerely,

Elyse

Comment: Should sign the full name.

Elyse Hillmer, MSW

Comment: No mention of the enclosures or if a copy has been sent to the client.

Comment: Where is the position title?

Comment if you kno person, b formal, as document official pu

Comment language vague.

Comment tone is ver casual. In case the l is a part o appeal pro which sho reference the letter. reference present. T are also m misspellin

Revised Business Letter

Topaz Multiservice Center

1111 MAIN STREET ✿ EVERYTOWN, XX 12345

555-555-5000 ✿ INFO@TOPAZMSC.ORG

June 23, 2017

Mr. Toby Wellner

Waiver Program

Everytown Medicaid Program

600 Main Street

Everytown, XX 12345

Dear Mr. Wellner:

RE: Mrs. Regina Palicetti's Application for Aging Waiver Services

Per our phone conversation yesterday, I am writing to request an expedited eligibility determination for Mrs. Regina Palicetti's Aging Waiver application in accordance with review policy A-705. Mrs. Palicetti and her family received a denial of eligibility (copy enclosed) claiming that they had not submitted required documents. They had submitted those documents, and a copy of the online confirmation (with the requested time stamp) is also enclosed. This family exhausted its savings (both Mrs. Palicetti's and that of her daughter Sophia Belton's family) because it was not aware of Waiver services even though she has, in all likelihood, been medically and financially eligible for six or more months. A recent layoff has left the family in jeopardy of losing its home, which would result in Mrs. Palicetti's being admitted to a nursing facility on Medicaid. They have already waited four weeks for this determination. As the finding seems to be based on an administrative oversight, I am requesting an expedited determination to prevent further financial strain and to prevent unnecessary nursing home admission. Please do not hesitate to contact me for additional information. Thank you in advance for your assistance in this matter.

Sincerely,

Elyse Hillmer

Elyse Hillmer, MSW

Service Coordinator

Enc: (1) denial letter and (2) online confirmation

cc: Mrs. Regina Palicetti

16

IN-DEPTH CASE ANALYSIS EXERCISES

This section of the book presents several in-depth case analyses that ask you to integrate and apply the knowledge and skills you have learned in class to real-life case scenarios. These are composite cases drawn from actual client situations, and they can be used in small break-out in-class group discussions, as in-class essay exams or take-home exams, or as papers. Each case is followed by several questions requiring good critical thinking.

1. "Not in My Backyard" is a case on the mission, ethics, and values of social work.

2. "A Breach of Confidentiality" addresses the core values, social work ethics, initial client engagement, and ways of helping.

3. "The Case of Jane: Version 1" is a case addressing the direct application of authenticity, use of empathic communication, and verbal following skills.

4. "The Case of Jane: Version 2" deals with social work values, dilemmas, exploration of client concerns, and assessment skills.

5. "A New Year's Eve Crisis" is a case about using verbatim application of empathy and verbal following skills.

6. "Neighborhood Conflict" is a community organizing scenario coupled with the application of micro interviewing skills.

7. "We Should Have Safety Personnel With Us" addresses core social work values, racial stereotypes, and the role of a social worker on a multidisciplinary team.

8. "A Crisis in Confidence" is a case addressing the application of ethics to a client situation.

9. "What Do I Do Now?" concerns the application of assessment and intervention skills.

CASE 1: NOT IN MY BACKYARD

You are a generalist practice social worker employed by the satellite office of a nonprofit community human services center. Your job involves a variety of roles and responsibilities including neighborhood mediation, community organizing, crisis intervention, and some short-term counseling with the families in the neighborhood area. Your referrals come from a variety of sources: directly from citizens within the neighborhood area (i.e., both individuals and community groups), from the police officers who walk the beat (a recent change from car patrol), and from other small local social service agencies. The main human services center is located in the center of a large urban area 15 miles away.

You live in the same small community where you work. Your neighborhood is racially mixed (African American, Hispanic, Eastern European immigrants, a few Asian and Caucasian families) and could be categorized as a working-class neighborhood. The citizens generally view themselves as hard-working people who value family, home, and their cultural and religious traditions. The neighborhood has taken considerable pride in its reputation as a stable and safe place to live—"not like the city." About a year ago, there was a slight increase in petty crime (e.g., car theft and burglary), and you successfully assisted the community in organizing a crime watch program run by community volunteers.

The current crisis stems from the announcement that the state is closing one of the large state mental hospitals located 50 miles from your community. This closing will result in the relocation of 300 mentally ill consumers into your county. Because your community is outside the city and is not subject to certain prohibitive zoning statutes, the state wants to build several sheltered care homes to house 75 of these consumers. The hospital plans to close in six months. The day following the announcement in the local paper, a small group of citizens comes to your office demanding that you do something to stop both the relocation of the consumers into your community and the development of the sheltered care facilities. They tell you that they are afraid that the presence of the mentally ill consumers will shatter the safe, relatively tranquil environment of their community and lower the property values of their homes. They want you to draw up a petition to stop the patient relocation plan immediately. You ask the group of six citizens to sit down, and you spend an hour and a half talking with the group.

Immediately after the group leaves, you receive a packet of memos from the central office regarding the hospital closing. In this packet a plan is outlined, which you read carefully. You discover that there are no plans for licensing the sheltered care facilities (they will simply go out to the lowest bid), there are no plans to professionally train the operators, and staff will not be required to have any more than a high school degree and one week of training. Furthermore, these consumers will be followed only once a month "if needed" by case managers who will be given only one month of training and, again, will only be required to have a high school degree. It appears as though the money saved from closing the hospital will not be put into developing community resources for the consumers. As an MSW social worker, you are extremely concerned about this because the plan outlined by the powers-that-be seems destined for failure. You place the packet of memos on your desk, sigh to yourself, and begin to think through what you should do.

Questions to Address in Your Essay or Discussion

1. What are the potential ethical challenges and/or dilemmas posed by this case? Describe them in detail.

2. As a professional social worker in this scenario, to whom and what are you responsible? Briefly describe all of your professional responsibilities in order of priority. Good sources for guidance include the NASW *Code of Ethics*, the overview of the purpose and mission of social work discussed in class and in your readings, and the roles and domain of social work practice (see Chapter 2 of this book).

3. Which of the six core values of social work are pertinent to this case? For each value cited, discuss specifically how it applies to this case.

CASE 2: A BREACH OF CONFIDENTIALITY

You are a social worker who is employed by a small community hospital located in a tiny town about 50 miles from a large urban area. You work with the families of hospitalized patients, help them find resources, and do discharge planning. In the past six months, you have personally seen six patients diagnosed with Acquired Immune Deficiency Syndrome (AIDS), which is more than you have seen in the past three years. Although this number can't compare with the statistics you've seen for the urban hospitals, you are concerned about the sudden increase; plus those six patients have all been suffering similar difficulties. They all stated that after they were diagnosed, somehow the information leaked out and subsequently each was evicted from his or her apartment and then had difficulty finding housing. Furthermore, they have all lost their jobs, and there is no support network of any kind for individuals with AIDS in your small town. You have talked to two of the doctors in your hospital about your observations and concerns, but they have brushed you off, stating that they "don't have time" to be bothered, and, furthermore, "AIDS is not a problem in this town." Soon after you return to your office, one of the patients, Joe Smith (who was discharged from the hospital a couple days ago), shows up unexpectedly. You ask him to sit down, and he says, "I have to talk to you. I know you tried to help me while I was in the hospital; please help me now. How did people in the town find out I was sick?"

Questions to Address in Your Essay or Discussion

1. What are your responsibilities as a social worker in this scenario?

2. Which of the core values of social work are pertinent to this case? For each value you cite, state how it is pertinent.

3. You met with Joe Smith for an hour. Using what you know so far about the knowledge and skills utilized in the initial phase of the helping process, discuss and describe in detail how you would engage Joe and explore his concerns. Specifically identify the knowledge and skills utilized.

4. List in order and describe in sufficient detail the first four steps you would take to respond to the situation as a professional social worker. These steps should be realistic, show good professional judgment, and be ethically defensible. Please note: you are not expected to completely resolve the situation in these four steps; this is just the beginning of what you would do.

CASE 3: THE CASE OF JANE: VERSION 1

Mr. and Mrs. Smith are the parents of Jane, a 30-year-old woman with a moderate intellectual disability (Intellectual Developmental Disorder). Jane has always lived with her parents and currently attends a part-time day treatment program at the local base service unit. Mr. Smith works as a car salesman, and Mrs. Smith has a small out-of-home crafts business, which she works on when Jane is at the day program.

About a month ago, Mrs. Smith noticed that Jane seemed to be getting heavier, particularly around the abdominal area. She took Jane to the family doctor, who told Mrs. Smith that he suspected Jane was pregnant. A pregnancy test confirmed this. After talking to Jane for some time, the doctor determined that Jane had had sexual relations with another intellectually disabled client at the day program numerous times and, in all likelihood, this led to the pregnancy. Jane, however, has no understanding of what "being pregnant" means, and the Smiths are in a quandary about what to do. The family doctor recommends that they make an appointment at the counseling service where you work "to talk to someone."

You greet Mr. and Mrs. Smith in the waiting room and invite them to come back to your office. After describing the situation with Jane, Mrs. Smith dabs at her eyes with a tissue and says anxiously, "Please help us; we don't know what to do about Jane. We're getting older, we both have health problems, we can't manage caring for a baby, and Jane can barely take care of her own basic needs, let alone take care of a child. What should we do?"

Tasks to Address in Your Essay or Discussion

1. Write a verbatim response to what Mrs. Smith said that clearly illustrates the use of authentic and empathic communication skills. Then discuss exactly why you chose the words you did and delineate exactly what issues you were trying to address in your response to Mrs. Smith.

2. Continuing from the response above, write a verbatim dialogue with the Smiths that includes five more responses on your part and five responses from either Mr. or Mrs. Smith. Each of your responses must clearly use one or more verbal following skills. For each response you make: (1) identify which verbal following skills are being used in the response and (2) describe exactly how that response will help further the development of rapport and explore the clients' concerns.

CASE 4: THE CASE OF JANE: VERSION 2

Mr. and Mrs. Smith are the parents of Jane, a 30-year-old woman with a moderate intellectual disability (Intellectual Developmental Disorder). Jane has always lived with her parents and currently attends a part-time day treatment program at the local base service unit. Mr. Smith works as a car salesman, and Mrs. Smith has a small out-of-home crafts business, which she works on when

Jane is at the day program. About a month ago, Mrs. Smith noticed that Jane seemed to be getting heavier, particularly around the abdominal area. She took Jane to the family doctor, who told Mrs. Smith that he suspected Jane was pregnant. A pregnancy test confirmed this. Jane has no idea she is pregnant, and the Smiths are in a quandary about what to do and so decided to come to the counseling service where you work "to talk to someone." Mr. and Mrs. Smith tell you that Jane is completely incapable of caring for a child, and Mrs. Smith, who is 59 years old, has heart problems and does not feel she is up to taking on the responsibility of a newborn. In fact, they are beginning to be concerned about how much longer they will be able to take care of Jane. They would like to either arrange for Jane to get an abortion or have her carry the baby to term and immediately place the baby for adoption without telling Jane. They are sure that Jane will never figure out that she is pregnant. After talking to Jane for some time, they determined that she probably had sexual relations with another client with an intellectual disability at the day program. The doctor also told the Smiths that with both parents having intellectual developmental disorders, the likelihood that the infant will have intellectual and/or developmental challenges as well is high. They want your advice about what to do.

Questions to Address in Your Essay or Discussion

1. What would be the initial avenues of exploration and assessment that you would pursue and why?

2. Who else besides Mr. and Mrs. Smith would likely be involved as clients, consultants, or collaterals?

3. What are the value dilemmas this case presents?

4. What would be the first three steps you would take in addressing these value dilemmas? Please note: you are not expected to completely resolve the situation in these three steps; this is just the beginning of what you would do.

CASE 5: A NEW YEAR'S EVE CRISIS

It is New Year's Eve and you are pulling the night shift at the community center crisis hotline. This hotline is a service supported by United Way, and in your moderately sized urban area, it is the only 24-hour hotline available. You and your colleagues receive a wide range of calls—everything from people who ask you how to get a cat out of a tree to callers who are seriously suicidal. A call comes in:

YOU: "Hello, Crisis Line, may I help you?"

CALLER: "Hi, um, (long pause with a sniffle) I . . . I don't know why I called. . . . I mean I've never done this before but . . . but . . . I don't know . . . I need help or something. I was looking forward to a real nice evening with my husband, I mean it's New Year's Eve and all and, well, it was great at first but then we started fighting and then (begins to cry and sniffle more) we said some bad things, and then he told me . . . he told me he's . . . he's been sleeping with my best friend. (Cries harder and keeps crying for a while) What am I going to do? I hate him! How could he do this to me?!"

Tasks to Address in Your Essay or Discussion

1. Write your first response—verbatim—to this caller using empathic communication. Then discuss why you chose the words you did and delineate exactly what issues you were trying to address your response to the caller.

2. Write a verbatim dialogue with this client that includes four more responses from the client and four responses on your part that demonstrate the use of verbal following skills. For each response you make, identify which verbal following skills are involved and what the aim of each response is; that is, how will that response help the client and further your ability to explore her problems?

CASE 6: NEIGHBORHOOD CONFLICT

You are a neighborhood mediator for the Crescent Heights section of a large urban area. In this particular neighborhood many changes have and are taking place. For decades, it has been a stable working class neighborhood. In the past few years, some of the old families have sold their homes, the homes have been torn down, and moderate- to low-income housing has been put up in its place. These housing units have mostly families with either young children or teenagers living in them. The teenagers hang around the street corners and in the park, and the older original residents are becoming very nervous about the situation. One elderly couple who you know quite well (you have helped them at other times with disputes with their neighbors) comes to your office and asks to talk with you.

YOU:	"Hello, Mr. and Mrs. Jackson. How are you today?"
MRS. JACKSON:	"Well, dear, we're managing about the same as always. My hip is bothering me a bit, you know. We're not here about that. . . . Well, George, you can tell it better than I can."
MR. JACKSON:	"Yes, well (clears throat), it's just those kids you know, hanging around all the time. We don't like to complain, and don't say we said anything, but something's got to be done. The missus and I don't feel safe no more even going to the store. We think the city should do something. Could you ask that there be a curfew at least so those kids are off the streets? It's not that we don't like kids, but it's like this ain't my neighborhood no more."

Tasks to Address in Your Essay or Discussion

1. Write your first response, verbatim, to Mr. and Mrs. Smith using empathic communication. Then discuss why you chose the words you did and delineate exactly what issues you were trying to address.

2. Write a verbatim dialogue with the Smiths that includes four more responses on their part and four responses on your part that demonstrate the use of verbal following skills. For each response you make, identify which verbal following skills are involved and what the aim of each response is; that is, how will that response help the clients and further your ability to explore their problems?

CASE 7: WE SHOULD HAVE SAFETY PERSONNEL WITH US

You are a social worker on a 30-bed inpatient psychiatric unit that provides care to adults. There are two other social workers on the unit. Each morning, the clinical staff convenes to receive the morning report from the charge nurse. The morning report is an overview of the clinical status of all patients on the unit. After the morning report, the treatment teams start morning rounds. Each patient has a treatment team, which generally consists of a psychiatrist, nurse, chief resident, and social worker.

A newly hired social worker will be shadowing you for the next two weeks. Your treatment team is preparing to start rounds, but the chief resident is late. The team decides to wait a few minutes for his arrival. Within five minutes, the chief resident arrives and is apologetic for being late. He is scheduled to take the lead in interviewing patients during rounds this morning. After reviewing the names and status of each patient, the team decides the order of each visit. Often new patients are seen last because it takes longer to review their cases. As the chief resident reads the names of patients, he pauses, looks at the nurse, and says, "We should have safety personnel with us when visiting Ralph Jones. I understand he is a big black man." The new social worker looks at you, shocked, after this statement. No one says anything, and the team proceeds to do morning rounds.

Ralph Jones is the last patient seen. The treatment team enters his room, and safety personnel stand by the door in the event the patient becomes hostile or threatening. What the team discovers is a man struggling with depression, trying to cope with multiple life-changing events, and expressing hopelessness.

Questions to Address in Your Essay or Discussion

1. Which core social work values are prominent in this case?

2. What stereotypes are reinforced concerning Ralph Jones?

3. What are the risks to Ralph Jones as a patient, based on what was said about him prior to rounds?

4. Should either social worker express concerns to the treatment team and/or to the chief resident about the statement regarding Mr. Jones?

5. Write a verbatim statement for how you would address your concerns to the treatment team and/or the chief resident.

CASE 8: A CRISIS IN CONFIDENCE

Maria Rossi (a 25-year-old woman of Mexican and Italian heritage) approaches ABC Community Agency (a general social services agency with services that include general case management, clinical case management, nutrition programs, recreational programs, energy assistance, and employment assistance services). She reports that she "might like to move out of her mom's home but doesn't know how to do that because she will probably fail if she tries." As she tells her initial story, you learn that she is the divorced mother of a 3½-year-old toddler, Ricky. After her divorce two years ago, she moved back into the small home of her parents, Marco and Josephina, because she "had no choice."

She describes her son as "a joy, full of energy, curiosity, and enthusiasm." She divorced her ex-husband, his father, because if his "drug use and temper." While he often called her names and occasionally hit her, the final straw was when he threatened Ricky. She has nothing to do with him now and can't recall the last time he saw Ricky. When she left him, she had never been more afraid in her life. She had "failed at marriage and picked the wrong guy," just like her dad said she would. Even though she still has a job, it pays a lot less than her ex-husband's did. The loss of income was hard, and she has never lived on her own. She says she "doesn't have any skills to get a better-paying job."

She says her parents are "supportive because they don't charge rent, and her mom watches Ricky while she works." She helps by buying food for the family and paying the electric bill. Her parents don't have much income because her dad had to retire early and go on disability for poor health; her mother has always been a "homemaker." In passing she says, "They aren't very happy people, and I don't know why they are still together." There is a lot of yelling in the house. Her dad smokes "all the time everywhere" and her mom "drinks a lot" plus is "verbally abusive." The house is small with only two bedrooms, so she shares her bedroom with Ricky.

Maria tried to get help and move out once before. She quit because she was "a failure as a client, too, never knowing what to say and couldn't even do the first assignment to find another apartment." She would like to feel better about her life and give her son a good life.

Questions to Address in Your Essay or Discussion

Apply the NASW *Code of Ethics* to analyze this case.

1. What might your responsibilities be in this situation as a social worker employed by ABC Community Agency?

2. Which values and standards apply from NASW's *Code of Ethics*? Are there other standards or requirements that apply? Connect them to the case.

3. Are there challenges related to ethics and/or ethical dilemmas present? Why?

4. How would you begin to practice in this situation to either stay at the level of an ethical or clinical challenge (see Chapter 4) or begin to resolve any existing ethical dilemmas?

CASE 9: WHAT DO I DO NOW?

Kiyo Andrews (a 38-year-old Japanese American woman) hesitantly approaches ABC Community Agency (a general social services agency with services that include general case management, nutrition programs, recreational programs, energy assistance, family support program, and emergency services) for help at the recommendation of her therapist. She tells you she will only talk to you under the condition that you not reveal her therapy to anyone. She is also reluctant to tell her family she has come to the agency. She has been seeing a therapist for about two weeks because she has been feeling anxious, sad, and overwhelmed. She is not quite sure what to do. Her neighborhood was evacuated about 5½ weeks ago due to a wildfire. Although the fire did not destroy her family's home, it caused significant damage, and they cannot live there until it is repaired. They have moved into her parent's home, and her stress levels are high. Her therapist suggested that her stress levels may reduce if she gets some practical assistance.

Kiyo's husband, Mark Andrews, is an engineer. Kiyo works as a legal secretary. They had a reasonably comfortable lifestyle prior to the fire but didn't have much of a financial cushion. Although they had insurance, it has become clear that not everything will be covered. Money has become extremely tight. Because other families were impacted, the price for services seems to have skyrocketed and wait times are long. They need to contribute to costs borne by her parents plus pay toward their own home. It has been hard to replace clothes and supplies and keep up with food costs. In addition, their commutes are much longer from her parents' home for their jobs and the children's schools and activities.

Kiyo and Mark have three children, ages 6, 9, and 12. Since the fire, they have been staying at her parents' home, which is smaller than their home and only has three bedrooms, so she and her husband are sleeping in the living room. Her parents, who immigrated to the United States before her birth, do not approve of the way Kiyo and Mark discipline the children. They find it too lax. They were never particularly crazy about Kiyo's choice of husband, but they all seemed to get along before this. Now Kiyo finds herself mediating between her parents, the kids, and her husband.

Your agency is working with quite a few other families displaced by the fire. The larger community has been impacted. Many are in similar circumstances—they have some resources but not quite enough and are living with relatives while awaiting repairs to their damaged homes. Your agency developed a variety of responses to the emerging and ongoing needs of these community members, including a support group. The agency is providing some services by itself and others in partnership with other groups, churches, and agencies.

Tasks to Address in Your Essay or Discussion

1. Select a level of system for intervention (individual, family, group, organization, or community) as your focus. Name and explain a rationale for your choice.

2. Complete an assessment.

    - Pull out and highlight the most relevant information you have.

    - What else do you need to know to complete the assessment?

    - How would you obtain it?

3. Set a mutually agreed-upon goal.

    - Only one goal, please. Select a priority to examine in depth, even though the case may suggest more than one goal.

4. Design and implement an intervention for the chosen goal.

    - Explain the intervention.

    - Explain how it will be implemented.

    - Select and explain techniques and skills to do this.

5. Other considerations

    - Are there cultural or other factors you need to consider?

    - Have you worked from a strengths perspective? Is it evident in the goal? How is it evident elsewhere?

REAL-WORLD
EXPERIENTIAL EXERCISES

This chapter provides a list of suggested experiences for students to try and then reflect on by journaling, giving a presentation to the class, writing a paper, or posting to an online discussion forum. The process of doing an activity and reflecting upon it can expose you to aspects of the social work profession that you might not encounter otherwise in your formal classes. These experiential exercises should assist in broadening your perspective on social work, enhancing your understanding of the social and environmental conditions experienced by clients, and seeing firsthand how agencies operate and offer services. These exercises may help you choose a social work specialization for future classes and your field placements. They also offer you an opportunity to apply the concepts that you are learning in the classroom to the real world.

To the instructor: There are many ways to use these exercises. Each of the authors has used them differently. The four suggestions below are simply ideas. Please be creative and fit your choices to your classes and program.

The Experiential Journal

- Review the list of experiences and select four to six of them to complete over the course of the term. After completing each one, write a two- to four-page journal entry describing your experience and connecting it to what you are learning about social work.

- Note: If you choose to view and approach the journal as simply "busywork," you will gain little from the experiences. However, if you approach it as an assignment that can enhance your experience and perception of the real world of social work, you will potentially gain a lot. In other words, you will get out of it what you put into it.

Class Presentations

- Review the list of experiences and select four to six of them to complete over the course of the term. Choose the single activity that was most meaningful or the richest learning experience, and then do a five-minute class presentation describing the experience and what you learned from it.

- Select an activity that can be done in a group of four people, like the community walk-about, and have the group give a 20-minute presentation on the experience.

Reflection Papers

- Review the list of experiences, select one, and write a three- to four-page reflection paper about it and connect it to the concepts being learned in class.

Online Discussion Posting

- Review the list of experiences and select three of them to complete over the course of the term. Post about the experiences and respond to the posts of other students, connecting themes and insights.

EXPERIENTIAL EXERCISE OPTIONS

1. **Attend a local meeting of the National Association of Social Workers (NASW).** Contact the representative of the local NASW region in your state for information about where and when the meetings take place. In smaller, less populated states, there may be a single chapter, but in larger states, such as New York and California, the state is broken up into regions. In your assignment, please summarize the issues discussed, comment on any decisions made during the meeting, and address the following questions: What were your general reactions to the meeting? Would you join NASW? Explain why or why not. Discuss how the experience changed or expanded your perspective on social work practice.

2. **Attend a public hearing concerned with a current issue relevant to social work.** In the assignment, summarize the issues discussed. Who were the client systems involved? How might *you* participate regarding the issues addressed? Discuss how the experience changed or expanded your perspective on social work practice.

3. **Attend a meeting of a community or neighborhood association.** In the assignment, discuss the issues of concern, how the group functions, what roles social workers do or could perform within the association, and what the social work profession could or should contribute. Discuss how the experience changed or expanded your perspective on social work practice.

4. **Attend a continuing education lecture, workshop, or seminar addressing issues related to social work practice** that is offered outside of your school or department of social work. Review and critique the lecture, workshop, or seminar, and discuss how it changed or expanded your perspective on social work practice.

5. **Attend a self-help or support group meeting.** Be certain that you attend an "open meeting," *not* a closed one (note: some open meetings may not be open to everyone, just those who experience the issue; try to call ahead to be sure you are welcome). Describe your experience and observations. What happened during the meeting? Do you think the group is helpful to its participants? Why or why not? Would you refer a client to the group? Why or why not? Discuss how the experience changed or expanded your perspective on social work practice.

6. **Attend a tenants' meeting in public or income-supported housing.** Summarize the issues discussed and identify the client systems involved and how social workers are playing or could play a helpful role. Discuss your reactions to the experience of attending the meeting and how the experience changed or expanded your perspective on social work practice.

7. **Attend an event of or visit a local educational project and describe how social workers are or could be involved** (e.g., drug and alcohol prevention programs such as the D.A.R.E. program, teen pregnancy prevention programs, cultural/racial/gender awareness programs, Gay-Straight Alliance events, Take Back the Night events, a poverty simulation). Summarize your findings. Discuss how the experience changed or expanded your perspective on social work practice in schools and education.

8. **Interview an agency administrator or program director about the Americans with Disabilities Act.** Explore how the agency's policies and/or programs fulfill the requirements of the Act. Do you think this particular agency or program has responded appropriately? Do they seem to be adequately in compliance, or do you detect some gaps still remaining? You should review the Act prior to your interview. Recall that physical accessibility is only one small portion of the Act. Employment and educational accommodation are also part of it.

9. **Interview a mental health or other social service administrator and discuss with that person how managed care impacts the services that are provided to the agency's clients.** Inquire about the degree that the plans serve clients, insurers, or agencies. Discuss the

impact from the perspective of an agency administrator, a direct services social worker, and a consumer of services.

10. **Interview an international student at your college or university.** Ask the student about how social work services are delivered in their home country and how social welfare needs are handled. Compare and contrast the student's country with the United States. Discuss how the conversation changed or expanded your perspective on global or international social work practice.

11. **Visit a local social service agency.** Identify the mission of the agency and discuss the duties and responsibilities of the social workers who work there (if the agency does not employ professionally trained social workers, choose a different agency). Would you want to work or do your field placement in that agency? Why or why not? Discuss how the experience changed or expanded your perspective on social work practice.

12. **Visit a mental health service; a children, youth, and families agency; or an agency serving older adults and interview one of the social workers.** Find out what the access points are for clients and their families. What are the roles and responsibilities of social workers who work there? Would you want to work for or do your field placement at that agency? Why or why not? Discuss how the experience changed or expanded your perspective on social work practice.

13. **Visit the office of a local legislator and request a copy of pending social services legislation.** Review and critique the bill and discuss its strengths and weaknesses in your analysis. Discuss how the office visit and review of the bill changed or expanded your perspective on both social work practice and policy.

14. **Visit a public welfare office.** First, instead of driving, take the bus or walk to the office, which is what many of our clients must do. Sit in the waiting room and observe what is happening and the atmosphere. Next, imagine that you are a client in need of services. How would you feel? What would your thoughts be? Then, ask for an application or get it online, fill it out in its entirety, and think about what that feels like. This is the type of situation many of your clients will have experienced. Please **do not** attempt to interview any of the staff or clients and **do not submit the application**. Address the following questions in the discussion of your experience:

    a. What did you observe and learn from this exercise?

    b. Did you have any difficulty completing the application form? If so, in what way?

    c. Did any of your perceptions of public welfare change?

15. **Volunteer to work for a day in a soup kitchen, home-delivered meals program, or food pantry.** Describe your experience, including what you did and who you met. What common needs do the clients appear to have? What diversity among the clients did you observe? Discuss how this experience changed or expanded your perspective on social work practice and social work services.

16. **Volunteer for Habitat for Humanity or another labor-intensive volunteer project in your community.** While participating, talk with the organizers of the activity and discuss its purpose and mission. Talk with your fellow volunteers about why they decided to volunteer and what their goals are. Discuss how the experience changed or expanded your perspective on social work practice and volunteerism in your community.

17. **Select a neighborhood and conduct a community walk-about, noticing the appearance of the community, the people living and working there, its accessibility, and its access to resources.** What services, businesses, residences, parks, and recreational facilities are present? Discuss what you saw and how you felt in that community. Discuss issues of concern, community strengths, and community needs and ways a social worker might be involved in this community. Explain how this experience changed your perspective on communities.

18. **Investigate and identify the full range of human services available in your community.** Describe and discuss the services. Are there any gaps in services? Is there adequate service

provision to special populations (e.g., women, persons with disabilities, low-income people, members of the LGBTQI community, veterans)? Do you think that your community is adequately served? Discuss how the experience changed or expanded your perspective on social work practice.

19. **Choose one of the following topics and follow it through the media for one month.** *Media* is defined as newspapers, magazines, radio, television programs, or online newsfeeds. Choose at least two liberal sources, two conservative sources, and two mainstream sources.

   - Child abuse and/or neglect

   - Domestic and/or world hunger

   - Elder abuse or exploitation

   - Globalization

   - HIV/AIDS

   - Health care reform

   - Homelessness

   - Immigration reform

   - Police brutality

   - PTSD and suicide in veterans

   - Racial/ethnic conflict/relations

   - Reform of social welfare programs

   - Reproductive rights

   - Sexual harassment/assault

   - Substance use disorders

   - Violence in families

   Summarize the social work practice and policy issues from the media information you have obtained and analyze how the media presents the topic. You must have a minimum of eight different sources and must provide appropriate citations within the text and a complete reference list in APA format.

20. **Call your state legislator to discuss an issue such as health care reform, funding for higher education, or mental health services—whatever particularly interests you related to social work practice.** Discuss your conversation with the legislator and what issues you addressed. Discuss how the experience changed or expanded your perspective on social work practice and policy.

21. **Create an assignment on a topic of your choice.** For a self-created choice, take the initiative to find out about the wide range of resources in your college or university and larger community. You can then choose an experience that addresses your particular interests. For example, you could attend a lecture or workshop at a local social service agency and then discuss and critique what you learned. You might also volunteer, interview, or explore some other agency, population, or social issues not mentioned here. You must discuss your idea with the instructor prior to commencing work and you must receive the instructor's approval.

ABOUT THE AUTHORS

Christina E. Newhill earned a PhD in social welfare from the University of California, Berkeley; an MSW from Syracuse University; and a BA in sociology from Harpur College, State University of New York, at Binghamton. Dr. Newhill is a professor of social work with a joint appointment with the Clinical and Translational Science Institute and teaches in the MSW and PhD programs. In 2008, she received the Chancellor's Distinguished Teaching Award, Pitt's highest teaching honor. Professor Newhill's primary research interests are community mental health services, the psychosocial treatment of individuals with serious and persistent mental illness, and improving the assessment of violent behavior. Newhill has more than 10 years of community mental health practice experience, primarily in psychiatric emergency and inpatient settings. She has conducted training workshops on client violence and social worker safety at the local, state, and national levels for many years and authored *Client Violence in Social Work Practice: Prevention, Intervention and Research* (Guilford Press, 2003). She is also the author of the textbook *Interventions for Serious Mental Disorders: Working with Individuals and Their Families* (Pearson/Allyn & Bacon, 2015). Newhill is a licensed clinical social worker in California and a licensed social worker in Pennsylvania.

Elizabeth A. Mulvaney earned her MSW from the University of North Carolina at Chapel Hill and a BA in psychology from the University of Virginia. She holds a clinical social work license in Pennsylvania and has 14 years of practice experience as a gerontological social worker. Current research and practice interests include geriatric workforce development, Alzheimer's disease and related dementias, ethics, palliative care, and problem gambling prevention for older adults. Serving as a lecturer since 2012 and prior to that as the coordinator for the University of Pittsburgh's HPPAE program, she primarily instructs MSW and BSW students in practice and behavior classes. She has taught generalist skills for over a decade.

Bobby F. Simmons earned his MSW in social work from the University of Pittsburgh. He has an MS from the University of Tennessee in vocational rehabilitation evaluation and a BA from Knoxville College in psychology. Simmons began working at the University of Pittsburgh after a long career in mental health where he held various clinical and administrative positions. Currently, he is director of career services and enjoys teaching in both the BASW and MSW programs.

REFERENCES

American Psychiatric Association. (2000). *Diagnostic and statistical manual of mental disorders* (4th ed., text rev.). Washington, DC: Author.

Anheier, H. K. (2014). *Nonprofit organizations*. New York, NY: Routledge.

Becvar, D. S., & Becvar, R. J. (2009). *Family therapy: A systematic integration* (7th ed.). Boston: Allyn & Bacon.

Borgman, D. & Yates, C. B. (2018). Community organizing vs. community development. *Culture and Youth Studies*. Retrieved from http://cultureandyouth.org/community-development/articles-community-development/community-organizing-vs-community-development/

Bovend'Eerdt, T. J. H., Botell, R. E., & Wade, D. T. (2009). Writing SMART rehabilitation goals and achieving goal attainment scaling: A practical guide. *Clinical Rehabilitation, 23*(4), 352–361. doi:10.1177/0269215508101741

Bowen, J., Mogensen, L., Marsland, E., & Lannin, N. (2015). The development, content validity and inter-rater reliability of the SMART-Goal Evaluation Method: A standardised method for evaluating clinical goals. *Australian Occupation Therapy Journal, 62*, 420–427. doi:10.1111/1440-1630.12218

Bowen, M. (2004). *Family therapy in clinical practice*. Oxford, UK: Rowman & Littlefield.

Boyd-Franklin, N., Cleek, E. N., Wofsy, M., & Mundy, B. (2013). *Therapy in the real world: Effective treatments for challenging problems*. New York, NY: Guilford Press.

Bransford, J. D., Brown, A. L., & Cocking, R. R. (Eds.). (2000). *How people learn: Brain, mind, experience and school*. Commission on Behavioral and Social Sciences and Education, National Research Council. Washington, DC: National Academy Press.

Brother, J., & Sherman, A. (2011). *Building nonprofit capacity: A guide to managing change through organizational lifecycles*. San Francisco, CA: John Wiley & Sons.

Carlson, M., & Donohoe, M. (2010). *The executive director's guide to thriving as a nonprofit leader*. San Francisco, CA: John Wiley & Sons.

Carrillo, T. E. (2007). *Home visiting strategies: A case management guide for caregivers*. Columbia, SC: University of South Carolina Press.

Centers for Disease Control and Prevention. (2013). *Community needs assessment participant workbook*. Retrieved from https://www.cdc.gov/globalhealth/healthprotection/fetp/training_modules/15/community-needs_pw_final_9252013.pdf

Compton, B. R., & Galaway, B. (1989). *Social work processes* (4th ed). Pacific Grove, CA: Brooks/Cole.

Compton, B. R., Galaway, B., & Cournoyer, B. R. (2004). *Social work processes* (7th ed.). Pacific Grove, CA: Brooks/Cole.

Corey, M. S., Corey, G., & Corey, C. (2015). *Groups: Process and practice* (9th ed). Belmont, CA: Thompson Brooks/Cole.

Coulton, C. (1979). A study of the person-environmental fit among the chronically ill. *Social Work in Health Care, 5*, 5–17. doi:10.1300/J010v05n01_01

Council on Social Work Education. (2015). *2015 educational policy and accreditation standards for baccalaureate and master's social work programs*. Washington, DC: Author. Retrieved from https://cswe.org/getattachment/Accreditation/Standards-and-Policies/2015-EPAS/2015EPASandGlossary.pdf.aspx

Cowger, C. D. (1994). Assessing client strengths: Clinical assessment for empowerment. *Social Work, 39*, 262–267. doi:10.1093/sw/39.3.262

Crenshaw, K. (1991). Mapping the margins: Intersectionality, identity politics, and violence against women of color. *Stanford Law Review, 43*(6), 1241–1299. doi:10.2307/1229039

Davis, M. H. (1983). Measuring individual differences in empathy: Evidence for a multidimensional approach. *Journal of Personality and Social Psychology, 44*, 113–126. doi:10.1037/0022-3514.44.1.113

Day, T., & Tosey, P. (2011). Beyond SMART? A new framework for goal setting. *The Curriculum Journal, 22*(4), 515–534. doi:10.1080/09585176.2011.627213

Doran, G. T. (1981). There's a S.M.A.R.T. way to write management's goals and objectives. *Management Review, 70*, 35–36.

Epstein, N., & Bishop, D. (1981). Problem-centred systems therapy of the family. In A. S. Gurman & D. P. Knisker (Eds.), *Handbook of family therapy*. New York, NY: Burnner/Mazel.

Fink-Samnick, E., & Powell, S. K. (2012). Professional resilience revisited. *Professional Case Management, 17*(4), 149–152. doi:10.1097/NCM.0b013e31825884e7

Fischer, J. (1973). An eclectic approach to therapeutic casework. In J. Fischer (Ed.), *Interpersonal helping: Emerging approaches for social work practice* (pp. 317–335). Springfield, IL: Charles C. Thomas.

Fisher-Borne, M., Cain, J. M., & Martin, S. L. (2015). From mastery to accountability: Cultural humility as an alternative to cultural competence. *Social Work Education, 34*(2), 165–181. doi:10.1080/0 2615479.2014.977244

Frankel, A. J., & Gelman, S. R. (2016). *Case management: An introduction to concepts and skills.* New York, NY: Oxford.

Freese, B. (2015, August 8). *What's the deal with online therapy?* Retrieved from https://www.socialworkhelper.com/2015/08/25/ whats-deal-online-therapy/

Glaser, B., & Suter, E. (2016). Interprofessional collaboration and integration as experienced by social workers in health care. *Social Work in Health Care, 55*, 395–408. doi:10.1080/00981389.2015 .1116483

Goldenberg, H., & Goldenberg, I. (2007). *Family therapy: An overview* (7th ed.). Mason, OH: Cengage.

Gordon, R. S. (1983). An operational classification of disease prevention. *Public Health Reports, 98*(2), 107–109.

Graybeal, C. (2001). Strengths-based social work assessment: Transforming the dominant paradigm. *Families in Society, 82*(3), 233–242. doi:10.1606/1044-3894.236

Grier, W., & Cobbs, P. (1968). *Black rage.* New York, NY: Basic.

Gucciardi, E., Espin, S., Morganti, A., & Dorado, L. (2016). Exploring interprofessional collaboration during the integration of diabetes teams into primary care. *BMC Family Practice, 17*(1), 1–12. doi:10.1186/s12875-016-0407-1

Harpur, P. (2012). From disability to ability: Changing the phrasing of the debate. *Disability & Society, 27*(3), 325–337. doi:10.1080/096 87599.2012.654985

Hartman, A. (1978). Diagrammatic assessment of family relationships. *Families in Society, 76*, 111–122.

Hartman, A., & Laird, J. (1983). The family in space: Ecological assessment. In *Family-centered social work practice* (pp. 157–186). New York, NY: The Free Press.

Hasenfeld, Y., & English, R. A. (1977). *Human service organizations.* Ann Arbor, MI: University of Michigan Press.

Hepworth, D. H., & Larsen, J. A. (1990). *Direct social work practice: Theory and skills* (3rd ed.). Belmont, CA: Wadsworth.

Hepworth, D. H., Rooney, R. H., Rooney, G. D., & Strom-Gottfried, K. (2013). *Direct social work practice: Theory and skills* (10th ed.). Belmont, CA: Brooks/Cole.

Hodge, D. R. (2005). Spiritual assessment in martial and family therapy: A methodological framework for selecting from among six qualitative assessment tools. *Journal of Marital and Family Therapy, 31*(4), 341–356. doi:10.1111/j.1752-0606.2005.tb01575.x

Institute of Medicine. (2011). *The health of lesbian, gay, bisexual, and transgender people: Building a foundation for better understanding.* Washington, DC: The National Academies Press.

International Federation of Social Workers. (2012). *Statement of ethical principles.* Retrieved from http://ifsw.org/policies/ statement-of-ethical-principles/

International Federation of Social Workers. (2014). *Global definition of social work.* Retrieved from http://ifsw.org/policies/ definition-of-social-work/

Kirschenbaum, H. (1992). A comprehensive model for values education and moral education. *Phi Delta Kappan, 73*(10), 771–776.

Kirst-Ashman, K. K., & Hull, G. H. (2015). *Understanding generalist practice* (7th ed.). Stamford, CT: Cengage.

Leavell, H., & Clark, E. (1958). *Preventive medicine for the doctor in his community: An epidemiologic approach.* New York, NY: McGraw-Hill.

Légaré, F., Stacey, D., Brière, N., Fraser, K., Desroches, S., Dumont, S., Sales, A., . . . Aubé, D. (2013). Healthcare providers' intentions to engage in an interprofessional approach to shared decision making in home care programs: A mixed methods study. *Journal of Interprofessional Care, 27*, 214–222. doi:10.3109/1356182 0.2013.763777

Levy, C. S. (1976). *Social work ethics.* New York, NY: Human Sciences Press.

Lewis, J. M., & Kreider, R. M. (2015, March). *Remarriage in the United States.* American community survey reports, ACS-30. Washington, DC: U.S. Census Bureau. Retrieved from https://www.census.gov/ content/dam/Census/library/publications/2015/acs/acs-30.pdf

Lowenberg, F., & Dolgoff, R. (1988). *Ethical decisions for social work practice* (3rd ed.). Belmont, CA: Brooks/Cole.

Lukas, S. (1993). *Where to start and what to ask: An assessment handbook.* New York, NY: W. W. Norton & Company.

Maluccio, A. N., & Marlow, W. D. (1974). The case for the contract. *Social Work, 19*(1), 28–36.

McGoldrick, M., Carter, B., & Garcia-Preto, N. (2011). *Individual, family, and social perspectives: The expanded family life cycle* (4th ed.). Boston, MA: Allyn & Bacon.

McGoldrick, M., Gerson, R., & Petry, S. (2008). *Genograms: Assessment and intervention.* (3rd ed.). New York, NY: Norton.

Miller, W. R., & Rollnick, S. (2013). *Motivational interviewing: Helping people change* (3rd ed.). New York, NY: Guilford Press.

Minuchin, S. (1974). *Families and family therapy.* Cambridge, MA: Harvard University Press.

Minuchin, S., & Fishman, H. C. (1981). *Family therapy techniques.* Cambridge, MA: Harvard University Press.

Murphy, P. W., & Cunningham, J. V. (2003). *Organizing for community controlled development: Renewing civil society.* Thousand Oaks, CA: SAGE.

National Association of Social Workers. (n.d.). *Social justice.* Retrieved from http://www.socialworkers.org/pressroom/features/Issue/peace.asp? print=1&

National Association of Social Workers. (2001). *NASW standards for cultural competence in social work practice.* Washington, DC: Author.

National Association of Social Workers. (2007). *Indicators for the achievement of the NASW standards for cultural competence in social work practice.* Washington, DC: Author.

National Association of Social Workers. (2008). *Code of ethics.* Washington, DC: Author.

National Association of Social Workers. (2012). *Social work speaks: National Association of Social Workers policy statements, 2012–2014* (9th ed.). Washington, DC: Author.

National Association of Social Workers. (2013). *NASW guidelines for social worker safety in the workplace.* Washington, DC: Author.

National Association of Social Workers. (2015). *Standards and indicators for cultural competence in social work practice.* Washington, DC: Author.

National Association of Social Workers. (2017a). *Code of ethics of the National Association of Social Workers.* Washington, DC: Author. Retrieved from https://www.socialworkers.org/About/Ethics/Code-of-Ethics/Code-of-Ethics-English

National Association of Social Workers (Producer). (2017b, January 31). Developing cultural humility in social work practice [Video webinar]. Retrieved from https://www.socialworkers.org

National Association of Social Workers, Association of Social Work Boards, Council on Social Work Education, & Clinical Social Work Association. (2017). *NASW, ASWB, CSWE, & CSWA standards for technology in social work practice.* Washington, DC: NASW Press. Retrieved from http://www.socialworkers.org/includes/newIncludes/homepage/PRA-BRO-33617.TechStandards_FINAL_POSTING.pdf

Newhill, C. E. (1990). The role of culture in the development of paranoid symptomatology. *American Journal of Orthopsychiatry, 60,* 176–185. doi:10.1037/h0079170

Newhill, C. E. (2015). *Interventions for serious mental disorders: Working with individuals and their families.* Boston, MA: Pearson/Allyn & Bacon.

Nickless, R. (2012, October 24). Business beware: Technology shortcuts brain power. *Australian Financial Review.* Retrieved March 8, 2017, from http://www.afr.com/technology/technology-companies/business-beware-technology-shortcuts-brain-power-20121023-j1l0k

O'Carroll, V., McSwiggan, L., & Campbell, M. (2016). Health and social care professionals' attitudes to interprofessional working and interprofessional education: A literature review. *Journal of Interprofessional Care, 30,* 42–29. doi:10.3109/13561820.2015.10516414

Ohmer, M. L., Teixeira, S., Booth, J., Zuberi, A., & Kolke, D. (2016). Preventing violence in disadvantaged communities: Strategies for building collective efficacy and improving community health. *Journal of Human Behavior in the Social Environment, 26*(7–8), 608–621. doi:10.1080/10911359.2016.1238804

Okun, B. F., & Kantrowitz, R. E. (2105). *Effective helping: Interviewing and counseling techniques.* Stamford, CT: Cengage Learning.

Pecukonis, E., Doyle, O., & Bliss, D. L. (2008). Reducing barriers to interprofessional training: Promoting interprofessional cultural competence. *Journal of Interprofessional Care, 22,* 417–428. doi:10.1080/13561820802190442

Pennsylvania Child Welfare Resource Center. (2013). *SMART goal worksheet.* Retrieved from http://www.pacwrc.pitt.edu/Curriculum/501_WritingEffctPerfStndrds/Hndts/HO11_SmrtGlWksht.pdf

Pennsylvania Department of Human Services. (n.d.). *Homeless assistance programs.* Retrieved from http://www.dhs.pa.gov/citizens/homelessassistance/index.htm

Pew Research Center. (2017, January 12). *Mobile fact sheet.* Retrieved from http://www.pewinternet.org/fact-sheet/mobile/

Pilsecker, C. (1978). Values: A problem for everyone. *Social Work, 23*(1), 54–57. doi:10.1093/sw/23.1.54

Rapp, C. A., & Goscha, R. J. (2012). *The strengths model: A recovery oriented approach to mental health services.* New York, NY: Oxford University Press.

Richmond, M. E. (1917). *Social diagnosis.* New York, NY: SAGE.

Rogers, C. (1961). *On becoming a person: A therapist's view of psychotherapy.* Cambridge, MA: Riverside.

Rooney, R. H. (Ed.). (2009). *Strategies for work with involuntary clients* (2nd ed.). New York, NY: Columbia University Press.

Saleebey, D. (2013). *The strengths perspective in social work practice* (6th ed.). Upper Saddle River, NY: Pearson.

Saleeby, P. W. (2007). Applications of a capability approach to disability and the International Classification of Functioning, Disability and Health (ICF) in social work practice. *Journal of Social Work in Disability & Rehabilitation, 6*(1–2), 217–232.

Simon, S. B., Howe, L. W., & Kirschenbaum, H. (1995). *Values clarification: A handbook of practical strategies for teachers and students.* New York, NY: Warner.

Siporin, M. (1980). Ecological systems theory in social work. *The Journal of Sociology & Social Welfare, 7*(4), 507–532. Retrieved from http://scholarworks.wmich.edu/jssw/vol7/iss4/4

Smith-Carrier, T., & Neysmith, S. (2014). Analyzing the interprofessional working of a home-based primary care team. *The Canadian Journal of Aging, 33,* 271–284. doi:10.1017/S071498081400021X

Soska, T. M. (2017). *Organizations.* Unpublished training materials.

Steinberg, D. M. (2010). Mutual aid: A contribution to best practice social work. *Social Work with Groups, 33,* 53–68. doi:10.1080/01609510903316389

Tichelaar, J., den Uil, S. H., Antonini, N. F., van Agtmael, M. A., de Vries, T. P. G. M., & Richir, M. C. (2016). A 'SMART' way to determine treatment goals in pharmacotherapy education. *British Journal of Clinical Pharmacology, 82,* 280–284. doi:10.1111/bcp.12919

Treacher, A. (1989). Termination in family therapy: Developing a structural approach. *Journal of Family Therapy, 11,* 135–147.

Tuckman, B. W. (1965). Developmental sequence in small groups. *Psychological Bulletin, 63*(6), 384–399. doi:10.1037/h0022100

Tuckman, B. W., & Jensen, M. A. C. (1977). Stages of small-group development revisited. *Group & Organization Management, 2*(4), 419–427. doi:10.1177/105960117700200404

U.S. Department of Veterans Affairs. (2017). *VA telehealth services.* Retrieved from https://www.telehealth.va.gov/

Walsh, F. (2006). *Strengthening family resilience* (2nd ed.). New York, NY: Guilford Press.

Walsh, J. (2015). *Theories for direct social work practice* (3rd ed.). Belmont, CA: Brooks/Cole Cengage.

Warren, R. (1983). Contexts: Community and organization. In R. M. Kramer & H. Specht (Eds.), *Readings in community organization practice* (3rd ed.; pp. 24–36). Englewood Cliffs, NJ: Prentice Hall.

Worth, J. (2009). *Nonprofit management.* Thousand Oaks, CA: SAGE.

Zimmerman, S. S. (1980). The family: Building block or anachronism? *Social Casework, 61,* 195–204.

INDEX

Note: Page numbers in **bold** refer to exercises.